Fusion Food Cook-book

Fusion Food Cookbook

Hugh Carpenter
& Teri Sandison

Food Styling by Erez and by Carol Cole

Artisan *New York*

Text editor: Melanie Falick

Production director: Hope Koturo

**Library of Congress Cataloging-
in-Publication Data**

Carpenter, Hugh.

Fusion food cookbook /

Hugh Carpenter & Teri Sandison;

food styling by Erez and Carol Cole.

Includes index.

ISBN 1-885183-00-3

1. Cookery, American. 2. Cookery,

International. I. Sandison, Teri. II. Title.

TX715.C274   1994

641.5973—dc20   94-19146

Published in 1994 by Artisan,

A Division of Workman Publishing

Company, Inc.

708 Broadway, New York, NY 10003

Printed in Japan

10 9 8 7 6 5 4 3 2 1

First Printing

Contents

Red Meats for Winter
Nights and Summer
Barbecues 134

Stars and
Supporting Roles
with Pasta,
Rice, and Breads 158

Magic with Vegetables
and Eggs 180

Chocolate Fantasies
for Life Fulfillment 200

Introduction

Fusion Food Cookbook celebrates a revolution that is occurring across North America. As never before, cooks are experimenting with techniques, ingredients, and presentation ideas from diverse culinary traditions to achieve new eating sensations. Intriguing seasonings from Asia, the American Southwest, the Caribbean, and the Mediterranean are enriching today's home cooking and entertaining. This exciting new "fusion cooking" means, for example, that a veal meat loaf is brushed with a traditional Caribbean jerk barbecue sauce as it bakes in the oven; a swirl of Southwestern Ancho Chile Jam is stirred into cream of asparagus soup before serving; and a classic basil pesto sauce is enhanced with serrano chiles, mint, and cilantro.

Although "fusion" is a new term in the cooking world (the word is widely used in the arts, particularly in glass art and contemporary jazz), culinary history is a series of fusion events. For example, in the years following the arrival of Columbus in America, the Spanish and Portuguese inaugurated a huge global interchange of foods. Ingredients native to the New World, including chiles, cocoa beans, corn, peanuts, potatoes, sweet potatoes, and tomatoes, were introduced to Europe, Africa, and Asia. In return the Spanish and the Portuguese brought into the Americas dozens of seasonings, foods, and farm animals, including cattle, goats, horses, pigs, sheep, spice plants, black-eyed peas, okra, watermelon, European grape varieties, herbs, and citrus fruits. Before 1492 there were no tomatoes in Mediterranean cooking, no chiles for the fiery foods of Thailand and Szechwan, and no cheeses for Mexican *chiles relleños*. This massive exchange of ingredients forever changed the cuisines of the world.

Now a second great flavor revolution, made possible by jet travel, mass media, new immigration, and a globe-trotting, affluent, and growing middle class, is changing and challenging our gastronomic lives. Ingredients from around the world arrive daily in major cities and are then spread, through sophisticated shipping systems, into the heartland of North America. Supermarkets offer an increasingly large variety of vegetables, fruits, herbs, ethnic seasonings, and bottled condiments. The new supermarket emporiums offer food courts with salad bars, sushi counters, and wok stations as well as complete lines of cookware and recipes accompanied by shopping lists generated by in-store computers. Local farmers' markets, now commonplace but not long ago a novelty, provide fresh seasonal produce, breads, preserves, and locally made cheeses.

The passion for flavor is fueled by chefs who work in both large coastal cities and small interior towns across North America. Tom Young at Expressions in the rural mountain town of Hendersonville, North Carolina, includes flavor accents such as papaya and basil purée and smoked shiitake sauce. Kurt Fleischfresser at The Coach House in Oklahoma City says, "Ten years ago there would have been no enthusiasm for such dishes as Grilled Buffalo Steak Marinated with Pineapple and Lemongrass, or Seafood Mixed Grill with Thai Basil Marinade. Today our clients love this food." Tom Lambing, chef-owner of Times Change in Jackson, Mississippi, serves Smoked Salmon Won Tons, Colorado Bison with Red-Chile Béarnaise, and Grilled Swordfish with Jalapeño-Lime Marmalade to enthusiastic patrons. Even bastions of French cuisine, such as Fleur de

Lys in San Francisco, Le Français in Wheeling, Illinois, Le Bec Fin in Philadelphia, and Le Bernardin in New York City, reach way beyond classical French commandments. "Armed with spice grinders, coconut graters, and rice papers, classically trained chefs are giving haute cuisine a decidedly Asian flavor," reports Florence Fabricant in the *New York Times* (March 25, 1992).

The popularity of these new flavors reflects the huge ethnic influx into North America from Asia, Mexico, Central America, and the Caribbean. In the year 2050, it is estimated that Asians will account for 10 percent of America's population, Latinos 22 percent. The foods, seasonings, and cooking styles of these immigrants permeate our gastronomic lives as witnessed by a succession of ethnic food fads that have swept across North America, including Mexican, Caribbean, Thai, and Chinese. Simultaneously, an avalanche of ethnic cookbooks fills our stores.

For this volume, we gathered the most exciting fusion recipes that we have been cooking at home during the last five years. Guiding us has been the following flavor evaluation system, which acts as a framework when we create recipes and helps improve our flavor memories when we taste them. We hope this system, which is referred to throughout the book, acts as a catalyst for increasing food appreciation and gives creative cooks the confidence to start developing their own fusion recipes.

"Smell"/"Aroma" is the response of our olfactory cells, which occupy about two square inches in the upper reaches of the nasal cavity. "Taste" refers to the sensations of the thousands of taste buds lining the surface of the tongue. Our taste buds differentiate sweet (tip of the tongue), salty (front edges of the tongue), sour (along the sides of the tongue), bitter (at the back of the tongue), and hot/spicy (front and sides of the tongue and along the top and back of the mouth).

"Flavor" is the sensory combination of smell plus taste. Many of the recipes refer to "flavor profile." This involves not only the sensory experiences of smell and taste, but also five terms created to more accurately evaluate food: "low," "middle," and "high" notes, "roundness," and "depth of flavor." Low notes are the deep, earthy, robust, lingering flavors that come from such foods as anchovies, beans, chocolate, dried mushrooms, fish sauce, garlic, and oyster sauce, and from cooking processes such as barbecuing, broiling, browning, smoking, and caramelizing. "Middle notes" are the more subtle flavors, neither as dominant nor as lingering as the low notes, such as those contributed by vegetables, salad greens, chicken, and most fish. "High notes" refer to flavors from citrus juice and its grated zest, chiles, and the fresh floral flavors of herbs and spices. A dish can have low, middle, and high notes yet still not have a "rounded" flavor, which is gained from ingredients such as butter, coconut milk, cream, reduced stocks, salt, and sugar. Used judiciously, these unify the other ingredients and cause the flavors to linger without adding their own dominant taste. "Depth of flavor" describes whether a dish has a broad range of "flavor notes."

For example, this is how we describe the flavor profile of Stir-Fried Coconut Curry Chicken with Bok Choy and Basil. The hoisin sauce, dark sesame oil, and toasted spices in the curry paste contribute rich, lingering low notes. The stir-fried chicken and bok choy provide the basic middle notes, while the basil, ginger, and chiles in the curry paste contribute intriguing high notes. Coconut milk gives the dish an appealing, rounded flavor with a long finishing taste to complete the requirements for a dish that has good depth of flavor.

As part of the overall evaluation of a dish, we take into account the eye appeal, the aroma, the initial taste, and the mouth feel of the food, both in terms of temperature and texture. Then we evaluate the flavor profile, noting if there is a rapid development of full flavor in the mouth and a good aftertaste (whether an appropriate quick drop-off of flavor or a lingering sensation).

We return throughout the book to certain magical flavor combinations and techniques. The blend of hoisin sauce, Dijon mustard, red wine, garlic, and rosemary adds a depth of flavor to many of the barbecue sauces. Sautéing fresh mushrooms over low heat until they become densely textured and intensely flavored is a preliminary cooking step we use to include low notes in stews and omelet fillings. Raw corn kernels, cut from just-picked white corn, add great texture and a sweet high note when included in salads, guacamole, ravioli fillings, and corn bread mixes, and when sprinkled as a garnish across sauces. A dash of low-note oyster sauce stirred into Italian tomato sauces intensifies all the flavors, just as adding freshly ground black pepper to any chocolate dessert adds a depth of flavor to the chocolate.

We have also given menu plans throughout the book. In our opinion, no social activity bonds individuals together, deepens friendships, acts as a catalyst for new adventures, or has a more civilizing effect than sharing food. Yet many home cooks feel intimidated by entertaining. Here are some guidelines that we have found helpful. Don't be influenced by complex "menu of the month" fantasies or the over-decorated table settings pictured in some magazines and entertaining cookbooks. Choose a menu that allows you to spend the most uninterrupted time with your guests. Limit hors d'oeuvres to only one selection. Involve friends by asking them to bring a course. Utilize neighborhood food resources, such as delicatessens, gourmet food shops, pastry stores, and ice cream parlors, to augment your menu. Involve your guests in a brief culinary activity upon arrival, such as folding dumplings, stuffing mushrooms, scattering toppings on pizza dough, filling spring rolls, or slicing *gravlax*. Serve champagne and watch the sense of unease among strangers vanish. Maintain exciting conversation by being prepared, if spirits lag, to ask everyone to either change seats for the next course or move into the living room for dessert and coffee. Hire a kitchen helper to wash dishes as they collect. Invite friends for Saturday and Sunday lunches rather than for dinner. This relieves you of the self-imposed "gourmet dinner menu syndrome," allows guests to arrive and leave during the light of day, gathers the group in a more casual setting, and gives special friends the opportunity to linger for an early supper.

The foregoing is meant only as a guide. Enjoy the cooking process with family and friends. Lean over the bubbling pot and savor the aroma. Think about the food as you eat it. Try to remember the flavors, textures, and visual look of the dish. Relish the experience.

For the Fun of It: Appetizers to Tease the Palate

Marinated Goat Cheese with Pepper Berries, Garlic, and Mint

In this recipe, just a few ingredients and a very simple preparation technique achieve a complex flavor profile. We have created many variations of this recipe by substituting, for example, fresh cilantro or basil for the mint, or by adding to the marinade chopped olives or a few dried tomatoes, softened in hot water and then thinly sliced. The marinated goat cheese also makes a magnificent crown when positioned in the center of a dinner salad. Simply place it under the broiler until slightly warm, about 2 minutes, then add it to the salad.

- Easy
- Serves 6 to 10 as an appetizer.

12-ounce log of goat cheese or 4 to 6
  2- to 3-ounce "rounds"
¾ cup extra-virgin olive oil
1 teaspoon black peppercorns
1 teaspoon white peppercorns
1 teaspoon pink peppercorns
1 teaspoon Szechwan peppercorns
  (optional)
½ teaspoon whole allspice
2 cloves garlic, finely minced
2 tablespoons very finely minced fresh
  ginger
⅓ cup slivered fresh mint leaves
Crackers or thin slices of pumpernickel
  bread

• advance preparation

If using a log of goat cheese, cut it into ½-inch-thick slices. Place the cheese in a single layer in a small, flat nonmetal dish.

In a small saucepan, combine the oil, peppercorns, and allspice. Place over medium-high heat and cook until the peppercorns begin to "pop," about 2 minutes. Immediately stir in the garlic, ginger, and mint, then pour the mixture over the cheese. Gently turn the cheese so that each slice is completely coated. Marinate in the refrigerator for at least 8 hours but for no longer than 3 days.

• last-minute assembling

Bring the cheese to room temperature. Serve with crackers or thin slices of pumpernickel bread.

• menu ideas

A very simple dinner for 4: Start with Marinated Goat Cheese with Pepper Berries, Garlic, and Mint, then follow with Barbecued Chicken Breasts Caribbean served with Pan-fried Potatoes with Rosemary, a tossed green salad, and a premium store-bought ice cream accented with Velvet Chocolate Sauce.

PRECEDING PAGES

Spicy Gravlax with Mango Salsa; Marinated
Goat Cheese with Pepper Berries, Garlic, and Mint;
and Beef Satay with Caribbean Jerk Sauce

Asian Barbecued Quail

Fresh quail, marinated in a spicy Asian herb sauce, then barbecued and cut into quarters, makes a delectable taste treat and adds a note of extravagance to a special party. There is such a big difference in taste between fresh and frozen quail that it is worth the extra effort to locate a butcher who can special-order fresh quail for you. Be sure to ask for boned quail (which means just the breast bones have been removed) because it cooks more quickly than quail that hasn't been boned and is easier to cut into quarters for appetizer portions. To eat, each person holds onto the end of a leg or wing while nibbling the tender, rich-tasting meat. Because roasting or broiling quail results in a rubbery texture, this recipe should be reserved for good weather—unless, of course, you have an indoor grill.

- Easy
- Serves 6 to 8 as an appetizer or 3 as an entrée.

6 fresh quail, preferably with breast bones removed
10 cilantro sprigs, for garnish

• marinade

6 tablespoons freshly squeezed lime juice
¼ cup light brown sugar
¼ cup fish sauce
¼ cup cooking oil
1 tablespoon Asian chile sauce
6 cloves garlic, finely minced
¼ cup finely minced green onions
¼ cup minced fresh mint leaves
¼ cup minced fresh basil leaves

• preparation and cooking

Using a sharp knife or poultry shears, split the quail in half. Rinse the quail, pat dry, and pull off and discard all pin feathers.

Set aside the cilantro sprigs. Combine all of the marinade ingredients.

Approximately 30 minutes prior to barbecuing, toss the quail with the marinade.

If using a gas barbecue or indoor grill, preheat to medium (350°F.). If using charcoal or wood, prepare the fire. When the coals or wood are ash-covered or the gas barbecue or indoor grill is preheated, brush the grill with cooking oil, then lay the quail on the grill, meat side up. Cook about 8 minutes, brushing on extra marinade; then turn the quail over and continue cooking until they just begin to feel firm to the touch, about 14 minutes total cooking time. Cut into the quail; the meat should be slightly pink.

Remove the quail from grill. Cut each one in half again so that each quail has been cut into quarters. Place on a serving platter. Garnish with cilantro sprigs and serve at once.

• menu ideas

For an intimate dinner for 6 friends, serve Asian Barbecued Quail, Shi-itake Mushroom Salad with White Corn and Crisp Rice Sticks, Mussel Soup with Cilantro and Serrano Chiles, and White Chocolate Mousse with Tropical Fruits.

Bruschetta East and West

Bruschetta East and West serves as a good example of the great flavor revolution that we are now experiencing. Innovative young chefs eager to create their own culinary styles, an affluent middle class that travels to far-flung lands, and a huge influx of Asian and Latin immigrants have all helped transform "classic" recipes from different countries into new sensory experiences. In this recipe, Italian *bruschetta,* slices of bread toasted on both sides, then rubbed with olive oil and garlic, serve as a fine platform for Southwestern and Chinese toppings. Other *bruschetta* toppings that we like are salsa, *gravlax,* carpaccio, marinated goat cheese, and stir-fried chicken livers.

- Easy
- Serves 8 to 12 as an appetizer.

Ancho Chile Jam (page 84) (optional)

1 red bell pepper
2 ears white corn, husks removed
1 ripe avocado
2 teaspoons Asian chile sauce
2 teaspoons freshly squeezed lime juice
¼ teaspoon salt
•
1 head Roasted Garlic (page 220) (optional)
2 Japanese eggplants or 1 very small European eggplant
3 small shallots, peeled and finely minced
¼ cup dry sherry
2 tablespoons oyster sauce
1 tablespoon dark sesame oil
½ teaspoon sugar
2 tablespoons cooking oil
Freshly ground black pepper, to taste
1 very narrow baguette (about 1½ inches in diameter)
Extra-virgin olive oil

• advance preparation

Make the Ancho Chile Jam.

Roast the red pepper: Turn the oven setting to broil. Cut off and discard the ends from the pepper. Cut the pepper so it can be flattened into large pieces. Discard the seeds and ribbing. Place the pepper, skin side up, directly on the oven rack. Place the oven rack 4 inches below the broiler heat and roast the pepper until the skin turns black, about 5 minutes. Remove the pepper from the oven and transfer to a plastic bag. After 5 minutes, using your fingers, rub the blackened skin off the pepper. Dice and set aside.

Stand the corn on end and cut off the kernels. Cut the avocado in half, remove the seed, then scoop out the flesh and dice. Combine the roasted red pepper, raw corn, avocado, chile sauce, lime juice, and salt. Taste and adjust seasonings.

Prepare the Roasted Garlic.

If using European eggplant, peel the eggplant. Cut the eggplant into ¼-inch cubes. Set aside the shallots. In a small bowl, combine the sherry, oyster sauce, sesame oil, and sugar. Place a wok or sauté pan over highest heat. Add the cooking oil. When the oil begins to smoke, add the eggplant and shallots. Sauté 15 seconds, then add the sherry mixture. Cover the wok, reduce the heat to medium, and cook the eggplant until it softens, about 4 minutes. During cooking, periodically remove the cover from the wok and stir the eggplant. If necessary, add a splash of dry sherry or water to moisten the eggplant. Taste and adjust seasonings, adding the freshly ground black pepper. Transfer to a plate, cool, and refrigerate if completed more than 30 minutes in advance of serving.

• last-minute cooking

Cut the bread into ¼-inch-thick slices.

Bring the eggplant to room temperature. Preheat the broiler. Place a single layer of bread on a baking sheet, transfer to the oven, and toast on both sides until golden.

Brush one side of the bread slices with olive oil. Spread a very thin layer of Ancho Chile Jam on the oiled side of half the bread slices. Top with the avocado mixture. Spread the roasted garlic and eggplant mixture on the oiled side of the remaining bread slices. Serve at once.

• menu ideas

Late-afternoon appetizers for a gathering of friends: Bruschetta East and West, Scallop and Avocado Tostadas, and Curried Lamb Coins.

Magical Chicken Wings

This recipe is dedicated to those fanatic chicken wing devotees who fasten their attention on how quickly a platter of chicken wings can disappear, regardless of whether napkins are provided or other guests are trying to engage in conversation. These chicken wings, which are glazed with hoisin sauce, chile sauce, garlic, lime juice, and fresh herbs, then roasted to a beautiful mahogany color, have a complex multilevel taste.

- Easy
- Serves 6 to 10 as an appetizer.

4 pounds chicken wings
1 cup hoisin sauce
¾ cup plum sauce
2 teaspoons grated or finely minced lime zest (colored part of skin)
⅓ cup freshly squeezed lime juice
⅓ cup fish sauce
⅓ cup honey
¼ cup dry sherry
1 tablespoon Asian chile sauce
½ cup chopped fresh cilantro
⅓ cup chopped fresh mint
10 cloves garlic, finely minced

• **advance preparation**

Cut off the tips of the chicken wings and save them for making stock. If serving wings in small pieces, cut each in half at the joint. In a bowl large enough to hold the wings, combine all of the remaining ingredients. Add the wings, mix thoroughly, and marinate in the refrigerator for 8 hours.

• **last-minute cooking**

Preheat the oven to 375°F. Line a shallow baking pan with foil. Coat a wire rack with cooking spray and place the rack in the baking pan. Drain the chicken and reserve the marinade. Arrange the wings on the rack and roast for 30 minutes. Baste the wings with the reserved marinade, turn them, and baste again. Continue roasting until the wings turn a mahogany color, another 20 to 30 minutes. Serve hot or at room temperature.

• **menu ideas**

A holiday appetizer party for 12: Magical Chicken Wings (double recipe), Spicy Gravlax with Mango Salsa (double recipe), Crisp Salmon Spring Rolls, and Spicy Red and White Dumplings.

Firecracker Shrimp

In this recipe, a marinade of cilantro, ginger, garlic, tangerine zest and juice, hoisin sauce, honey, and Asian chile sauce is fitted between large shrimps and their shells. The cooked shrimp meat, protected by its armor during barbecuing, boasts an intense shrimp flavor, a sweet tenderness that would be lacking if the shells were removed prior to cooking, and an exciting depth of taste and aroma.

- Easy
- Serves 6 to 10 as an appetizer.

1 pound raw large shrimp, shells on

• **tangerine firecracker marinade**

¼ cup minced green onion
¼ cup chopped fresh cilantro
2 tablespoons finely minced garlic
1 tablespoon finely minced fresh ginger
1 teaspoon grated or finely minced tangerine zest (colored part of skin)
½ cup freshly squeezed tangerine juice
¼ cup hoisin sauce
2 tablespoons thin soy sauce
2 tablespoons honey

1 tablespoon dark sesame oil
1 tablespoon white wine vinegar
1 tablespoon Asian chile sauce
1 tablespoon white sesame seeds, lightly toasted

• **advance preparation and serving**

Using scissors, cut the shrimp shells along the back, then rinse away the veins. In a bowl, combine all of the marinade ingredients and stir well. Set aside ¼ cup marinade to sprinkle over the cooked shrimp.

your fingers, insert the ...ade under the ... marinate 1 hour.
...cue, preheat to ...using charcoal or ...e. When the ...sh-covered or ...preheated, ...rack with oil and ...it. Grill about 2

minutes on each side, brushing on more marinade throughout the cooking process, until the shells turn pink and the shrimp feel firm. Be sure not to overcook the shrimp.

Remove the shrimp from the grill. If serving the shrimp hot, toss with the reserved marinade and serve at once. If serving the shrimp chilled, place in the refrigerator. Remove the shells if you wish. The recipe to this point can be completed up to 8

hours in advance of serving. Just prior to serving, toss the chilled shrimp with the reserved marinade. Transfer to a decorative plate or bowl and serve.

• **menu ideas**

Meal for 2 on a hot summer night: Firecracker Shrimp served with Baby Greens with Blue Cheese-Pecan Dressing, Any Kind of Bread, and Chocolate Sorbet with Mangoes.

Scallop and Avocado Tostadas

What characterizes all successful appetizers is visual power, intriguing textures, and aggressive flavors that heighten everyone's eagerness for later gastronomic triumphs. In this recipe, the high notes of the spicy chile, the sourness of the lime, and the herbaceous taste of the chopped cilantro contribute great depth of flavor. This salsa also makes an excellent filling for papaya and avocado halves, or for omelets.

• Easy
• Serves 6 to 10 as an appetizer.

• **dressing**

¼ cup chopped fresh cilantro or mint leaves
1 whole green onion, finely minced
1 clove garlic, finely minced
3 tablespoons freshly squeezed lime juice
3 tablespoons extra-virgin olive oil
2 tablespoons light brown sugar
1 teaspoon Asian chile sauce
¼ teaspoon salt
•

2 tablespoons cooking oil
1 tablespoon very finely minced fresh ginger
½ pound fresh bay scallops
1 red bell pepper
2 small ripe avocados
Squeeze of lemon or lime juice
30 unsalted tortilla chips
1 whole nutmeg

• **advance preparation**

Combine all of the dressing ingredients and stir well.

Place the cooking oil and finely minced ginger in a 12-inch sauté pan set over high heat. When the ginger begins to sizzle, add the scallops and sauté over high heat until they just begin to feel firm and they lose their raw outside color. Immediately transfer the scallops to a large dinner plate and spread in a thin layer. Cool the scallops to room temperature, then cover and refrigerate.

Stem and seed the red pepper, then chop the flesh into ¼-inch cubes. Cut around the avocado seeds, then twist the avocados to separate each one into 2 halves. Remove the seeds, and, with a large spoon, scoop out the flesh. Squeeze the lemon or lime juice over the avocado flesh, wrap

airtight, and refrigerate. The recipe can be completed to this point up to 4 hours in advance of serving.

• **last-minute assembling**

Place the tortilla chips on a decorative platter. Cut the avocado flesh into ¼-inch cubes. In a medium bowl, combine the scallops, red pepper, avocado, and dressing. Stir to combine evenly, then taste and adjust seasonings. Spoon the salsa onto the tortilla chips. Grate a dusting of nutmeg over the salsa. Serve at once.

• **menu ideas**

Appetizers for an outdoor summer music concert: Scallop and Avocado Tostadas, Magical Chicken Wings, and Barbecued Shrimp Brushed with Creole Butter.

Tuna Carpaccio with Capers, Chiles, and Ginger

In this recipe, seasonings from three different cuisines—Mediterranean, Creole, and Japanese—are fused to achieve a dynamic new flavor combination and visual look. Borrowing from Japanese culinary tradition, very fresh raw tuna is thinly sliced and arranged on a platter. The fish is then dotted with a spicy Ginger Creole Mayonnaise and sprinkled with chopped parsley, lemon zest, and capers. If you can't buy sashimi-grade tuna, called "Number 1 Grade Tuna," at your local market, ask the chef at a good Japanese restaurant to arrange tuna, or other types of raw fish, such as yellowtail, on one of your own decorative platters, then keep the platter refrigerated until ready to serve. Alternatively, in place of the raw tuna, substitute 1 pound cooked and chilled seafood, such as shrimp, crab, or lobster tail meat. As for the Ginger Creole Mayonnaise, use it as a New World tartare sauce for barbecued fish and cooked and chilled seafood, and as the starting point for new kinds of salad dressings.

- Easy
- Serves 6 to 10 as an appetizer.

• ginger creole mayonnaise

1 cup mayonnaise
2 tablespoons Grand Marnier
1 tablespoon freshly squeezed lime juice
2 teaspoons Worcestershire Sauce
1 teaspoon Asian chile sauce
1 tablespoon very finely minced fresh ginger
1 teaspoon finely grated or minced orange zest (colored part of skin)
2 tablespoons chopped fresh cilantro
½ teaspoon salt

•

1 pound raw sashimi-grade tuna filet
¼ cup chopped fresh parsley
2 tablespoons lemon zest threads (colored part of skin)
2 tablespoons capers, rinsed and drained

• advance preparation

In a small bowl, combine all of the ingredients for the Ginger Creole Mayonnaise and mix well. Cover and refrigerate for no longer than 3 days.

Using a very sharp, thin-bladed knife, cut the fish into ¼-inch-thin rectangular slices, each about 1½ inches long and ½ inch across. Keeping the knife blade wet helps prevent the fish from tearing. Arrange the fish on a serving platter. Cover with plastic wrap and refrigerate. The recipe to this point can be completed up to 6 hours in advance of serving.

• last-minute assembling

Set aside the parsley, lemon zest threads, and capers. Place approximately 1 teaspoon Ginger Creole Mayonnaise in the center of each piece of tuna. Sprinkle on the parsley, lemon zest, and capers. Serve at once.

• menu ideas

For a seafood feast: Tuna Carpaccio with Capers, Chiles, and Ginger, Seafood Salad with Fresh Chiles, Anise Seed, and Lime, Sautéed Filet of Sole with Champagne Herb Sauce served with wild rice, and Black and White Bread Pudding for dessert.

Thai Meatballs with Green Curry Sauce

For this recipe we created dramatic contrasts of flavor, color, and texture that intensify appetites for subsequent courses. The meatball ingredients include pork, which is used because of its rich flavor and fat content; cilantro, grated orange zest, and chile sauce, which contribute high floral notes; and oyster sauce, which rounds out, accents, and intensifies the flavors of all the other ingredients. The tender meatballs are dusted with cornstarch and panfried until golden, then placed in a brilliantly colored, spicy Thai green curry sauce.

- Easy
- Serves 6 to 10 as an appetizer.

½ pound ground beef

½ pound ground pork

2 whole green onions, finely minced

¼ cup chopped fresh cilantro, plus
   cilantro sprigs for garnish

4 cloves garlic, finely minced

½ teaspoon grated or finely minced
   orange zest (colored part of skin)

2 tablespoons oyster sauce

1 tablespoon Asian chile sauce

¾ teaspoon freshly grated nutmeg

1 egg

¼ cup cooking oil

¼ cup Thai Green Curry Paste (page 100)

¾ cup coconut milk

½ cup cornstarch

• advance preparation

In a large bowl, combine the beef, pork, green onions, cilantro, garlic, orange zest, oyster sauce, chile sauce, nutmeg, and egg. Mix thoroughly to combine evenly. Rub a little cooking oil on your hands, then, using your hands, form the mixture into 20 small meatballs. Place on a lightly oiled plate and refrigerate.

Prepare the Thai Green Curry Paste: Combine ¼ cup curry paste with the coconut milk and set aside. The recipe to this point can be completed up to 8 hours in advance of serving.

• last-minute cooking

Spread the cornstarch in an even layer on a baking sheet. Add the meatballs and jiggle the baking sheet so that the meatballs turn over and become evenly coated with the cornstarch; then gently shake off all excess cornstarch from each meatball. Place a 12-inch sauté pan over medium-high heat. When the pan becomes hot, add the cooking oil. When the oil just begins to give off a wisp of smoke, add the meatballs. Panfry the meatballs, turning them over in the oil, until they become golden on the outside and are no longer pink in the center, about 4 minutes.

Meanwhile, place the curry paste-coconut milk mixture in a small saucepan and bring to a low simmer. Taste and adjust the seasonings, especially for salt. Pour the sauce into a flat serving dish. Place the meatballs on top of the sauce. Garnish with cilantro sprigs. Serve at once.

• menu ideas

As part of a holiday appetizer party: Thai Meatballs with Green Curry Sauce, Spicy Gravlax with Mango Salsa, Magical Chicken Wings, and Five-Cheese Pizza with Grilled Peppers.

note: For variation, in place of this recipe's meatball mixture, try one of the dumpling fillings from Chapter 2, such as the scallop-ground chicken filling on page 38. Or, for a more radical departure, mix 1 cup bread crumbs into a quadrupled portion of the meat filling, place in a loaf pan, brush on a generous amount of Secret Asian Barbecue Sauce, and bake in a 400°F. oven for approximately 30 minutes. Finish by broiling the meat loaf for 2 minutes in order to caramelize the sauce. What was once a spicy meatball appetizer metamorphoses into a memorable fusion meat loaf.

Hot-and-Sour Chicken Livers

The rich taste and soft texture of chicken livers serve as a perfect platform for culinary adventure. While the following recipe uses garlic, oyster sauce, chile sauce, grated orange zest, and a sprinkling of vinegar to create an "Asian" taste profile, other choices that work well are the Caribbean flavorings of ginger, chiles, nutmeg, allspice, cinnamon, and rum, or the Southwestern Ancho Chile Jam from page 84. The key to this dish is to cook the livers briefly in a blazing hot pan and serve them tender and slightly pink in the center. These livers are delicious in omelets or positioned piping hot on top of a leafy green salad glistening with an extra-virgin olive oil and balsamic vinegar dressing.

- Easy
- Serves 6 to 10 as an appetizer.

1 pound fresh chicken, duck, rabbit, or turkey livers
3 cloves garlic, finely minced
2 small shallots, finely minced
3 tablespoons cognac
2 tablespoons oyster sauce
2 teaspoons dry mustard
2 teaspoons Asian chile sauce
1 teaspoon sugar
½ teaspoon grated or very finely minced orange zest (colored part of skin)
¼ teaspoon five-spice powder
1 tablespoon red wine vinegar, or to taste
20 asparagus tips, 2 small vine-ripened tomatoes, or 1 ounce rice sticks
2 tablespoons cooking oil
Fresh cilantro sprigs, for garnish

• advance preparation

Trim all of the fat from the livers. Cut the livers into bite-sized pieces. Set aside the garlic and shallots. In a small bowl, combine the cognac, oyster sauce, dry mustard, chile sauce, sugar, orange zest, and five-spice powder. Set the vinegar aside.

For the asparagus tips, in a 4-quart saucepan, bring 12 cups water to a vigorous boil. Add the asparagus tips, then as soon as they brighten, transfer to a bowl filled with cold water and ice, chill, then pat dry and set aside. If using tomatoes, remove the stems, cut the tomatoes into ¼-inch slices, then cut each slice in half. If using rice sticks, follow the cooking instructions on page 58. The recipe to this point can be completed up to 8 hours in advance of last-minute cooking.

• last-minute cooking

Place a wok or 12-inch sauté pan over highest heat. When very hot, add the cooking oil and roll around the sides of the pan. When the oil just begins to smoke, add the garlic and shallots. Sauté about 10 seconds, then add the livers. Stir and toss the livers until they lose all raw outside color, then add the cognac sauce. Cook 15 more seconds, then sprinkle on the vinegar. Continue cooking the livers until they take on a slight softness when you press them with a finger, or are still pink in the center, about 2 minutes. Taste and adjust the flavors for sweet (sugar), sour (vinegar), and spice (chile sauce). Transfer the livers to a serving plate and decorate with the cilantro sprigs. Radiate the asparagus outward from the livers, or ring the livers with sliced tomato or crisp rice sticks. Serve at once.

• menu ideas

Since not everyone is equally enthusiastic about chicken livers, serve these with another appetizer, such as Spicy Gravlax with Mango Salsa or Scallop Dumplings in Coconut-Basil Sauce.

Endive Filled with Crab and Fresh Shiitake Mushrooms

These endive cups mounded with fresh crab and shiitake mushrooms provide great visual appeal and flavor impact. The crunchy texture and the slight bitterness of the endive and the richness and low notes of the mushrooms combine to form an intriguing foil to the sweet taste of fresh crab. Either place the filling in the center of a round platter and fan the endive cups around the outside edge so that the guests can help themselves, or for larger parties, fill the endive cups in the kitchen for convenient serving. If fresh crab is unavailable, select one of the easy variations provided at the end of the recipe.

- Easy
- Serves 6 to 10 as an appetizer.

1 freshly cooked, cleaned, and cracked Dungeness crab or ½ pound fresh lump crab meat

¼ pound fresh shiitake mushrooms

2 whole green onions, chopped

2 large heads Belgian endive

1 teaspoon finely minced fresh ginger

3 tablespoons dry sherry

1 tablespoon oyster sauce

2 teaspoons dark sesame oil

½ teaspoon cornstarch

¼ teaspoon sugar

⅛ teaspoon finely ground black pepper

2 tablespoons cooking oil

• **advance preparation**

Remove the crab meat from the shell in large pieces. Check for any small bits of shell, then pull any very large pieces of crab meat into smaller pieces.

Cut off and discard the mushroom stems. Overlap the caps and cut into ¼-inch-thick strips; then combine the strips with the green onions. Cut the ends off the endive and pull apart the leaves. In a small bowl, combine the ginger, sherry, oyster sauce, sesame oil, cornstarch, sugar, and pepper. The recipe to this point can be completed up to 8 hours in advance of serving.

• **last-minute cooking**

Place a sauté pan or wok over highest heat. When the pan becomes very hot, add the oil and tilt the pan so the oil coats the inside surface.

Add the mushrooms and green onions. Sauté 1 minute, then add the crab meat and sauce. Stir and toss the ingredients until the crab is piping hot, about 1 minute. Transfer the crab to a decorative serving plate. Surround with endive cups. Serve at once.

• **menu ideas**

Asian appetizers for a reunion of 8 old friends: Endive Filled with Crab and Fresh Shiitake Mushrooms, Asian Barbecued Quail, and Tricolor Pasta Salad with Asian Peanut Dressing.

note: The key to this dish is always to use fresh crab meat. If unavailable, substitute ½ pound raw shrimp, shelled and deveined. Cut the shrimp widthwise into very thin slices. Alternatively, special-order 1 whole duck breast, boned and skinned, from your butcher; cut the duck into very thin shreds and marinate with 1 tablespoon each oyster sauce and dry sherry. When completing the last-minute cooking stage, first stir-fry or sauté the raw shrimp or duck; set it aside temporarily while cooking the mushrooms and green onions; then return the shrimp or duck to the pan during the last few seconds of cooking.

Crisp Salmon Spring Rolls

Paper-thin Chinese spring roll skins, which are found only in Asian markets and are always sold frozen, bear no resemblance to the thick egg roll skins sold by most supermarkets. The latter, which are made from the same dough as won ton skins, do not work well in this recipe and should not be used. Luckily, spring roll skins are very durable and can be thawed and frozen repeatedly without any deterioration in quality. Chinese chefs usually make a filling from cooled, stir-fried shredded vegetables and meat, but we long ago abandoned this laborious technique and now substitute a raw meat or seafood filling instead. Rolled into long cylinders and double-fried to make them crisper, these spring rolls make extraordinary appetizer-size treats.

• Moderate
• Serves 6 to 10 as an appetizer.

6 dried Asian mushrooms
4 cups loosely packed spinach leaves,
    about 6 ounces
2 whole green onions, ends trimmed
1 pound salmon filet, skin and bones
    removed
1/3 pound ground pork or veal
2 tablespoons thin soy sauce
1 tablespoon dry sherry
1 tablespoon dark sesame oil
1 teaspoon Asian chile sauce
2 tablespoons finely minced fresh ginger
1 tablespoon grated or finely minced
    lemon zest (colored part of skin)
10 sheets spring roll skins
2 eggs, well beaten
Southwest Ketchup (double portion,
    page 42) or Spicy Apricot Sauce
    (page 118)
2 cups cooking oil

• **advance preparation**

Cover the dried mushrooms with very hot water and soak until softened, about 30 minutes. Cut off and discard the stems, then mince the caps. Thoroughly wash the spinach leaves. In a 2½-quart saucepan, bring 1 inch water to a vigorous boil. Add the spinach and turn it in the boiling water until it wilts, about 30 seconds; drain, rinse with cold water, and drain again. Using your hands, press all of the water from the spinach, then mince. Mince the green onions. Chop the salmon into very fine pieces. In a bowl, combine the mushrooms, spinach, green onions, salmon, pork or veal, soy sauce, sherry, sesame oil, chile sauce, ginger, and lemon zest. Mix with your fingers until combined.

Separate the spring roll skins and cut them in half diagonally from corner to corner. Position a spring roll skin so the longest edge is closest to you and the tip is pointing away from you. Form about 1/3 cup filling into a 4-inch-long cylinder shape along the edge closest to you. Using a pastry brush or your fingers, moisten the edges of the spring roll skin with beaten egg. Fold the side corners over the filling. Roll the filling towards the opposite tip, sealing the tip with extra egg. Be sure to roll the spring rolls tightly. Fill and roll the remaining spring rolls. Place on a baking sheet lined with nonstick cooking (parchment) paper and refrigerate, uncovered, for up to 10 hours.

Make one of the dipping sauces.

• **last-minute cooking**

Place a 12-inch frying pan over highest heat. Add the cooking oil. When a piece of spring roll skin or paper-thin slice of fresh ginger bounces across the surface when added to the oil, add 10 spring rolls. Fry on both sides until the spring rolls become light golden, about 2 minutes. During cooking regulate the heat so that the oil is always sizzling but never smoking. Transfer the spring rolls to a wire rack set over a layer of paper towels. Fry the remaining spring rolls.

If the heat is not on high, raise it to high and heat the oil about 1 minute, until very hot but not smoking, about 400°F. Fry the spring rolls a second time, in 2 batches, until they are dark golden, about 1 minute. Drain. Serve immediately with dipping sauce.

• **menu ideas**

Outdoor lunch for 6 on a warm summer day: Crisp Salmon Spring Rolls accompanied by Candied Walnut Salad with Goat Cheese and large bowls of Chilled Tomato and Crab Soup with Avocado Crown.

Spicy Gravlax with Mango Salsa

There is no more elegant or sensual way to begin an evening of festivities than with chilled caviar, freshly shucked raw oysters, or cured fish, such as this spicy *gravlax* balanced atop water crackers or toast points. In this recipe, salmon is cured for 3 days with vodka and the Southeast Asian seasonings of mint, basil, ginger, lime, and fish and chile sauces to achieve a complex flavor profile. The fish is then thinly sliced and accented by the wonderful high notes of the chopped fresh Mango Salsa.

• Moderate
• Serves 8 to 10 as an appetizer.

½ pound salmon filet, skin on
¼ cup chopped fresh mint
¼ cup chopped fresh basil
¼ cup finely minced fresh ginger
4 cloves garlic, finely minced
Grated zest (colored part of skin) of 1
   lime
¼ cup vodka
2 tablespoons fish sauce
2 tablespoons Thai chile sauce
1 tablespoon sugar
1 tablespoon salt
2 ounces cream cheese
30 water crackers

• mango salsa

Flesh from 2 small mangoes, chopped
2 whole green onions, chopped
½ cup chopped fresh cilantro
3 tablespoons freshly squeezed lime
   juice
2 tablespoons brown sugar
2 tablespoons fish sauce
1 teaspoon Asian chile sauce

• advance preparation
  (3 days before serving)

Remove all bones from the salmon. Combine the mint, basil, ginger, garlic, lime zest, vodka, fish sauce, chile sauce, sugar, and salt. Place the salmon and marinade in a small plastic food bag. Seal airtight and place on a tray. Fill an 8-quart pot with cold water and place the pot on top of the salmon. Refrigerate for 3 days, turning the salmon over each day. The ready-to-eat *gravlax* can be stored, uncut, in the refrigerator for up to 1 week.

Prepare the Mango Salsa the day you plan to serve the *gravlax*. In a small bowl, combine all of the ingredients for the salsa.

Up to 4 hours prior to serving the appetizer, scrape most of the marinade off the salmon. Very thinly slice the salmon, keeping the blade wet so the fish does not tear and angling the knife so that no skin is included in each slice. Wrap the slices airtight in plastic wrap and refrigerate.

• last-minute assembling

Spread a very thin layer of cream cheese across each water cracker. Top each water cracker with a slice of *gravlax*, then top with a little Mango Salsa. Serve within 30 minutes.

• menu ideas

For a seafood appetizer and champagne party for 12 hungry friends (double all the recipes): Spicy Gravlax with Mango Salsa, Barbecued Shrimp Brushed with Creole Butter, Crisp Salmon Spring Rolls, and Crab Dumplings with Jade Sauce.

Five-Cheese Pizza with Grilled Peppers

We like rolling pizza dough into a paper-thin sheet, adding a layer of flavorful toppings, baking the pizza in a 550°F. oven so that the crust becomes very crisp, and then serving the dramatically flavored pizza to welcome our dinner guests. In this recipe, dried red chile flakes and chopped fresh basil are added to the pizza dough so that with every bite there is an extra jolt of flavor. The dough can be made 4 hours in advance of serving, then left to slowly rise in the refrigerator. As soon as the dinner guests arrive, roll out the dough and encourage them to help sprinkle on the toppings. For best results, purchase the largest pizza stone that will fit in your oven. The very hot surface of the stone vaporizes all moisture from the dough, which is the only way to produce a perfectly crisp crust.

- Moderate
- Serves 6 to 8 as an appetizer or 2 as a main entrée.

1 teaspoon active dry yeast
2 teaspoons sugar
½ cup warm water (105° to 115°F.)
2 tablespoons extra-virgin olive oil
1 teaspoon salt
2 tablespoons coarsely chopped fresh basil leaves
1 teaspoon crushed red chile flakes
1½ cups bread flour
Flour and cornmeal, for dusting

- toppings

2 Asian eggplants
approximately ¼ cup white wine or dry sherry, 2 tablespoons thin soy sauce, and 2 tablespoons olive oil, for marinating eggplants
1 red bell pepper
1 orange bell pepper
2 tablespoons extra-virgin olive oil
3 cloves garlic, peeled
2 ounces low-moisture, part-skim mozzarella, grated
1 ounce Asiago cheese, grated
1 ounce Provolone, grated
2 ounces soft goat cheese, crumbled
1 teaspoon grated or finely minced lime zest (colored part of skin)
2 tablespoons chopped fresh basil leaves
2 tablespoons imported Parmesan cheese, grated

- advance preparation

Prepare the dough: Sprinkle the yeast and sugar over the warm water. When bubbles appear on the top (after about 5 minutes), the yeast has been activated. (If this does not occur, begin again with a new package of yeast.) Stir in the olive oil and salt. Combine the basil, chile flakes, and flour. Stir the yeast mixture into the flour. Turn the dough onto a lightly floured board and knead until the dough is no longer sticky and has a smooth surface, about 5 minutes.

Lightly oil a bowl, then rotate the dough in the bowl so that it picks up a film of oil. Cover the bowl with a towel and let rise about 1 hour, until doubled in size. The dough can be made 4 hours in advance, but the bowl of dough should be placed in the refrigerator so the dough rises more slowly.

Prepare the eggplant: Cut off and discard the eggplant stems. Cut the eggplant crosswise into ¼-inch "rounds."

Place the white wine or dry sherry, thin soy sauce, and olive oil in a flat dish. Stir, then add the eggplant and turn in the marinade. Marinate for 1 hour, turning the eggplant over every 15 minutes. After 1 hour, turn the oven setting to broil. Line a baking sheet with foil, then spread the eggplant in a single layer on the foil. Place the eggplant 4 inches from the broiler heat, and broil until golden, about 5 minutes. Turn the eggplant over and broil on the other side until golden and soft, about 3 more minutes. Remove the eggplant from the oven, cool to room temperature, and set aside. Makes about ¾ cup.

Grill the peppers. Turn the oven setting to broil. Cut off and discard the ends from the peppers. Cut the peppers so they can be flattened into large pieces. Discard the seeds and ribbing. Place the peppers, skin side up, directly on an oven rack. Place the oven rack 4 inches below the broiler heat. Roast the peppers until the skin turns black, about 5 minutes. Remove the peppers from the oven and transfer to a plastic bag. After 5 minutes, using your fingers, rub the blackened skin off the peppers. Cut the peppers into bite-sized strips, rectangles, or triangles. Set aside.

Set aside the olive oil. Press the garlic through a garlic press, or smash and mince the garlic until it becomes a paste. Set aside the mozzarella, Asiago, Provolone, and goat cheese.

• last-minute assembling and cooking

Preheat the oven to 550°F. (If using a pizza stone, preheat it in the oven for 45 minutes.) Set aside the grated lime zest, chopped basil, and grated Parmesan. Place the pizza dough on a well-floured surface. Using a rolling pin, roll the dough into a 16-by-10-inch rectangle. If using a pizza stone, transfer the dough to a wood pizza paddle (or a sturdy cardboard sheet) that is lightly dusted with flour and cornmeal. Or transfer the dough to a heavy baking sheet lightly dusted with flour and cornmeal.

Spread the toppings evenly across the entire dough, right to the edge, as follows: Gently spread the olive oil across the dough, then add the garlic paste. Sprinkle on the mozzarella, Asiago, and Provolone. Add the eggplant and peppers, then sprinkle on the crumbled goat cheese. Slide the pizza onto the pizza stone, if necessary. Bake the pizza until the dough turns golden and the cheese bubbles, about 12 minutes.

Remove the pizza from the oven. Sprinkle the lime zest, basil, and Parmesan over the surface. Cut pizza into wedges, rectangles, or small appetizer squares. Serve at once.

Curried Lamb Coins

This recipe is another example of how cooking traditions from around the world can be fused to achieve new flavors. A filling made with ground lamb, curry powder, oyster sauce, and ginger is spread along one edge of phyllo dough. The filling and phyllo are then rolled into a cylinder and sliced into bite-sized pieces.

Arranged on a baking sheet lined with nonstick cooking paper, these "coins" can be refrigerated for up to 6 hours prior to baking. Phyllo dough, once available only in specialty markets, is now sold frozen by most supermarkets. Be sure to defrost the package overnight in the refrigerator, and cover the sheets, once unwrapped, with a dry kitchen towel.

- Easy
- Serves 6 to 10 as an appetizer.

6 sheets phyllo dough

½ small red onion

6 cups loosely packed spinach leaves, about 8 ounces

½ pound ground lamb

2 tablespoons finely minced fresh ginger

4 cloves finely minced garlic

1 tablespoon oyster sauce

1 tablespoon curry powder

1 teaspoon sugar

1 teaspoon Asian chile sauce

1 egg

½ cup unsalted butter

• **advance preparation**

If the phyllo dough is frozen, thaw according to the package directions. Peel and mince the onion. Stem and wash the spinach. Thoroughly wash the spinach leaves. In a 2½-quart saucepan, bring 1 inch water to a vigorous boil. Add the spinach and turn it in the boiling water until it wilts, about 30 seconds. Transfer the spinach to a colander to drain, then rinse with cold water and drain again. Using your hands, press all of the water from the spinach, then mince. In a bowl, combine the onion, spinach, lamb, ginger, garlic, oyster sauce, curry powder, sugar, chile sauce, and egg. Mix thoroughly.

Melt the butter. Place 1 sheet of phyllo dough lengthwise in front of you. Lightly brush the entire top of the sheet with butter, then lay a second sheet directly on top and brush lightly with butter. Place a third sheet on top. Add half the meat filling in a long, thin cylinder along the edge closest to you.

Gently roll the phyllo into a cylinder, brushing on a little butter along the top edge in order to seal the cylinder closed.

Lightly brush the top and sides of the cylinder with butter. Using a serrated knife, gently cut the cylinder into 16 1-inch coins. Keeping the coins together, transfer the cylinder, seam side down, to a baking sheet lined with nonstick cooking (parchment) paper. Repeat the process with the remaining phyllo dough and filling. The coins can be refrigerated for up to 6 hours prior to baking.

• **last-minute baking**

Preheat the oven to 375°F. Bake the coins until golden, about 15 minutes. Transfer to a heated serving plate and serve at once.

• **menu ideas**

Super Bowl Appetizer Party for 20 served in front of the big screen (double all recipes): Curried Lamb Coins, Crisp Salmon Spring Rolls, Marinated Goat Cheese with Pepper Berries, Garlic, and Mint, Barbecued Shrimp Brushed with Creole Butter (served chilled), and Magical Chicken Wings.

Beef Satay with Caribbean Jerk Sauce

Skewers of meat or seafood, known as "satays" in Indonesia, are found worldwide. The preparation is done hours in advance, and the last-minute cooking takes only a few minutes. In this recipe, the satay technique is combined with a uniquely Jamaican barbecue sauce called "jerk." The word "jerk" refers to the flavoring mixture of allspice, nutmeg, cinnamon, and fresh chiles, which in Jamaica is rubbed on meat that is then cooked over green all-spice branches. While Jamaicans usu-ally use pork for their jerk, leg of lamb, beef tenderloin, and chicken thigh meat all work well, as do large shrimp that have been split open but left unshelled. Whatever the choice, for a dramatic presentation, gather the cooked skewers, meat end down, cross them into a tepee shape, and position them upright on a round plate.

- Easy
- Serves 6 to 10 as an appetizer.

16 4-inch-long bamboo skewers
1 pound beef tenderloin, trimmed of all fat

• jerk sauce

4 whole green onions, ends trimmed
2 tablespoons fresh thyme leaves
1 teaspoon ground allspice
1 teaspoon salt
1 teaspoon freshly ground black pepper
½ teaspoon freshly ground nutmeg
½ teaspoon ground cinnamon
4 cloves garlic, finely minced
1 tablespoon very finely minced fresh ginger
3 fresh serrano chiles, very finely minced (including seeds)
½ cup hoisin sauce
¼ cup cooking oil
2 tablespoons thin soy sauce
1 tablespoon cider vinegar

• advance preparation

Cover the skewers with hot water and soak for 1 to 24 hours. Trim all fat from the meat. Cut the meat crosswise into ¼-inch-thick slices. Cut the slices in half; there should be approximately 16 pieces.

Preheat a gas grill to 350°F. or pre-heat the oven to 450°F. Grill the green onions until lightly charred, about 4 minutes; or once the oven is preheated, turn the oven setting to broil, place the green onions 4 inches from the broiler heat, and cook on both sides until charred, about 2 minutes. Let the green onions cool to room temperature, then chop.

In a small mixing bowl, combine the green onions with the remaining Jerk Sauce ingredients. Mix well.

Thread one piece of meat onto the end of each skewer. Rub the meat with marinade and refrigerate for 1 to 4 hours.

• last-minute cooking

If using a gas barbecue or indoor grill, preheat to medium (350°F.). If using charcoal or wood, prepare a fire. When the gas barbecue or indoor grill is preheated or the coals or wood are ash-covered, brush the grill with oil, then grill the meat about 2 minutes on each side until it is still a little rare in the center. If broiling the meat, position the broiler rack as close to the heat source as possible, then preheat the oven to 550°F. When the oven is pre-heated, turn the setting to broil. Lay the skewers on a baking sheet and cover the bamboo ends with foil. Then broil the meat about 2 to 4 minutes. Transfer to a serving plate and serve at once.

• menu ideas

Simple dinner for 4: Serve Beef Satay with Caribbean Jerk Sauce and Southwest Caesar Salad with Chile Croutons accompanied by Any Kind of Bread Rolls. Conclude the dinner with store-bought premium ice cream topped with Raspberry Essence.

Wild About Dumplings

Southwestern Panfried Veal Dumplings

Shiu mai, won tons, ravioli, piroshki, *pelmeni,* and kreplach, by whatever name, whatever the filling, or whatever the cooking technique, whether served as an appetizer, an elegant first course, or a main entrée, dumplings are marvelously versatile, stimulate the appetite, and foster conversation. Because high-quality dumpling skins are sold fresh by most supermarkets under the name won ton or gyoza skins, there is never a need to remove the pasta machine from the cupboard. Make the dumpling filling in a few minutes using the food processor and leave the glories of dumpling-folding to your dinner guests. Enlisting them as helpers greatly reduces the preparation time.

- Moderate
- Serves 6 to 10 as an appetizer or 4 as a main entrée

1 red bell pepper
6 cups loosely packed spinach leaves, about 8 ounces
1 ear white corn, husk removed
2 small whole green onions
¼ cup chopped fresh cilantro
¾ pound ground veal
2 cloves garlic, finely minced
1 egg
1 tablespoon oyster sauce
2 teaspoons Asian chile sauce
Southwest Salsa (page 93)
36 won ton skins, preferably round
Cornstarch, for dusting
2 tablespoons cooking oil

PRECEDING PAGE
*Scallop Dumplings
in Coconut-Basil Sauce*

• **advance preparation**

Roast the red pepper: Turn the oven setting to broil. Cut off and discard the ends from the pepper. Cut the pepper so it can be flattened into large pieces. Discard the seeds and ribbing. Place the pepper, skin side up, directly on the oven rack. Place the oven rack 4 inches below the broiler heat and roast the pepper until the skin turns black, about 5 minutes. Remove the pepper from oven and transfer to a plastic bag. After 5 minutes, using your fingers, rub the blackened skin off the pepper. Chop and set aside.

Thoroughly wash the spinach leaves. In a 2½-quart saucepan, bring 1 inch water to a vigorous boil. Add the spinach and turn it in the boiling water until it wilts, about 30 seconds. Transfer the spinach to a colander to drain, rinse with cold water and then drain again. Using your hands, press all of the water from the spinach. Cut the kernels off the corn cob. In a food processor, separately mince the spinach, green onions, and red pepper. In a bowl, combine the spinach, corn, green onions, red pepper, cilantro, veal, garlic, egg, oyster sauce, and chile sauce. Mix with your fingers until thoroughly combined. Prepare the salsa and set aside.

Within 5 hours of cooking, fold the dumplings: If the won tons are square, trim into circles. Add 2 teaspoons filling to the center of each won ton skin. Bring the edges of the skin up around the filling. Place the dumpling in the soft hollow of one hand between your thumb and index finger. Squeeze the "waist"

gently with that same index finger, while also pressing the top and the bottom of the dumpling with the other index finger and thumb. The dumplings should be flat on the bottom. Line a tray with nonstick cooking (parchment) paper, dust the paper with cornstarch, place the dumplings on the paper, and refrigerate uncovered.

• **last-minute cooking**

Combine ½ cup water with ½ cup of the salsa. Reserve the remaining salsa. Place a 12-inch nonstick sauté pan over high heat. Add the cooking oil and immediately add the dumplings. Fry the dumplings until the bottoms turn dark golden, about 2 minutes. Add the salsa-water mixture. Immediately cover the pan, reduce the heat to medium, and steam the dumplings until they are firm to the touch, about 2 minutes.

Remove the cover. Over high heat, continue frying the dumplings until the sauce thickens, about 30 seconds, turning the dumplings over so that they are completely coated with the salsa. Tip the dumplings out onto a heated serving platter, individual appetizer plates, or dinner plates. Serve at once, accompanied by a small dish of the remaining salsa for guests to spoon over the dumplings if they wish.

• **menu ideas**

Appetizers for 8 before testing the newest restaurant in town: Southwestern Panfried Veal Dumplings and Tuna Carpaccio with Capers, Chiles, and Ginger.

Lobster Dumplings
with Chile and Cilantro Accents

For this dish, one of the most beautiful and complex-tasting in this book, lobster dumplings are glazed in a saffron-ginger cream sauce and garnished with dots of Thai chile sauce and a sprinkling of chopped cilantro. After the lobster is steamed, the meat is removed, cut into small pieces, and mixed with ground chicken to bind it into a compact filling. Begin with a live lobster rather than trying to substitute one of the rubbery, overcooked lobsters sold at fish markets.

- Challenging
- Serves 8 to 12 as an appetizer or 4 as a main entrée.

1 1½-pound live lobster
6 cups loosely packed spinach leaves, about 8 ounces
⅓ cup chopped jicama
2 whole green onions, minced
½ pound ground chicken
1 tablespoon finely minced fresh ginger
2 tablespoons thin soy sauce
1 tablespoon dry sherry
¼ teaspoon freshly ground white pepper
40 won ton skins, preferably round
Cornstarch, for dusting

• **sauce**

2 cups whipping cream
½ cup white wine
2 teaspoons dark sesame oil
½ teaspoon salt
Large pinch of saffron
1 tablespoon very finely minced fresh ginger

• **garnish**

¼ cup Thai chile sauce
½ cup chopped fresh cilantro

• **advance preparation**

Over highest heat, bring 4 inches water to a vigorous boil in a large pot. Add the lobster, head first, then cover the pot and steam until the lobster turns bright red, about 6 minutes. Remove the lobster from the water and cool to room temperature. Cut the lobster in half lengthwise with a heavy knife or poultry scissors. Remove all the meat. Crack the claws and remove the meat. Cut the lobster meat into pieces small enough to fit inside the dumplings.

Thoroughly wash the spinach leaves. In a 2½-quart saucepan, bring 1 inch water to a vigorous boil. Add the spinach and turn it in the boiling water until it wilts, about 30 seconds. Transfer the spinach to a colander to drain, then rinse with cold water and drain again. Using your hands, press all of the water from the spinach, then mince. In a large bowl, combine the lobster, spinach, jicama, green onions, chicken, ginger, soy sauce, sherry, and white pepper. Mix with your fingers until thoroughly combined.

Within 5 hours of cooking, fold the dumplings: If the won tons are square, trim into circles. Add 2 teaspoons filling to the center of each won ton skin. Moisten the edges with water and fold the won ton in half over the filling, then pinch the edges together firmly. Moisten each end of the dumpling, then touch the ends together so that the dumplings look like caps. Place the dumplings in a single layer on a baking sheet lined with nonstick cooking (parchment) paper and dusted with cornstarch. Refrigerate uncovered.

Make the sauce: In a small bowl, combine the cream, wine, sesame oil, salt, and saffron, then refrigerate. Separately set aside the ginger and the garnishes.

• **last-minute cooking**

Bring 6 quarts water to a vigorous boil. Add the dumplings and give them a gentle stir. When the dumplings float to the surface, after about 3 minutes, gently tip them into a colander to drain.

While the dumpling water is coming to a boil and the dumplings are cooking, place the sauce in a 12-inch sauté pan. Bring to a vigorous boil over high heat and cook until the sauce thickens enough to lightly coat a spoon, about 2 minutes. Stir in the minced ginger. Taste and adjust seasonings, especially for salt and pepper. Transfer the dumplings to a bowl, add the sauce, and toss gently.

Place the dumplings and sauce on a heated serving platter, appetizer plates, or dinner plates. Garnish the edge of the sauce with dots of chile sauce. Sprinkle on the cilantro and serve at once.

• **menu ideas**

Champagne dinner for 8: Crunchy Wild Rice Salad (double recipe), Lobster Dumplings with Chile and Cilantro Accents (double recipe), and, for dessert, Angels in Heaven accompanied by Far Niente's glorious dessert wine, called Dolce.

Pork and Corn Dumplings in Cilantro Cream

This dish has an intriguing flavor profile and a striking look. Dumplings are filled with ground pork and tender fresh corn kernels, then panfried, placed on a cilantro-and-ginger-infused cream sauce, and garnished with a sprinkling of raw corn kernels. The tender dumplings, which if served alone would taste one-dimensional, need the contrasting high notes from the sauce to create a rounded flavor that lingers long after the last bite. The key is keeping all the ingredients in balance so that no single flavor dominates.

• Moderate
• Serves 6 to 10 as an appetizer or 4 as a main entrée.

2 ears white corn, husks removed
2 whole green onions, minced
2 cloves garlic, finely minced
¾ pound ground pork
1 egg
1 tablespoon oyster sauce
2 teaspoons dry sherry
2 teaspoons dark sesame oil
1 teaspoon Asian chile sauce
36 won ton skins, preferably round
Cornstarch, for dusting
2 tablespoons cooking oil

• **sauce**

1 small bunch cilantro, large stems removed, about 1 cup
1 tablespoon finely minced fresh ginger
1 clove garlic, finely minced
3 serrano chiles, stemmed and minced (including seeds)
¼ cup Homemade Chicken Stock (page 70)
¾ cup whipping cream
1 teaspoon cornstarch
½ teaspoon salt

• **advance preparation**

Stand the corn cobs on end and cut off the kernels. In a bowl, combine half the corn kernels, the green onions, garlic, pork, egg, oyster sauce, dry sherry, sesame oil, and chile sauce. Mix with your fingers until thoroughly combined.

Within 5 hours of cooking, fold the dumplings: If won tons are square, trim into circles. Add 2 teaspoons filling to the center of each won ton skin. Bring the edges of the skin up around the filling. Place the dumpling in the soft hollow of one hand between your thumb and index finger. Squeeze the "waist" gently with that same index finger, while also pressing the top and the bottom of the dumpling with the other index finger and thumb. The dumplings should be flat on the bottom. Line a tray with nonstick cooking (parchment) paper, dust the paper with cornstarch, place the dumplings on the paper, and refrigerate uncovered.

Make the sauce: Place the cilantro, ginger, garlic, chiles, chicken stock, cream, cornstarch, and salt in an electric blender and blend at highest speed until completely liquefied. Set aside.

• **last-minute cooking**

Place the sauce in a 2½-quart saucepan or small sauté pan set over high heat and bring to a vigorous boil. Boil the sauce, stirring, until it thickens enough to lightly coat a spoon, about 2 minutes. Keep the sauce warm.

Place a 12-inch nonstick sauté pan over high heat. Add the cooking oil, then immediately add the dumplings. Fry the dumplings until the bottoms turn dark golden, about 2 minutes. Add ¾ cup water, immediately cover the pan, reduce the heat to medium, and steam the dumplings until they are firm to the touch, about 1 minute. Place the sauce on a heated platter, add the dumplings, scatter the remaining raw corn kernels over them, and serve at once.

• **menu ideas**

Green is the Theme: Pork and Corn Dumplings in Cilantro Cream as a main entrée, then Grilled Vegetable Salad with Tortilla Threads, and, for dessert, a premium mint ice cream topped with Velvet Chocolate Sauce.

Scallop Dumplings in Coconut-Basil Sauce

Panfried dumplings are one of the most memorable taste sensations. Called pot stickers by the Chinese, these dumplings are traditionally filled with ground pork, then panfried and served with dipping sauces of black vinegar and chile oil. The following recipe fuses Asian and contemporary American cooking techniques by replacing the traditional filling with a mixture of diced scallops, ground chicken, and Asian mushrooms. After panfrying the dumplings until their bottoms turn a deep golden, a splash of coconut-basil sauce is added to the pan, then during the last few seconds of cooking, the pan is jostled so that the dumplings capsize and become completely coated with the sauce.

- Moderate
- Serves 6 to 10 as an appetizer or 4 as a main entrée.

6 large dried Asian mushrooms
6 cups loosely packed spinach leaves, about 8 ounces
2 small whole green onions
⅔ pound raw fresh scallops
⅓ pound ground chicken or veal
1 tablespoon finely minced fresh ginger
1 tablespoon oyster sauce
2 teaspoons dry sherry
2 teaspoons dark sesame oil
½ teaspoon Asian chile sauce
36 won ton skins, preferably round
Cornstarch, for dusting
3 tablespoons cooking oil

• coconut-basil sauce

1 tablespoon minced fresh basil leaves
1 small whole green onion, minced
¼ cup Homemade Chicken Stock (page 70)
¼ cup coconut milk
2 tablespoons dry sherry
1 tablespoon oyster sauce
½ teaspoon sugar
½ teaspoon Asian chile sauce

• advance preparation

Cover the dried mushrooms with very hot water and soak until softened, about 30 minutes. Then cut off and discard the stems. Thoroughly wash the spinach leaves. In a 2½-quart saucepan, bring 1 inch water to a vigorous boil. Add the spinach and turn it in the boiling water until it wilts, about 30 seconds. Transfer the spinach to a colander to drain, then rinse with cold water and drain again. Using your hands, press all of the water from the spinach. In a food processor, mince separately the mushrooms, spinach, and green onions. Coarsely chop the scallops. In a bowl, combine the vegetables, scallops, chicken (or veal), ginger, oyster sauce, sherry, sesame oil, and chile sauce. Mix with your fingers until thoroughly combined.

Within 5 hours of cooking, fold the dumplings: If the won tons are square, trim into circles. Add 2 teaspoons filling to the center of each won ton skin. Moisten the edges with water and fold the won ton in half over the filling, then pinch the edges together firmly so that the dumplings look like caps. Place the dumplings in a single layer on a baking sheet lined with nonstick cooking (parchment) paper and dusted with the cornstarch. Refrigerate uncovered.

Combine all of the sauce ingredients and mix well.

• last-minute cooking

Place a 12-inch nonstick sauté pan over high heat. Add the cooking oil and immediately add the dumplings. Fry the dumplings until the bottoms turn dark golden, about 2 minutes. Pour in the sauce. Immediately cover the pan, reduce the heat to medium, and steam the dumplings until they are firm to the touch, about 2 minutes.

Remove the cover. Over high heat, continue cooking the dumplings until the sauce reduces completely, about 1 minute. While cooking, shake the pan so that the dumplings "capsize" and are glazed all over with the sauce. Tip the dumplings out onto a heated serving platter, individual appetizer plates, or dinner plates. Serve at once.

Crab Dumplings with Jade Sauce

In Chinese cooking, dumplings, whether panfried, deep-fried, steamed, or boiled, are served unadorned so that diners can season them according to their own taste with various table condiments. We often stray from that culinary tradition and toss dumplings with salsa, one of the salad dressings from Chapter 3, or a homemade pesto sauce thinned with balsamic vinegar and olive oil. In this recipe, the dumplings are boiled, then combined with a "jade" green sauce that is, all at once, tart, hot, and herbaceous, thanks to such ingredients as vinegar, chile sauce, and mint, cilantro, and basil. Always make the sauce in a blender, which liquefies the ingredients better than a food processor.

- Moderate
- Serves 6 to 10 as an appetizer or 4 as a main entrée.

¾ pound fresh lump crab meat
⅓ pound raw shrimp, shelled and
   deveined
1 egg white
6 dried Asian mushrooms
6 cups loosely packed spinach leaves
1½ tablespoons finely minced fresh
   ginger
1 tablespoon oyster sauce
2 teaspoons dark sesame oil
½ teaspoon Asian chile sauce
¼ teaspoon sugar
36 won ton skins, preferably round
Cornstarch, for dusting
1 tablespoon white sesame seeds

• **sauce**

1 clove garlic, finely minced
1 teaspoon finely grated orange zest
   (colored part of skin)
¼ cup fresh mint leaves
¼ cup fresh cilantro sprigs
8 large fresh basil leaves
1 small whole green onion, chopped
2 tablespoons dry sherry
2 tablespoons white distilled vinegar
2 tablespoons dark sesame oil
1 tablespoon thin soy sauce
2 teaspoons hoisin sauce
2 teaspoons sugar
½ teaspoon Asian chile sauce

• **advance preparation**

Pull the lump crab meat apart into small pieces and discard all shells. Combine the shrimp and egg white in a food processor and process until finely minced. In a medium bowl, combine the crab and shrimp.

Cover the mushrooms with very hot water and soak until soft, about 30 minutes, then cut off and discard the stems. Mince the mushrooms. Remove all the stems from the spinach and thoroughly wash the leaves. Set aside 1 cup spinach leaves. In a 2½-quart saucepan, bring 1 inch water to a vigorous boil. Add the remaining spinach and turn it in the boiling water until it wilts, about 30 seconds. Transfer to a colander to drain, then rinse with cold water and drain again. Add the minced mushrooms, chopped blanched spinach, half the minced ginger, the oyster sauce, sesame oil, chile sauce, and sugar to the crab-shrimp mixture. Using your fingers, thoroughly mix the filling.

Within 5 hours of cooking, fold the dumplings: If the won tons are square, trim into circles. Add 2 teaspoons filling to the center of each won ton skin. Moisten the edges with water and fold the won ton in half over the filling, then pinch the edges together firmly so that the dumplings look like caps. Place the dumplings in a single layer on a baking sheet lined with nonstick cooking (parchment) paper and dusted with cornstarch. Refrigerate uncovered.

Toast the sesame seeds in an ungreased sauté pan until golden; then tip out seeds and set aside.

Make the Jade Sauce: In an electric blender, place the remaining spinach leaves and minced ginger, garlic, orange zest, mint, cilantro, basil, green onion, sherry, vinegar, sesame oil, soy sauce, hoisin sauce, sugar, and chile sauce. Blend until completely liquefied, then refrigerate.

• **last-minute cooking**

Bring the Jade Sauce to room temperature. Bring 6 quarts water to a vigorous boil over highest heat. Add all the dumplings at the same time and stir gently. When all the dumplings float to the surface, after about 2 minutes, gently tip them into a colander. Shake the colander to remove excess water, then transfer the dumplings to a mixing bowl. Gently toss the dumplings with the Jade Sauce, then transfer to a heated serving platter, individual appetizer plates, or dinner plates. Sprinkle on the toasted sesame seeds. Serve at once.

Spicy Red and White Dumplings

More and more Americans are able to travel throughout the world and observe authentic regional cooking techniques. For example, at the famous Lemon Grass Restaurant in Bangkok, we watched the chef rhythmically mince a mound of raw freshwater shrimp with a large number of egg whites until the mixture almost resembled a soufflé. Chopping in green onions, ginger, and a dash of oyster sauce, he used the shrimp filling to create that night's feathery light yet crunchy dumplings. Their color and texture contrasted dramatically with the brilliant red curry sauce with which they were served.

If you do not own a multitiered Chinese steamer, follow the dumpling-folding and cooking instructions described in the recipe for Crab Dumplings with Jade Sauce on page 39.

- Moderate
- Serves 6 to 10 as an appetizer or 4 as a main entrée.

6 cups loosely packed spinach leaves, about 8 ounces

1 medium carrot

2 whole green onions

1 pound raw shrimp, shelled and deveined

3 egg whites

1 tablespoon finely minced fresh ginger

1 tablespoon oyster sauce

1 tablespoon cornstarch

36 won ton skins, preferably round

Cornstarch, for dusting

1 cup Red Curry Sauce (page 126)

1 tablespoon cooking oil

¼ cup chopped fresh cilantro, basil, mint, or chives

• advance preparation

Thoroughly wash the spinach leaves. In a 2½-quart saucepan, bring 1 inch water to a vigorous boil. Add the spinach and turn it in the boiling water until it wilts, about 30 seconds. Transfer the spinach to a colander to drain, then rinse with cold water and drain again. Using your hands, press all of the water from the spinach, then mince in a food processor. Set aside. In a food processor, separately mince the carrot and green onions and set aside. Place the shrimp and egg white in the food processor and pulse on and off several times until the shrimp is finely chopped but still has some texture. Transfer to a bowl and add the spinach, carrot, green onions, ginger, oyster sauce, and cornstarch. Mix with your fingers until thoroughly combined.

Within 5 hours of cooking, fold the dumplings: If the won tons are square, trim into circles. Add 2 teaspoons filling to the center of each won ton skin. Moisten the edges with water and fold the won ton in half over the filling, then pinch the edges together firmly so that the dumplings look like caps. Line a tray with nonstick cooking (parchment) paper, dust the paper with cornstarch, place the dumplings on the paper, and refrigerate uncovered.

Prepare and set aside the Red Curry Sauce. Set aside the herbs.

• last-minute cooking

Place 2 inches water in a Chinese steamer and bring to a vigorous boil. Line the steamer tray with a layer of foil, leaving a few holes around the edges uncovered so that the steam can circulate. Rub cooking oil over the foil, then place the dumplings on the foil. Fit the steamer tier over the pot of boiling water, cover, and steam the dumplings until they feel just firm to the touch, about 3 minutes.

Meanwhile, bring the Red Curry Sauce to a very low simmer, then evenly coat a heated serving platter, individual appetizer plates, or dinner plates with the sauce. Place the dumplings side-by-side on the sauce, sprinkle on the chopped herbs, and serve at once.

Asian Pot Stickers with Southwest Ketchup

We call the sauce that accompanies these dumplings Southwest Ketchup, and it is one of the most versatile in this book. Made with chipotle chiles and tomatoes, it is excellent zigzagged across a plate of barbecued chicken, stirred into sour cream or mayonnaise, or rubbed across pork loin prior to barbecuing. Think about spreading it on toasted hamburger buns, packing it under the shells of jumbo shrimp, or using it to perk up a dull salad dressing. Southwest Ketchup will last for at least a month in a tightly sealed glass jar in the refrigerator.

- Moderate
- Serves 6 to 10 as an appetizer or 4 as a main entrée.

⅓ ounce dried morels or porcini
   mushrooms
3 green onions, white part only
½ pound raw shrimp, shelled and
   deveined
1 egg white
½ pound ground veal
2 tablespoons oyster sauce
1 tablespoon dry sherry
1 teaspoon Asian chile sauce
½ teaspoon sugar
36 won ton skins
Cornstarch, for dusting
¼ cup cooking oil
¼ cup chopped fresh chives or cilantro,
   for garnish
½ cup sour cream or crème fraîche

• southwest ketchup

¼ cup canned chipotle chiles in adobo
   sauce
1¼ cups seeded and finely chopped
   vine-ripened tomatoes, about 4
   medium tomatoes
4 cloves garlic, finely minced
2 shallots, peeled and minced
2 tablespoons cooking oil
2 tablespoons white distilled vinegar
2 tablespoons light brown sugar
¼ teaspoon salt
⅛ teaspoon ground allspice

• advance preparation

Place the dried mushrooms in a small bowl and cover with 2 cups boiling water. When the mushrooms soften, after about 20 minutes, remove them from the water and mince.

Preheat the broiler. Place the green onions on a baking sheet and place 4 inches from the broiler heat. Cook the green onions on both sides until they become slightly charred, about 2 minutes per side, then remove from the oven and mince.

Combine the shrimp and egg white, then mince finely in a food processor. In a medium bowl, combine the mushrooms, green onions, shrimp, veal, oyster sauce, dry sherry, chile sauce, and sugar. Mix with your fingers until thoroughly combined.

Within 5 hours of cooking, fold the dumplings: If won tons are square, trim into circles. Add 2 teaspoons filling to the center of each won ton skin. Bring the edges of the skin up around the filling. Place the dumpling in the soft hollow of one hand between your thumb and index finger. Squeeze the "waist" gently with that same index finger, while also pressing the top and the bottom of the dumpling with the other index finger and thumb. The dumplings should be flat on the bottom. Line a tray with nonstick cooking (parchment) paper, dust the paper with cornstarch, and place the dumplings on the paper. Refrigerate uncovered.

Make the Southwest Ketchup: Purée the chipotle chiles and their liquid in a blender, then force all the pulp through a sieve and discard the seeds. Set aside the tomatoes, garlic, and shallots. Place a 12-inch sauté pan over medium-high heat. Add the 2 tablespoons cooking oil, garlic, and shallots. Sauté briefly, then add the chipotle pulp, tomatoes, vinegar, sugar, salt, and allspice. Bring to a rapid boil and cook until 1 cup remains. Taste and adjust seasonings. Transfer to a glass jar, seal tightly, and refrigerate for up to 1 month.

• last-minute cooking

Set the fresh herbs aside. Place a 12-inch nonstick sauté pan over high heat. Add the ¼ cup cooking oil and immediately add the dumplings. Fry the dumplings until the bottoms turn dark golden, about 2 minutes. Add 1 cup water, immediately cover the pan, reduce the heat to medium, and steam the dumplings until they are firm to the touch, about 2 minutes.

Meanwhile, place the Southwest Ketchup in a small saucepan and bring to a very low simmer. If the sauce is very thick, thin it with chicken stock or white wine so that it is just thick enough to lightly coat a spoon. Taste and adjust seasonings. Spoon the sauce across a heated serving platter, individual appetizer plates, or dinner plates. Place the dumplings in the center of each plate. Place dots of sour cream around the outside edge of the platter or plates, sprinkle on the fresh herbs, and serve at once.

• **menu ideas**

Serve the Asian Pot Stickers with Southwest Ketchup as the main entrée, accompanied by a range of Mexican beers and Southwest Caesar Salad with Chile Croutons.

Creole Salmon Dumplings

In this recipe, a good example of fusion cooking, dumpling skins are filled with salmon, panfried, then steamed in a mildly spicy Creole sauce infused with the flavors of thyme, oregano, garlic, and Cajun hot sauce. Buy the brightest colored fresh salmon and chop it coarsely so that some of the salmon texture is maintained. Because salmon has minimal fat, panfry the dumplings only until they just feel firm to the touch, or the salmon filling will be very dry. One option to consider is adding $\frac{1}{4}$ pound ground pork to the mixture, which helps to keep the dumpling filling moist yet does not lessen the wonderful flavor of salmon.

• Moderate
• Serves 6 to 10 as an appetizer or 4 as a main entrée.

6 dried Asian mushrooms
6 cups loosely packed spinach leaves, about 8 ounces
$\frac{1}{2}$ cup chopped jicama or carrot
2 whole green onions
$\frac{3}{4}$ pound fresh salmon filet, bones and skin removed
1 tablespoon finely minced fresh ginger
1 tablespoon thin soy sauce
1 egg
36 won ton skins, preferably round
Cornstarch, for dusting
2 tablespoons cooking oil

• **sauce**

1 medium-sized vine-ripened tomato
$\frac{1}{4}$ cup whipping cream
2 tablespoons dry vermouth
1 tablespoon oyster sauce
$\frac{1}{2}$ teaspoon Cajun hot sauce
1 tablespoon chopped fresh oregano leaves
1 teaspoon fresh thyme leaves
2 cloves garlic, very finely minced

• **advance preparation**

Cover the dried mushrooms with hot water and soak until softened, about 30 minutes, then discard the stems. Thoroughly wash the spinach leaves. In a 2½-quart saucepan, bring 1 inch water to a vigorous boil. Add the spinach and turn it in the boiling water until it wilts, about 30 seconds. Drain, then rinse with cold water and drain again. Using your hands, press all of the water from the spinach, then mince. In a food processor, separately mince the mushrooms, jicama or carrot, and green onions. Coarsely chop the salmon so some pieces remain in $\frac{1}{4}$-inch cubes. In a bowl, combine the mushrooms, spinach, jicama, green onions, salmon, ginger, soy sauce, and egg. Mix with your fingers until thoroughly combined.

Within 5 hours of cooking, fold the dumplings: If the won tons are square, trim into circles. Add 2 teaspoons filling to the center of each won ton skin. Bring the edges of the skin up around the filling. Place the dumpling in the soft hollow of one hand between your thumb and index finger. Squeeze the "waist" gently with that same index finger, while also pressing the top and the bottom of the dumpling with the other index finger and thumb. The dumplings should be flat on the bottom. Line a tray with nonstick cooking (parchment) paper, dust the paper with cornstarch, place the dumplings on the paper, and refrigerate uncovered.

Make the sauce: Stem, seed, and chop the tomato. In a small bowl, combine the tomato, cream, vermouth, oyster sauce, hot sauce, oregano, thyme, and garlic.

• **last-minute cooking**

Place a 12-inch nonstick sauté pan over high heat. Add the cooking oil and immediately add the dumplings. Fry the dumplings until the bottoms turn dark golden, about 2 minutes. Add the sauce, immediately cover the pan, reduce the heat to medium, and steam the dumplings until they are firm to the touch, about 1 minute. Tip out onto a heated serving platter, individual appetizer plates, or dinner plates. Serve at once.

Spicy Giant Ravioli with Tomatoes, Basil, and Pine Nuts

The key ingredient in the sauce for these ravioli is vine-ripened tomatoes. If good fresh tomatoes are not available, substitute canned chopped tomatoes, preferably the tomato purée imported from Italy and sold in 1-quart cardboard containers. When you make this challenging dish, keep the rest of the menu simple.

• Challenging
• Serves 4 as a main entrée.

3 whole green onions, minced
¾ pound ground chicken or veal
½ pound raw shrimp, shelled, deveined, and cut crosswise into paper-thin slices
2 tablespoons very finely minced fresh ginger
1 tablespoon grated or very finely minced lemon zest (colored part of skin)
1 tablespoon thin soy sauce
1 tablespoon oyster sauce
½ teaspoon freshly ground black pepper
40 egg roll skins
3 eggs, well beaten
1 tablespoon cooking oil

• **sauce**

2 tablespoons olive oil
6 cloves garlic, finely minced
3 shallots, finely minced
½ pound button mushrooms, thinly sliced
1½ pounds vine-ripened tomatoes, seeded and chopped
½ cup chopped fresh basil leaves
1 cup white wine
1 tablespoon oyster sauce
1 teaspoon sugar
1 teaspoon cornstarch

½ teaspoon Asian chile sauce
½ cup pine nuts
4 ounces imported Parmesan cheese, freshly grated

• **advance preparation**

In a mixing bowl, combine the green onions, chicken, shrimp, ginger, half the minced lemon zest, soy sauce, oyster sauce, and pepper; then mix with your fingers until thoroughly combined.

Within 5 hours of cooking, fold the dumplings: Place an egg roll skin on the counter. Add 2 tablespoons filling to the center of the skin. Brush the outside of the skin with beaten egg. Lay another skin on top, then very firmly press the skins together around the outside, making sure there are no air pockets trapped inside the ravioli. Using a knife or a fluted cutter, cut the ravioli into 4-inch circles. Line a tray with nonstick cooking (parchment) paper, rub the paper with 1 tablespoon oil, then place the ravioli on the paper and refrigerate uncovered. Do not stack or overlap ravioli or the pieces will stick together. You should have 20 ravioli.

Make the sauce: Place a 12-inch sauté pan over high heat. When hot, add 2 tablespoons olive oil, the garlic, and shallots. Sauté until the garlic sizzles, then add the mushrooms, tomatoes, and basil. Sauté until the mushrooms lose their volume, about 8 minutes. Add the wine, oyster sauce, sugar, cornstarch, chile sauce, and remaining lemon

zest. Reduce the heat to medium and cook until the sauce thickens slightly. Remove from the heat. If prepared ahead, transfer to a bowl and refrigerate for up to 3 days.

Preheat the oven to 325°F. When heated, toast the pine nuts until golden, about 8 minutes. Set aside the Parmesan cheese.

• **last-minute cooking**

Bring 6 quarts water to a vigorous boil in a pan that is wide enough to enable you to gently lift the ravioli out of the boiling water when done, such as a stew or roasting pan. Lightly salt the boiling water, then gently add all the ravioli. Cook the ravioli until they float to the surface, about 2½ minutes.

While the ravioli water is boiling and the ravioli are cooking, reheat the sauce. If the sauce is thick, thin it with a little white wine or chicken stock. Taste and adjust the seasonings, especially for salt and pepper.

When ready, gently lift the ravioli out of the water with a slotted spoon and place on 4 heated dinner plates. Spoon the sauce over the dumplings, then add the Parmesan cheese and pine nuts. Serve at once.

Ricotta Ravioli with Champagne Mushroom Sauce

Whether the dumpling recipe is Italian or Asian, always buy egg roll skins, won ton wrappers, or gyoza skins instead of making the skins yourself with a pasta machine. Not only will you be spared hours of tedious labor, but these store-bought wrappers will fool even the most educated palate.

- Challenging
- Serves 4 as a main entrée.

20 sun-dried tomatoes
6 cups loosely packed spinach leaves, about 8 ounces
4 whole green onions, minced
¼ cup chopped fresh basil leaves
¼ pound prosciutto, chopped
¾ pound ricotta cheese
⅓ cup freshly grated imported Parmesan cheese
2 tablespoons thin soy sauce
¼ teaspoon freshly ground black pepper
40 egg roll skins
3 eggs, well beaten
1 tablespoon cooking oil

• sauce

2 cloves garlic, finely minced
1 red bell pepper, stemmed and seeded
¼ pound fresh shiitake mushrooms
2 tablespoons slivered fresh basil leaves
2 tablespoons chopped fresh cilantro
¼ cup pine nuts
3 cups dry champagne
1 tablespoon oyster sauce
2 teaspoons dark sesame oil
¼ teaspoon sugar
2 teaspoons cornstarch
2 tablespoons cooking oil

• advance preparation

Cover the sun-dried tomatoes with boiling water and set aside until softened, about 20 minutes, then drain and chop. Thoroughly wash the spinach leaves. In a 2½-quart saucepan, bring 1 inch water to a vigorous boil. Add the spinach and turn it in the boiling water until it wilts, about 30 seconds; drain, rinse with cold water, and drain again. Using your hands, press all of the water from the spinach, then mince. In a bowl, combine the tomatoes, spinach, green onions, basil, prosciutto, ricotta, Parmesan, soy sauce, and pepper. Mix with your fingers until thoroughly combined.

Within 5 hours of cooking, fold the dumplings: Place an egg roll skin on the counter. Add 2 tablespoons filling to the center of the skin. Brush the outside edges of the skin with beaten egg. Lay another skin on top, then very firmly press the skins together around the outside, making sure there are no air pockets trapped inside the ravioli. Using a knife or fluted cutter, cut the ravioli into 4-inch circles. Line a tray with nonstick cooking (parchment) paper, rub the paper with 1 tablespoon oil, then place the ravioli on the paper and refrigerate uncovered. Do not stack or overlap the ravioli or the pieces will stick together.

Prepare the sauce: Preheat the oven to 325°F. Set aside the garlic. Sliver the red pepper. Discard the mushroom stems, overlap the caps, and cut into slivers. Set aside the basil and cilantro. Place the pine nuts in the preheated oven and toast until light golden, about 8 minutes. Place the champagne in a 2½-quart saucepan, bring to a rapid boil, and boil until reduced to 1 cup. Transfer the champagne to a small bowl and add the oyster sauce, sesame oil, sugar, and cornstarch.

• last-minute cooking

Bring 6 quarts water to a vigorous boil in a pan that is wide enough to allow you to gently lift out the ravioli when done, such as a stew or roasting pan. Lightly salt the boiling water, then gently add all the ravioli. When the ravioli float to the surface, after about 2½ minutes, gently lift them out of the water with a perforated spoon and place in the center of 4 heated dinner plates.

While the ravioli water is coming to a boil and the ravioli are cooking, place a 12-inch sauté pan over high heat. Add 2 tablespoons cooking oil and the garlic. When the garlic sizzles, add the red pepper and mushrooms. Sauté 1 minute, then add the sauce.

Bring the sauce to a vigorous boil and cook until thickened, about 1 minute, then remove the sauté pan from the heat. Stir in the basil and cilantro. Spoon the sauce over the ravioli, sprinkle on the pine nuts, and serve at once.

Crisp Won Tons
with Shiitake Cream Sauce

Japanese-born chef Hiro Sone is one of the many young chefs whose fusion food is inspiring home cooks. At his well-known Napa Valley restaurant, Terra, he juxtaposes deep-fried won tons filled with squab livers with a shiitake mushroom cream sauce. Through the surprising contrast of the nutty and resilient won ton skins, the rich pâté-like filling, and the unctuous mushroom-infused cream sauce, he achieves multiple layers of flavor and texture. Fresh, firm livers are essential for this dish.

• Moderate
• Serves 6 to 10 as an appetizer or 4 as a main entrée.

½ pound fresh chicken, rabbit, or turkey liver
2 whole green onions
5 cloves garlic, finely minced
1 shallot, finely minced
1 tablespoon plus 2 cups cooking oil
1 tablespoon oyster sauce
¼ teaspoon sugar
¼ teaspoon freshly ground black pepper
30 won ton skins
2 eggs, well beaten
Cornstarch, for dusting
¼ cup unsalted butter
¼ pound fresh shiitake mushrooms
1 bunch chives, chopped
1 cup whipping cream
½ cup white wine
2 tablespoons thin soy sauce
½ teaspoon Asian chile sauce

• **advance preparation**

Trim all fat from the livers. Cut the large livers in half. Mince the green onions and set aside with 2 finely minced cloves of garlic and the shallot. Place a 12-inch sauté pan over medium-high heat. Add 1 tablespoon of the cooking oil and the green onion mixture. Sauté for about 15 seconds, until the garlic begins to sizzle, then add the livers. Sauté until the livers just feel firm to the touch but are still pink in the center, about 1 minute. Stir in the oyster sauce, sugar, and pepper, then transfer the livers to a plate to cool.

When the livers are cool, cut them into 30 pieces. Place a won ton skin on a work surface so one tip is pointing towards you. Add 1 piece of liver in the upper third of the won ton skin. Brush beaten egg on the won ton skin around the liver. Fold the won ton skin over the liver, then press the won ton skin together so that the liver is completely sealed.

Moisten each end of the long side of the won ton with egg, then touch the 2 ends together. Repeat with the remaining won tons. Lay a single layer of won tons on a baking sheet lined with nonstick cooking (parchment) paper and dusted with cornstarch. Refrigerate, uncovered, for up to 8 hours prior to cooking.

In a small bowl, set aside the butter and remaining garlic. Cut off and discard the mushroom stems. Overlap the mushrooms and cut into ¼-inch-thin strips. In a separate bowl, set aside the chopped chives. In another bowl, combine the cream, wine, soy sauce, and chile sauce.

• **last-minute cooking**

Place a 12-inch sauté pan over highest heat and add the butter-garlic mixture. When the garlic begins to sizzle, add the mushrooms. Sauté a few seconds, then add the sauce. Bring the sauce to a rapid boil and cook over highest heat until the sauce thickens and you can see the surface of the pan while stirring. Remove from the heat.

Meanwhile, place the 2 cups cooking oil in a 12- or 14-inch frying pan and place over highest heat. When the oil becomes hot enough for a slice of ginger to skip across the surface, add half the won tons. Fry the won tons on both sides until golden, about 4 minutes, then remove and drain on a wire rack placed over a layer of paper towels. Fry the remaining won tons.

Spoon the sauce across the surface of 6 to 10 heated appetizer plates. Place the won tons in the center of the sauce. Sprinkle with the chopped chives and serve at once.

• **menu ideas**

A lunch of appetizers for 8: Crisp Won Tons with Shiitake Cream Sauce, Spicy Gravlax with Mango Salsa, Endive Filled with Crab and Fresh Shiitake Mushrooms, and, for dessert, Chocolate Sorbet with Mangoes.

Fusion Salads for Any Occasion

Tropical Salad
with Citrus-Herb Dressing

Home cooks are the beneficiaries of the recent increase in availability of fresh, exotic tropical fruits. Rushed to our supermarkets by a sophisticated transportation system, the choices include lychee, passion fruit, guava, mango, papaya, star fruit, and kiwi. Always choose fruit at the peak of ripeness, except for papaya, which has a more pleasing texture in salads when still quite firm.

• Easy
• Serves 4 to 6 as a salad when accompanying a main entrée.

1 firm papaya
1 ripe avocado
1 pint very small fresh strawberries or other berries
6 cups baby lettuce greens or mixed torn lettuce greens
20 won ton skins
2 cups cooking oil

• **citrus-herb dressing**

1 clove garlic, very finely minced
2 tablespoons very finely minced fresh ginger
¼ cup chopped fresh cilantro
¼ cup chopped fresh mint leaves
1 teaspoon grated lime zest (colored part of skin) and 2 tablespoons freshly squeezed lime juice
1 teaspoon grated orange zest (colored part of skin) and ¼ cup freshly squeezed orange juice
2 tablespoons thin soy sauce
2 tablespoons light brown sugar
¼ cup safflower oil
1 teaspoon Asian chile sauce
¼ teaspoon salt

• **advance preparation**

Remove the papaya skin with a potato peeler; cut the papaya in half, scoop out and discard the seeds, and cut the flesh into cubes. Cut around the avocado seed, then twist the avocado to separate it into 2 halves; remove the seed, then with a large spoon, scoop out the flesh, and cut into bite-sized pieces. If done more than 10 minutes prior to serving, sprinkle the avocado with 1 tablespoon lime or lemon juice, cover snugly with plastic wrap, and refrigerate. Stem the strawberries; if large, cut in half. Wash and pat dry the lettuce.

Cook the won tons. Cut the won tons into ¼-inch-thin strips. Add the cooking oil to a 10-inch skillet set over medium-high heat and heat until a strip of won ton bubbles around the edges and floats across the surface when added to the oil. Scatter half the won ton strips across the oil and cook until very light golden, about 30 seconds. Drain on paper towels, then cook the remaining won tons. Combine all of the ingredients for the salad dressing, then taste and adjust the seasonings. The recipe to this point can be completed up to 4 hours in advance of serving.

• **last-minute assembling**

Place the papaya, avocado, strawberries, and greens in a large bowl. Add only enough salad dressing to moisten the greens, then gently fold in the won tons. Serve at once.

• **menu ideas**

Tropical Salad with Citrus-Herb Dressing, Chinois Butterflied Leg of Lamb, Chocolate Meltdown Cookies with a premium store-bought ice cream.

PRECEDING PAGE
Candied Walnut Salad with Goat Cheese

Baby Greens with Blue Cheese–Pecan Dressing

Easy-to-prepare, flavor-intense food is especially satisfying after a hard day at work. Many a night we have converted a simple salad, similar to this one, into a main entrée by tossing the greens with meat or seafood hot from the wok or barbecue, then accompanied the salad with nothing more than fresh sourdough rolls and glasses of wine. The easy transformation of this salad into a main entrée means a vacation for the cook . . . at least for one night.

• Easy
• Serves 4 to 6 as a salad when accompanying a main entrée.

4 cups baby lettuce greens or torn mixed
    lettuce greens
3 ounces enoki mushrooms
1 red bell pepper, stemmed and seeded
2 whole green onions
¼ cup raw pecans

• blue cheese–pecan dressing

¼ cup crumbled blue cheese
6 tablespoons extra-virgin olive oil
3 tablespoons balsamic vinegar
1½ tablespoons thin soy sauce
¼ teaspoon freshly and finely ground
    black pepper
¼ teaspoon salt, or to taste

• advance preparation

Preheat the oven to 325° F. Wash and dry the lettuce. Cut off and discard the dirty mushroom ends, then separate the mushroom threads. Do not wash. Sliver the red pepper and green onions. Place the pecans on a baking sheet and toast in the preheated oven for 15 minutes. Cool to room temperature, then finely chop and set aside. In a small bowl, combine all of the dressing ingredients, then taste and adjust the seasonings. The recipe to this point can be completed up to 8 hours in advance of serving.

• last-minute assembling

In a large bowl, combine the greens, mushrooms, pepper, and onions. Stir the dressing, then add only enough dressing to the salad to moisten the greens. Sprinkle on the chopped pecans and toss the salad to combine evenly. Taste the greens and adjust the seasonings for salt and pepper. Serve at once.

Watermelon and Sweet Red Onion Salad

John Ash, cookbook author and talented chef for Fetzer Vineyards, created this brilliantly visual and refreshing salad. We tasted it for the first time on a blazing hot day after a tour of the Fetzer organic vegetable garden, from which John, just moments previously, had gathered all of the ingredients. The contrasting tastes and textures of watermelon triangles and thin crisp red onion rings, heightened by a fresh raspberry vinaigrette, served as the perfect beginning to a dinner that included carrot risotto, grilled Sonoma duck, and a summer fruit tart. Although John used anise hyssop, a special type of mint, any fresh mint works well in this salad.

• Easy
• Serves 6 as a salad accompanying a main entrée.

• **raspberry salad dressing**

6 tablespoons Raspberry Essence (page 204)
¼ cup raspberry vinegar
2 tablespoons finely minced shallots
1 tablespoon honey
¼ cup safflower oil
1 teaspoon Asian chile sauce
¼ teaspoon salt
•
2 medium-sized red onions
2 bunches watercress
3 pounds fresh watermelon, preferably both red and yellow
¼ cup anise hyssop or other fresh mint leaves
Fresh berries, for garnish

• **advance preparation**

In a medium bowl, combine all of the dressing ingredients, then taste and adjust the seasonings.

Peel the onions, then cut into ⅛-inch-thin slices and separate into individual rings. Toss the onion rings with the salad dressing and marinate for 2 hours in the refrigerator, turning every 30 minutes.

Remove and discard the woody stems from the watercress, then refrigerate the sprigs. Cut enough watermelon into 1- to 2-inch cubes,

rectangles, triangles, or other shapes, knocking away the seeds, to yield 8 cups. Refrigerate the watermelon. Cut the mint leaves into shreds and set aside. The recipe to this point can be completed up to 8 hours in advance of serving.

• **last-minute assembling**

Arrange a bed of watercress on 6 chilled plates and top with watermelon slices. Arrange the onions attractively on the watermelon. Drizzle the salad dressing over the melon and onions. Garnish with the mint and fresh berries and serve at once.

• **menu ideas**

Summer barbecue for 8: Watermelon and Sweet Red Onion Salad, Thai Barbecued Squab with Banana Salsa (double recipe) accompanied by Any Kind of Bread Rolls and Steamed White Corn with Szechwan Butter Glaze (double recipe), and, for dessert, Chocolate Meltdown Cookies.

Cal-Asian Salad
with Red Sweet Ginger Dressing

A complex-flavored salad dressing featuring red ginger slices in syrup, one of our favorite ingredients, accents the buttery, rich avocado slices, crunchy cucumber, sweet cherry tomatoes, pine forest-scented enoki mushroom threads, and slightly bitter lettuce greens in this salad. Look for red ginger in syrup at Asian markets, but if you can't find it, substitute grenadine and double the amount of minced fresh ginger.

• Easy
• Serves 4 to 6 as a salad accompanying a main entrée.

1 large ripe avocado
Juice from half a lemon
½ hothouse cucumber
2 cups very small cherry tomatoes
3 ounces enoki mushrooms
1 tablespoon white sesame seeds
6 cups baby lettuce greens or torn mixed lettuce greens

• **red sweet ginger dressing**

3 tablespoons red wine vinegar
2 tablespoons juice from jar of red ginger slices in syrup
2 tablespoons safflower oil
1 tablespoon very finely minced fresh ginger
1 teaspoon orange zest (colored part of skin), grated or finely minced
½ teaspoon Asian chile sauce
½ teaspoon salt

• **advance preparation**

Cut around the avocado seed, then twist the avocado to separate into 2 halves. Remove the seed and, with a large spoon, scoop out the flesh. Cut the flesh into thin slices and sprinkle with the lemon juice. Cut the cucumber into ⅛-inch-thin slices, then overlap the slices and cut into ⅛-inch-thin matchsticks. Stem the tomatoes, and if they are not very small, cut in half. Cut off and discard the root ends of the enoki mushrooms, then separate the mushroom stems. Do not wash. Place the sesame seeds in an ungreased sauté pan and toast over medium heat until golden, then tip out and set aside. Wash and pat dry the lettuce.

Combine all the dressing ingredients in a small jar and shake vigorously. Taste and adjust seasonings. The recipe to this point can be completed up to 8 hours in advance of serving.

• **last-minute assembling**

Place the avocado, cucumber, tomatoes, mushrooms, and lettuce in a large salad bowl. Shake the salad dressing, then add only enough dressing to the salad to lightly coat the greens; toss all of the ingredients to combine evenly. Taste the salad and adjust the seasonings, especially for salt and pepper. Sprinkle on the toasted sesame seeds and serve at once.

• **menu ideas**

As a small dish that enhances the assertive flavors of the other courses, serve this with Caribbean Soup with Grilled Prawns and the white chocolate soufflé called Angels in Heaven.

note: For variation, just before serving, toss 1 ounce rice sticks cooked as described on page 58 into the salad, or turn this into an entrée by adding 1 pound cooked, chilled shrimp or fresh crab meat.

Fusion Salads for Any Occasion

Grilled Vegetable Salad with Tortilla Threads

Grilled vegetables, brushed with an oil and vinegar salad dressing, offer many exciting flavor possibilities for cooks. They contribute deep low notes when added to sandwiches, stirred into soups, rolled inside tortillas with grilled meat, and especially when used as an accent in salads. Although the grilled vegetables in this recipe are seasoned with a Chinese marinade, you can create a different type of flavor profile by substituting Southwest Jicama Salad Dressing or the Thai salad dressing from Wok-Seared Beef Salad.

- Moderate
- Serves 4 to 6 as a salad accompanying a main entrée.

2 red or other color bell peppers, stemmed and seeded
1 bunch asparagus
2 zucchini
4 whole green onions
6 cups baby lettuce greens or torn mixed lettuce greens
2 8-inch flour tortillas
2 cups cooking oil

• grilled vegetable salad dressing

2 cloves garlic, very finely minced
2 tablespoons very finely minced ginger
1/4 cup finely minced green onion
1/2 cup finely minced fresh cilantro
1/2 cup balsamic vinegar
1/4 cup thin soy sauce
3 tablespoons dark sesame oil
3 tablespoons safflower oil
4 teaspoons sugar
2 teaspoons Asian chile sauce

• advance preparation

Cut the peppers into long, 1-inch-wide strips. Snap off and discard the tough asparagus ends. Trim off and discard the zucchini ends. Cut each zucchini into 4 long pieces. Trim the ends off the green onions. Wash and pat dry the lettuce.

Cut the tortillas in half, then cut into 1/8-inch-wide strips. Add the cooking oil to a 10-inch skillet set over medium-high heat and heat until a strip of tortilla, when added to the oil, bubbles around the edges and floats across the surface of the oil. Scatter half the tortilla strips across the oil and cook until very light golden, about 30 seconds. Drain on paper towels, then cook the remaining tortillas.

In a rectangular dish, combine all of the dressing ingredients. Up to 8 hours prior to serving the meal, add the peppers, asparagus, zucchini, and green onions, and marinate 2 hours, rotating the vegetables every 30 minutes. Pour off the dressing and set aside half to use as a grilling sauce and half to use as the salad dressing.

If using a gas barbecue or indoor grill, preheat to medium (350°F.). If using charcoal or wood, prepare a fire. When the coals or wood are ash-covered or the gas barbecue or indoor grill is preheated, brush the grill with oil. Grill the vegetables about 5 minutes on each side, until softened and seared with grill marks, brushing on more marinade throughout the cooking process. Cut the vegetables into bite-sized pieces and set aside at room temperature for up to 2 hours, or refrigerate for up to 8 hours.

• last-minute assembling

If the grilled vegetables are refrigerated, bring them to room temperature. In a large salad bowl, combine the grilled vegetables and lettuce greens. Toss the salad ingredients with enough salad dressing to lightly coat them. Add the tortilla threads and gently toss with the salad. Taste and adjust seasonings. Serve at once.

note: Serve this salad with barbecued chicken or fish, or transform it into a main entrée for 4 people by adding 1 1/2 pounds chilled, cooked seafood.

Southwest Jicama Salad

Crunchy white flesh and refreshing sweetness make jicama (Hí kǎ mǎ) an ideal ingredient in salads, an easy appetizer when cut into strips and served with a dipping sauce, and a great texture enhancer when chopped into small pieces and added to dumpling fillings. Although jicama grows to over 20 pounds, it is sold by most supermarkets in 1- to 5-pound sizes.

• Easy
• Serves 4 as a salad accompanying a main entrée.

1½ pounds jicama
6 cups torn mixed lettuce greens

• ancho chile salad dressing

1 dried ancho, mulato, New Mexico, or
   pasilla chile
2 cloves garlic, finely minced
1 small shallot, minced
½ cup chopped fresh cilantro
½ cup extra-virgin olive oil
Grated zest (colored part of skin) from 1
   lime, plus ¼ cup freshly squeezed lime
   juice
1 tablespoon honey
½ teaspoon salt
¼ teaspoon freshly ground black pepper

• advance preparation

Using a knife, cut the skin away from the jicama. Cut the jicama into ⅛-inch-thin slices. Overlap the slices, cut into ⅛-inch-thin matchsticks, each about 2 inches long, and set aside. Wash and pat dry the lettuce.

Prepare the dressing: Stem and seed the dried chile. Place the dried chile in a small bowl, cover with boiling water, and let sit for 20 minutes. Remove the chile from the water, reserving the liquid, place the chile in an electric blender with 2 tablespoons of the soaking liquid, and blend until completely puréed. If necessary, add a few more tablespoons of the liquid so that the flesh is completely puréed. Add the remaining ingredients. Blend, then taste and adjust the seasonings. The recipe to this point can be completed up to 6 hours in advance of serving.

• last-minute assembling

In a large bowl, toss the salad greens with a third of the dressing. Transfer the lettuce to 4 salad plates. Place the jicama in a bowl and toss with only enough dressing to moisten it. Mound the jicama on top of the lettuce in the center of each salad plate. Serve at once.

• menu ideas

Serve this salad on a hot day accompanied by Barbecued Veal Chops with Chinese Herb Marinade, Popovers Scented with Garlic, Cilantro, and Chile, and White Chocolate Mousse with Tropical Fruits.

Shiitake Mushroom Salad with White Corn and Crisp Rice Sticks

Sautéing fresh shiitake mushrooms transforms them into a densely textured, meaty sensation. In this salad everything is prepared in advance with only the brief sautéing of the mushrooms completed at the last moment. Positioned on top of the salad, the mushrooms provide a dramatic flavor, texture, and temperature contrast to the toasted walnuts, sweet raw corn kernels, slightly bitter lettuce greens, and white, extraordinarily crisp rice sticks.

- Moderate
- Serves 4 to 6 as a salad with accompanying a main entrée.

½ pound fresh shiitake mushrooms

3 ears white corn

8 cups baby lettuce greens or torn mixed lettuce greens

1 cup walnut pieces

2 ounces rice sticks

2 cups cooking oil

2 shallots, finely minced

2 cloves garlic, finely minced

1 tablespoon very finely minced fresh ginger

¼ cup unsalted butter

• **cilantro-balsamic salad dressing**

¼ cup chopped fresh cilantro

¼ cup dry sherry

2 tablespoons oyster sauce

1 tablespoon honey

2 teaspoons dark sesame oil

½ teaspoon Asian chile sauce

3 tablespoons walnut oil from France

3 tablespoons balsamic vinegar

• **advance preparation**

Discard the mushroom stems. Overlap the mushroom caps and cut into ⅛-inch-wide strips. Stand the corn on end and cut off the kernels. Wash and pat dry the lettuce. Roast the walnuts as described on page 222.

Cook the rice sticks. Add the cooking oil to a 10-inch skillet set over medium-high heat and heat until the end of a rice stick expands within 2 seconds when placed in the oil. Cook a few rice sticks at a time. As soon as they expand, turn them over and push back into the hot oil to cook 5 more seconds. Drain on paper towels. Store at room temperature. This can be completed up to 5 hours prior to serving.

Combine the shallots, garlic, and ginger, then set aside. In a small bowl, combine the cilantro, dry sherry, oyster sauce, honey, sesame oil, and chile sauce. Stir vigorously. Combine ¼ cup of this mixture with the walnut oil and balsamic vinegar and set aside to use as the salad dressing. Set the remaining mixture aside for cooking the mushrooms. The recipe to this point can be completed up to 8 hours in advance of serving.

• **last-minute assembling**

Place the butter in a 12-inch sauté pan set over high heat. When the butter melts, add the shallots, garlic, and ginger. Sauté until the garlic sizzles, then add the mushrooms. Sauté the mushrooms about 1 minute, then add the sherry-oyster sauce mixture (not the salad dressing). Continue cooking over high heat until the mushrooms soften, about 2 minutes. If the mushrooms become very dry during cooking, moisten them slightly with a splash of dry sherry, white wine, or water.

Place the lettuce, corn, and walnuts in a large bowl. Add just enough dressing to moisten the greens, then toss the salad. Using your fingers, gently fold in the rice sticks. Place the salad on 4 salad plates, then top each one with sautéed mushrooms. Serve at once.

• **menu ideas**

Dinner party for 8: Double the recipes for Creole Salmon Dumplings, Shiitake Mushroom Salad with White Corn and Crisp Rice Sticks, and Santa Fe Corn Bread. Make a single recipe of Chocolate Ginger Mousse with Raspberry Essence for dessert.

Crunchy Wild Rice Salad

A great range of visual and flavor sensations are created in this recipe when wild rice and baby lettuce greens, ingredients not normally associated with Asian food, are matched with crisp won ton strips, rice sticks, and an Asian sweet-sour-spicy dressing. The nutty low-note flavor and slightly resilient texture of the wild rice invite other possible additions to the salad, such as smoked chicken cut into matchstick pieces, enoki mushrooms, grilled bell peppers, and cilantro sprigs.

• Easy
• Serves 6 as a salad accompanying a main entrée.

½ cup wild rice
1 teaspoon salt
4 cups baby lettuce greens or torn mixed
   lettuce greens
½ cup slivered almonds
16 won ton skins
1 ounce rice sticks
2 cups cooking oil

• asian salad dressing

2 tablespoons very finely minced fresh
   ginger
2 cloves garlic, very finely minced
¼ cup red wine vinegar
2 tablespoons thin soy sauce
2 tablespoons dark sesame oil
1 tablespoon plus 1 teaspoon sugar
1 tablespoon hoisin sauce
1 teaspoon dry mustard
1 teaspoon Asian chile sauce
½ teaspoon salt

• advance preparation

Bring 8 cups water to a vigorous boil. Rinse the wild rice, then stir the wild rice and salt into the water. When the water returns to a low boil, reduce the heat to low, cover, and simmer until two thirds of the wild rice grains have puffed, about 40 minutes. Tip the rice into a sieve, then rinse briefly under cold water to prevent further cooking; drain thoroughly and set aside.

Preheat the oven to 325°F.

Wash and pat dry the lettuce. Toast the almonds on a baking sheet in the oven until golden, about 15 minutes.

Cook the won tons and rice sticks: Cut the won tons into ¼-inch-thin strips. Add the cooking oil to a 10-inch skillet set over medium-high heat, and heat until a strip of won ton, when added to the oil, bubbles around the edges and floats across the surface of the oil. Scatter half the won ton strips across the oil and cook until very light golden, about 30 seconds. Remove the won ton strips with tongs or chopsticks, drain on paper towels, then cook the remaining won tons. Test the oil temperature for the rice sticks. When placed in oil, the end of a rice stick should expand within 2 seconds. Cook a few rice sticks at a time. As soon as they expand, turn the rice sticks over and push back into the hot oil to cook 5 more seconds. Remove from the oil with tongs or chopsticks, then drain on paper towels. Store at room temperature.

In a small bowl, combine the dressing ingredients. Stir well, then taste and adjust seasonings. The recipe to this point can be completed up to 5 hours in advance of serving.

• last-minute assembling

Place the greens and wild rice in a large mixing bowl. Add just enough dressing to coat the greens, then toss to combine evenly. Add the nuts, won tons, and rice sticks, gently tossing with the greens. Taste and adjust seasonings. Serve at once.

• menu ideas

For a luncheon party: Crunchy Wild Rice Salad followed by Chilled Tomato and Crab Soup with Avocado Crown, and, for dessert, Ginger Banana Cream Tart Lined with Chocolate.

note: You can easily transform this salad into a main entrée for 4 by adding 1½ pounds cooked, chilled seafood (such as salmon, scallops, shrimp, and crab), or a combination of cooked, chilled seafood and smoked chicken.

Papaya and Avocado Salad

When creating a dish with ingredients from two or more cultures, it is important to keep the flavors in balance. This papaya and avocado salad succeeds because the Ginger Citrus Dressing does not overwhelm the delicate tropical flavor of the fruits. When creating your own salad dressing, test the flavor profile and refine the blend of herbs and spices by dipping a piece of fruit into it, then tasting.

- Easy
- Serves 4 to 6 as a salad when accompanying a main entrée.

1 firm papaya
1 large ripe avocado
Juice from half a lemon
4 cups baby lettuce greens or torn mixed lettuce greens
1 cup pecans
2 ounces rice sticks
2 cups cooking oil

• ginger citrus dressing

2 tablespoons very finely minced fresh ginger
1/3 cup chopped fresh basil leaves
1 teaspoon grated orange zest (colored part of skin) and 1/4 cup freshly squeezed orange juice
1/4 cup balsamic vinegar
1/3 cup light-grade olive oil
1 tablespoon thin soy sauce
1/2 teaspoon Asian chile sauce

• advance preparation

Preheat the oven to 325°F. Using a potato peeler, peel the papaya; then split the papaya in half, scoop out the seeds, and cut the flesh into 1/2-inch cubes. Cut around the avocado pit, then twist the avocado to separate into 2 halves. Remove the pit and, with a large spoon, scoop out the avocado flesh. Cut the avocado into 1/2-inch cubes, sprinkle with the lemon juice, and set aside. Wash and pat dry the lettuce. Toast the pecans on a baking sheet in the preheated oven for 15 minutes. Remove the pecans from the oven and chop.

Place the rice sticks in a paper bag and pull into small bundles of 10 to 14 noodles. Add the cooking oil to a 10-inch skillet set over medium-high heat and heat until the end of a rice stick expands within 2 seconds when placed in the oil. Cook a few rice sticks at a time. As soon as they expand, turn them over and push back into the oil to cook for 5 more seconds. Drain on paper towels. Store at room temperature. This can be completed up to 5 hours prior to serving.

In a small bowl, combine the dressing ingredients. Stir well, then taste and adjust seasonings. The recipe to this point can be completed up to 5 hours in advance of serving.

• last-minute assembling

Using your hands, crumble the rice sticks slightly, then spread across 4 salad plates. Place the papaya, avocado, lettuce, and pecans in a large bowl. Add just enough dressing to lightly coat the greens and toss to combine evenly. Place the salad on top of the rice sticks and serve immediately.

• menu ideas

A complete do-ahead dinner for 8: Start with Spicy Gravlax with Mango Salsa, then serve this salad (double recipe) followed by Veal Stew with Basil, Cilantro, and Baby Carrots (double recipe) accompanied by Jasmine Steamed Rice. Finish with Chocolate Sorbet with Mangoes.

Candied Walnut Salad with Goat Cheese

Nothing lends more of a sense of elegance and sophistication to entertaining than serving a limited menu whose every dish provides the perfect counterpoint and complement to the surrounding courses. For example, begin a dinner with fresh caviar served on thin slices of toasted and buttered baguette; follow with this salad, then Braised Beef with Mushrooms, Thyme, and Asian Accents (made a day in advance) accompanied by Polenta Madness; for dessert, serve fresh berries at their peak of sweetness.

- Easy
- Serves 4 to 6 as a salad when accompanying a main entrée.

1 pound walnut halves
¼ cup honey
¼ cup sugar
¼ teaspoon salt
5 cups baby lettuce greens or torn mixed lettuce greens
2 cups torn arugula leaves
1 small red bell pepper, seeded, stemmed, and slivered
1½ ounces soft goat cheese, crumbled

• herb and walnut oil salad dressing

1 small shallot, peeled and chopped
2 cloves garlic, chopped
2 tablespoons finely minced fresh ginger
2 tablespoons chopped fresh cilantro or basil
¼ cup walnut oil from France
3 tablespoons balsamic vinegar
2 tablespoons thin soy sauce
2 tablespoons white wine
Salt and freshly ground black pepper, to taste

• advance preparation

Preheat the oven to 350°F. Line 2 baking sheets with foil and spray the foil with nonstick cooking spray. Place the walnuts in a small saucepan and cover with hot water. Place the saucepan over high heat and boil the walnuts for 5 minutes. Immediately tip the walnuts into a colander to drain. Place the honey, sugar, ¼ cup water, and the salt in a 2½-quart saucepan. Bring to a boil over medium heat, then add the walnuts and stir until the mixture becomes dry, about 4 minutes. Transfer the nuts to one of the baking sheets, spread in an even layer, place the baking sheet in the preheated oven, and cook the nuts until they turn a light mahogany color, about 12 minutes, turning the nuts over every 5 minutes. Remove the nuts from the oven and transfer to the second baking sheet to cool.

As soon as the nuts are cool enough to handle, after about 4 minutes, separate one from another by rolling them between your fingers for 3 more minutes. When completely cool, set aside ¾ cup candied walnuts for the salad. Transfer the remaining walnuts to an airtight bag and freeze indefinitely.

Wash and pat dry the lettuce. Set aside separately the arugula leaves, red bell pepper, and goat cheese.

Place the dressing ingredients in an electric blender. Blend, then taste and adjust the seasonings. The recipe to this point can be completed up to 8 hours in advance of serving.

• last-minute assembling

In a large bowl, combine the lettuce, arugula, red pepper, and walnuts. Add just enough salad dressing to lightly coat the greens, add the crumbled goat cheese, and toss to mix evenly. Taste and adjust seasonings, then serve at once.

Wok-Seared Beef with Baby Lettuce Greens

The contrast between the hot and cold ingredients in this recipe creates an exciting sensory surprise with every bite. Its success depends on searing very thinly sliced beef in a heavy cast-iron skillet for just a few seconds, then placing the slices on top of lettuce greens, asparagus, and rice sticks that have been tossed in a spicy Thai herb salad dressing. While this recipe calls for a large number of ingredients, it can be pared down and made with just the meat, a simple lettuce mix, and the dressing. In place of the beef, any of the following can be used: thinly sliced chicken breast, leg of lamb, duck breasts, swordfish, salmon, tuna, bay or sea scallops, or squid.

- Easy
- Serves 2 as a main entrée or 4 to 6 as a side dish.

1 pound beef tenderloin, trimmed of all fat
3 cloves garlic, finely minced
½ teaspoon grated or finely minced orange zest (colored part of skin)
2 tablespoons hoisin sauce
2 teaspoons Asian chile sauce
6 cups baby lettuce greens or torn mixed lettuce greens
1 bunch pencil-thin asparagus
2 ounces rice sticks
2 cups cooking oil
1 whole nutmeg

• spicy thai herb salad dressing

2 cloves garlic, finely minced
¼ cup minced fresh mint leaves
¼ cup minced fresh basil leaves
2 tablespoons chopped fresh cilantro
3 tablespoons safflower oil
3 tablespoons freshly squeezed lime juice
2 tablespoons brown sugar
1½ tablespoons fish sauce
1 teaspoon Asian chile sauce

• advance preparation

Cut the meat into very thin bite-sized pieces, about 1 inch long and $\frac{1}{16}$ inch thin. In a small bowl, combine the meat, minced garlic, orange zest, hoisin sauce, and chile sauce, and marinate at least 15 minutes but for no longer than 8 hours.

Wash and pat dry the lettuce. Snap the tough ends off the asparagus. Bring 8 cups water to a rapid boil in a 4-quart saucepan. Add the asparagus. When the asparagus turn bright green, after about 30 seconds, tip them into a colander, then transfer to a bowl filled with cold water and ice. Chill the asparagus, then pat dry. Cut the asparagus into 1-inch lengths.

Cook the rice sticks: Add the cooking oil to a 10-inch skillet set over medium-high heat and heat until the end of a rice stick expands within 2 seconds when placed in the oil. Cook a few rice sticks at a time. As soon as they expand, turn the rice sticks over and push back into

the hot oil to cook 5 more seconds. Drain on paper towels. Store at room temperature.

In a small bowl, combine the dressing ingredients. Stir well, then taste and adjust the seasonings. The recipe to this point can be completed up to 5 hours in advance of serving.

• last-minute assembling

Place the lettuce greens and asparagus in a large bowl. Shake the dressing, add just enough to the salad to lightly coat the greens, and toss to combine evenly. Add the rice sticks and toss gently. Divide the salad among 4 plates.

Place a 12-inch cast-iron skillet over highest heat. Add 1 tablespoon of cooking oil. When the oil just gives off a wisp of smoke, add the beef and stir and toss until it loses its raw outside color, about 1 minute. Immediately position the beef on top of the salad. Grate a fine sprinkling of nutmeg over each serving. Serve at once.

• menu ideas

Romantic dinner for 2: Freshly shucked oysters with Creole Mayonnaise followed by Wok-Seared Beef with Baby Lettuce Greens served with sourdough rolls, and, for dessert, Kahlúa Passion Tiles. Accompany with champagne late into the night.

Seafood Salad with Fresh Chiles, Anise Seed, and Lime

This salad produces bursts of flavor surprises with every bite. Sweet fresh sea scallops, deeply flavored roasted red pepper, buttery, nutty-tasting avocado, slightly salty feta cheese, and herbaceous fresh basil leaves are overlapped, then glazed in a South-western anise salad dressing made with finely minced fresh serrano chiles, garlic, lime juice, and extra-virgin olive oil. Variations we have enjoyed include substituting other oil and vinegar dressings from this chapter, using crab meat or chilled shrimp in place of the scallops, and leaving the seafood out to make a vegetarian salad. Serve this salad and the others in this chapter with chilled Sauvignon Blanc. Its balance of fruiti-ness and acidity makes it one of the few wines that can stand up to the acidity of most salad dressings.

- Easy
- Serves 6 as a first course or 2 as a main entrée.

¾ pound sea scallops
2 red bell peppers
2 ripe avocados
4 ounces feta cheese
30 small fresh basil leaves
6 lime wedges

• southwestern anise salad dressing

1 serrano chile, finely minced (including seeds)
1 clove garlic, finely minced
½ teaspoon grated or finely minced orange zest (colored part of skin)
½ teaspoon grated or finely minced lime zest (colored part of skin) plus ¼ cup freshly squeezed lime juice
2 tablespoons thin soy sauce
2 tablespoons extra-virgin olive oil
1 teaspoon light brown sugar
1 teaspoon ground anise seed

• advance preparation

Bring 6 cups water to a vigorous boil in a 2½-quart saucepan. Add the scallops, reduce the heat to low, and simmer until barely cooked in the center, about 4 minutes. Immedi-ately transfer the scallops to a bowl filled with cold water and ice. When thoroughly chilled, pat the scallops dry and cut into ⅛-inch-thin slices.

Cut the ends off the red peppers. Remove the seeds and ribbing, then flatten the peppers. Turn the oven to broil. Place the peppers, skin side up, on a wire oven rack and place the rack 3 inches from the broiler heat. Broil until the pepper skin turns black, about 5 minutes, then remove the peppers from the oven, cool, and rinse off the black skin. Cut the peppers into 1-inch cubes.

Cut around each avocado seed, twist the avocado to separate it into 2 halves, and remove the seed. Scoop out the flesh with a large spoon and cut into ½-inch slices. If done more than 30 minutes in advance of serving, moisten the avocado with a little lime or lemon juice to prevent discoloration. Cut the feta into 16 small thin squares (about ¾ inch square and ¼ inch thick). Set aside the basil leaves. Set aside the lime wedges.

Within 3 hours of serving, on 6 small plates or 2 dinner plates, overlap the scallops, red pepper, avocado, feta, and basil leaves. Refrigerate.

In a small bowl, combine the dressing ingredients. Stir well, then taste and adjust seasonings.

• serving

Stir the dressing, then drizzle over the top of the salad. Serve with lime wedges.

• menu ideas

Dinner for 6 featuring a fusion of Southwestern-Asian flavors: Pork and Corn Dumplings in Cilantro Cream, Seafood Salad with Fresh Chiles, Anise, and Lime, South-western Pasta with Grilled Vegeta-bles and Goat Cheese, and, for dessert, Chocolate Meltdown Cookies with fresh strawberries.

Tricolor Pasta Salad with Asian Peanut Dressing

This versatile salad, accompanied by Southwestern Fried Chicken or chilled Barbecued Shrimp Brushed with Creole Butter, is an ideal choice for outdoor summer concerts and picnics. It can also be transformed into a main entrée by adding barbecued chicken cut into bite-sized pieces, or chilled cooked shrimp.

- Moderate
- Serves 4 to 6 as a salad when accompanying a main entrée.

½ pound dried, tricolor spiral pasta
1 tablespoon safflower oil
½ bunch pencil-thin asparagus
1 medium carrot
1 small red bell pepper
1 cup matchstick-cut fennel root
½ cup matchstick-cut Japanese or hothouse cucumber
¼ cup raw hazelnuts

• asian peanut dressing

6 tablespoons chunky peanut butter
¼ cup boiling water
½ cup coconut milk
Finely grated or minced zest (colored part of skin) from 1 lime, plus 3 tablespoons lime juice
2 tablespoons heavy soy sauce
1 tablespoon dark sesame oil
1 teaspoon Asian chile sauce
¼ teaspoon salt
½ cup chopped fresh cilantro
2 tablespoons very finely minced fresh ginger
2 cloves garlic, very finely minced

• advance preparation

Preheat the oven to 325°F. Drop the pasta into 6 quarts lightly salted, rapidly boiling water. Over highest heat, cook according to the manufacturer's instructions, about 8 minutes, until firm but no longer raw-tasting. Tip the pasta into a colander and rinse under cold water, then drain thoroughly. Stir the oil into the pasta to prevent sticking.

Snap off and discard the asparagus ends. Bring 2 quarts water to a boil, stir in the asparagus, and cook until they brighten; immediately transfer to a bowl filled with cold water and ice. Leave the hot water in the pot. When the asparagus are cool, cut into 2-inch lengths.

Peel the carrot and cut on a sharp diagonal into ⅛-inch-thin slices; overlap the carrot slices and cut into ⅛-inch-thin matchsticks. Place the carrots in a sieve and pour the boiling water that the asparagus were cooked in over them; immediately transfer the carrots to a bowl of ice water. When chilled, pat the carrots dry with paper towels and set aside. Stem, seed, and cut the bell pepper into ⅛-inch-thin matchsticks. Set aside the fennel root and cucumber. Place the hazelnuts on a baking sheet and place in the preheated oven for about 15 minutes, until golden. Then cool and set aside.

Make the dressing: In a bowl, combine the peanut butter with the boiling water and stir until evenly mixed. Add all of the remaining salad dressing ingredients, stir well, then taste and adjust the seasonings. The recipe to this point can be completed up to 8 hours in advance of serving.

• assembling

Bring all the salad ingredients and the dressing to room temperature. Combine the pasta, vegetables, and nuts so they are evenly mixed. Add the dressing and mix again. Serve at room temperature.

• menu ideas

As part of an outdoor picnic, serve this salad with Magical Chicken Wings, Barbecued Shrimp Brushed with Creole Butter, and Valrhona Cocoa Truffles with fresh fruit.

Southwest Caesar Salad with Chile Croutons

It may be that Caesar ate salad every day in ancient Rome, but it wasn't until nearly two thousand years later that his descendant, Caesar Cardoni, finally decided to add the name "Caesar" to a salad. According to legend, on a busy night in 1922 at Caesar Cardoni's restaurant in the Mexican border town of Tijuana, he tossed baby romaine lettuce leaves with an olive oil and lemon dressing thickened with raw egg yolks, and finished his creation with a few twists of freshly ground black pepper and freshly grated Parmesan cheese. While the question of whether anchovies were included in the original salad is one of the major mysteries facing culinary historians today, we know Caesar would have used hot chile croutons were it not for the timid tastes of his American tourist clientele.

• Easy
• Serves 4 to 6 as a salad when accompanying a main entrée.

2 cups ½-inch bread cubes from good-quality French or sourdough bread, crusts on
¼ cup olive oil
3 cloves garlic, finely minced
1 teaspoon kosher salt
2 teaspoons Asian chile sauce
¼ cup chopped fresh cilantro
2 heads romaine lettuce
3 ears white corn
1 red bell pepper, stemmed and seeded
1 cup freshly grated imported Parmesan cheese

• southwest caesar salad dressing

⅓ cup freshly squeezed lemon juice
1 tablespoon light brown sugar
1 tablespoon thin soy sauce
1 tablespoon mayonnaise
2 tablespoons finely minced chives
½ cup extra-virgin olive oil
Salt and freshly ground black pepper, to taste

• advance preparation

Preheat the oven to 350°F. Set aside the bread cubes. Place the olive oil and 2 cloves of the minced garlic in a small saucepan set over medium heat and cook until the garlic begins to sizzle in the oil, about 30 seconds. Pour the oil into a medium bowl and add the salt, chile sauce, and cilantro. Add the bread cubes and toss to coat evenly with the oil. Transfer the bread cubes to a baking sheet, spread in a single layer, and bake in the preheated oven until quite golden, about 20 minutes. Remove from the oven, transfer the croutons to a second baking sheet, and cool. Croutons can be stored in an airtight container for 1 week, or frozen indefinitely.

Remove the large outside romaine leaves and reserve for another recipe. Tear the inner romaine leaves into bite-sized pieces, then set aside. Remove the corn husks. Stand the corn on end and cut off the kernels; set aside. Mince the red pepper and set aside. Set aside the Parmesan cheese.

Make the dressing: In an electric blender, combine the remaining garlic clove and all the dressing ingredients except the extra-virgin olive oil and salt and pepper. Blend well, then with the motor running, add the olive oil in a thin stream. Taste and adjust seasonings, adding salt and pepper to taste. The recipe to this point can be completed up to 8 hours in advance of serving.

• last-minute assembling

Place the romaine lettuce and raw corn in a large mixing bowl. Add the dressing, croutons, and half the grated cheese; then toss gently with the greens. Taste and adjust seasonings, especially for salt and freshly ground black pepper. Transfer the greens to 4 salad plates. Sprinkle on the red pepper and the remaining grated Parmesan cheese. Serve at once.

• menu ideas

Begin a dinner with this Caesar salad, follow with Creole Sea Scallops with Crab and Asparagus accompanied by Cajun Asian Dirty Rice, and conclude with Fantastic Raspberry Ice Cream with Velvet Chocolate Sauce.

New Wave *Soups* for *Main* Entrées

Homemade Chicken Stock

Homemade chicken stock, which is the foundation for all of the soups in this book as well as one of the basic building blocks for many sauces, is easy to make at home. Over a period of months, stockpile in the freezer all poultry, pork, and veal scraps. Use these scraps, plus fresh chicken wings, and follow the simple procedures outlined here. Always include chicken wings, because it is the wings that contribute more flavor than any other part of the bird. Add no seasonings, including salt, and keep additions such as onion and garlic to a minimum or the stock will become a vegetable soup. Chicken stock can be frozen and thawed repeatedly without any deterioration in quality.

Nowhere in this book do recipes, whether for beef stews or seafood soups, use beef or fish stock. It is an utter waste of time to complete the arduous process of roasting trays of beef shins or dragging pounds of fish heads around the kitchen when chicken stock works just as well. Your dinner guests will devour the food without ever noticing anything different, and you will be spared preparation tasks better suited to restaurant chefs.

If you do not have any homemade chicken stock for recipes calling for a small amount of stock, rather than using canned broth, soak a few dried mushrooms in boiling water, and after the mushrooms soften, use the liquid as a substitute. Make a note to get chicken wings the next time you go to the market, and ready your stockpot for action.

- Easy

5 pounds chicken wings
Poultry, pork, and/or veal scraps (optional)
5 paper-thin slices fresh ginger
2 unpeeled cloves garlic, smashed

• advance preparation

Place the chicken wings and poultry, pork, and/or veal scraps (if using) in a large stockpot. Add enough cold water to cover the wings and scraps by 2 inches. Place over high heat and bring to a very low boil. Reduce the heat to low and skim off the foam that rises to the surface. Add the ginger and garlic. Simmer the stock, partially covered, for 8 hours. Periodically stir the stock, adding more water if necessary to keep the wings covered.

Pour the stock through a colander lined with dampened cheesecloth into a bowl. Discard the solids. The chicken meat will be useless because all the flavor will have escaped into the stock. Set the bowl aside and let the stock cool to room temperature before refrigerating overnight.

After refrigerating the stock overnight, scrape off and discard the hard layer of fat on the surface. Because the stock is highly perishable (stock will spoil after about 4 days of refrigeration), place 1-cup portions of the stock in plastic food bags and freeze. The stock can be thawed and frozen repeatedly.

PRECEDING PAGE

*Chilled Tomato and Crab Soup
with Avocado Crown*

Chicken Soup for All Seasons

It takes boldness and style to make soup the focal point of a dinner. Unfortunately, soups are usually relegated to restaurant dining, perhaps because we mistakenly believe that making soup is difficult, or because of memories of late-night frustration trying to fit soup bowls into the dishwasher along with appetizer and dinner plates. Yet soups often require little or no last-minute attention and vastly simplify every aspect of entertaining. For example, serve one of the dumplings from Chapter 2 as an appetizer, follow with a soup served in large bowls accompanied by plenty of bread, then present a salad course and dessert. Make one or more flavor infusions, such as New World Pesto or Ancho Chile Jam, and place in small bowls on the dining table so that guests can swirl them into their broth. Before long the murmurs of praise at the dining table will rise to a crescendo.

- Easy
- Serves 4 as a main entrée.

4 cloves garlic, finely minced
1 small yellow onion, finely minced
8 small red potatoes
½ pound button mushrooms
1 bunch small carrots
14 sun-dried tomatoes
1 cup parsley sprigs
1 bunch fresh basil leaves, about 1 cup
10 cups Homemade Chicken Stock (page 70)
2 tablespoons oyster sauce
1 tablespoon dark sesame oil
¼ cup New World Pesto (page 103) or Ancho Chile Jam (page 84), optional
¼ cup light-grade olive oil or unsalted butter
6 whole chicken legs, cut in half and skinned

• advance preparation

Combine the garlic and yellow onion. Cut the potatoes into quarters. Wipe the mushrooms with a damp paper towel. Leaving the stems on, cut the mushrooms into quarters. Scrub or peel the carrots. Cut the carrots on a sharp diagonal, rolling each carrot one-quarter turn after every cut. In a large bowl, combine the sun-dried tomatoes, parsley, basil, chicken stock, oyster sauce, and sesame oil.

If using New World Pesto or Ancho Chile Jam, prepare now.

Place the olive oil or butter in a 5-quart stockpot over medium-high heat. When hot, add the garlic and onion and sauté until the onion sizzles and becomes soft, about 8 minutes. Add the potatoes, mushrooms, and carrots, then sauté 5 minutes.

Add the chicken stock mixture, bring to a low simmer, and add the chicken pieces. Simmer until the chicken is cooked, about 30 minutes. Remove the chicken pieces from the soup and cool to room temperature. Remove the meat, cut into bite-sized pieces, and return to the soup. If made more than 3 hours in advance, cool the soup and refrigerate. The recipe to this point can be made up to a day in advance.

• last-minute cooking

Bring the soup to a low simmer. Taste and adjust the seasonings, adding pepper and salt to taste (approximately 2 teaspoons salt). Ladle the soup into 4 large heated bowls. If using one of the flavor infusions, place little spoonfuls around the edge of the soup. Serve at once.

• menu ideas

A meal for 4 on a snowy winter night: Chicken Soup for All Seasons served with Grilled Vegetable Salad with Tortilla Threads and Chocolate Nut Tart.

Caribbean Soup with Grilled Prawns

This Jamaican soup is infused with the flavors of allspice, curry, chiles, and slivered mint leaves and is embellished with barbecued large shrimp (also known as prawns) that are packed with a seasoned butter mixture before they are grilled. Cooking the shrimp with the herb butter trapped under the shell keeps them moist and adds an intense flavor. Once the shrimp are cooked, either slip them out of the shell or add directly to the soup and provide everyone at the table with knives and forks to make shelling easier. Either way, serve the soup in large shallow bowls so your guests can marvel at the size of the shrimp.

- Moderate
- Serves 4 as a main entrée.

1½ pounds large raw shrimp (prawns), about 16 shrimp, shells on

10 cloves garlic

⅔ cup chopped fresh cilantro

½ pound unsalted butter, at room temperature

¼ cup plus 2 tablespoons thin soy sauce

1 tablespoon Asian chile sauce

1 teaspoon ground cinnamon

1 teaspoon ground cloves

2 serrano chiles, stemmed and minced

2 cloves garlic, finely minced

2 shallots, finely minced

3 bell peppers (1 red, 1 yellow, 1 green)

½ pound butternut squash

4 small red-skinned potatoes

2 teaspoons curry powder

1 teaspoon allspice berries, finely ground

4 cups Homemade Chicken Stock (page 70)

1¾ cups coconut milk

1 tablespoon cornstarch

¼ cup fresh mint leaves

⅓ cup fresh cilantro sprigs

Salt, to taste

1 whole nutmeg

• **advance preparation**

Using kitchen scissors, cut the shell along the top length of each shrimp and rinse away the vein. Place the cutting blade in the food processor, and with the motor running, add the garlic through the feed tube. Remove the processor top and add the cilantro, butter, ¼ cup of the soy sauce, the chile sauce, cinnamon, and cloves. Turn the processor on and off in brief pulses until the butter mixture is completely smooth. Set aside ¼ cup seasoned butter.

Pack the remaining butter underneath the shrimp shells. Refrigerate the shrimp.

In a small bowl, combine the chiles, garlic, and shallots. Discard the seeds and stems from the bell peppers. Cut the peppers into ¼-inch cubes. Peel the squash, then cut into ¼-inch cubes. Leave the skin on the potatoes and cut into ¼-inch cubes. In a bowl, combine the peppers, squash, and potatoes.

In a small dish, combine the curry powder and allspice. In a large bowl, combine the chicken stock, coconut milk, and the remaining 2 tablespoons soy sauce.

Place a 4-quart saucepan over medium-high heat. Add the reserved ¼ cup seasoned butter, plus the chiles, garlic, and shallots, and sauté until the garlic sizzles. Add the vegetables and sauté briefly, then add the curry powder and allspice. Sauté the vegetables until the peppers brighten, about 5 minutes. Add the stock mixture and bring to a low simmer. The soup can be made up to 8 hours in advance of last-minute cooking. Cool to room temperature, then refrigerate.

• **last-minute cooking**

Combine the cornstarch with an equal amount of cold water. Shred the mint leaves.

If using a gas barbecue or indoor grill, preheat to medium (350°F.). If using charcoal or wood, prepare a fire. When the coals or wood are ash-covered or the gas barbecue or

indoor grill is preheated, brush the grill with oil, then grill the shrimp about 2 minutes on each side, until the shells turn pink and the shrimp feel firm to the touch and are white in the center.

Reheat the soup, simmering it until the squash and potatoes soften,

about 10 minutes. Stir the corn-starch into the soup. Taste and adjust the seasonings, adding about 2 teaspoons of salt.

Ladle the soup into shallow, wide soup bowls. Place 4 shrimp in each bowl. Sprinkle on the mint and cilantro. Grate a little nutmeg across the surface of each serving. Serve at once.

• menu ideas

For a Jamaican feast: Beef Satay with Caribbean Jerk Sauce followed by big bowls of this soup served with Tropical Salad with Citrus-Herb Dressing, then, for dessert, Chocolate Sorbet with Mangoes.

Hot and Spicy Salmon Soup with Grilled Vegetables

We subscribe to food magazines, buy cookbooks, and dine out often in hopes of discovering recipes with complex flavors that can play starring roles in our future menus. At Southwestern restaurants we learned the wonderful effect grilling can have on vegetables, concentrating their sugar and adding slightly charred, low-note flavors. Before long we put this knowledge to work in this recipe by stirring grilled salmon and vegetables into a hot-spicy broth just prior to serving.

- Easy
- Serves 4 as a main entrée.

2 Japanese eggplants
1 red bell pepper
1 yellow bell pepper
16 spears asparagus
2 medium zucchini
2 ears white corn
1½ pounds salmon filet
East West Marinade (page 186)
6 cups Homemade Chicken Stock
  (page 70)
2 tablespoons cornstarch
Salt

• advance preparation

Trim the stems from the eggplants and discard. Cut each eggplant into 4 long pieces. Seed and stem the bell peppers. Leaving them in large pieces, flatten the peppers so they will lay flat on the grill. Snap off and discard the tough asparagus ends. Cut each zucchini into 3 long pieces. Husk the corn. Remove the bones from the salmon.

Place the East West Marinade in a large bowl. Set aside ½ cup marinade to use for seasoning the soup. Add all of the vegetables and the salmon to the remaining marinade and toss gently to coat evenly. Marinate for 2 hours in the refrigerator, gently tossing the ingredients every 30 minutes.

If using a gas barbecue or indoor grill, preheat to medium (350°F.). If using charcoal or wood, prepare a fire. When the coals or wood are ash-covered or the gas barbecue or indoor grill is preheated, brush the grill with oil, then grill the salmon and vegetables. Grill the salmon about 4 minutes on each side, brushing on more marinade as it cooks. It is better to slightly undercook the salmon because it can finish cooking when added to the soup. Grill the vegetables until they brighten in color, soften, and acquire very light golden grill marks. Do not grill the vegetables until they acquire a heavy char or the soup will taste burned.

Cool the salmon and vegetables to room temperature. Then, using your fingers, pull the salmon into bite-sized pieces, checking to make sure there are no bones. Cut the eggplant, peppers, asparagus, and squash into bite-sized pieces. Stand the corn on its end and cut off the kernels. Set the salmon and vegetables aside, refrigerating if prepared more than 30 minutes ahead of serving. The recipe to this point can be completed up to 8 hours in advance of last-minute cooking.

• last-minute cooking

Bring the chicken stock to a low boil. Stir in the salmon and vegetables. Combine the cornstarch with an equal amount of cold water. When the soup returns to a low boil, stir in the cornstarch. Stir in ⅓ to 1/2 cup East West Marinade, depending on how spicy you want the soup. Taste and adjust seasonings, especially for salt (about 2 teaspoons are needed). Ladle the soup into large bowls and serve at once.

• menu ideas

Highlight this soup with Popovers Scented with Garlic, Cilantro, and Chile, Shiitake Mushroom Salad with White Corn and Crisp Rice Sticks, and, for dessert, fresh berries with Chocolate Meltdown Cookies.

note: Enthusiasts of grilled vegetables, who at the spur of the moment decide to add them to practically everything, should purchase a cast-iron pan that will fit across 2 gas or electric stove burners. These heat up quickly and produce wonderful grilled vegetables without the fuss of setting up the outdoor barbecue.

Wild Mushroom Soup with Puff Pastry Tent

In this recipe, individual bowls of rich-tasting wild mushroom soup are covered with golden puff pastry cut into stars or other fanciful shapes. Even the most restrained guests won't be able to resist peaking under the pastry for a glimpse of the mysterious-looking soup and to savor the aroma. The soup can be prepared a day in advance, leaving only a simple reheating and the baking of the puff pastry to be completed at the last minute. Although using just one type of mushroom produces an acceptable soup, expanding the variety of mushrooms to those with a very firm texture, such as chanterelles, portabellos, and shiitakes, transforms it from the ordinary to the sublime.

- Moderate
- Serves 4 as a main entrée.

½ cup wild rice

½ teaspoon salt, plus more to taste

½ pound small fresh button mushrooms

⅓ pound fresh shiitake mushrooms

⅓ pound fresh chanterelle or portabello mushrooms

1 bunch asparagus

Half a smoked chicken

1 bunch chives, chopped

2 cloves garlic, minced

2 shallots, minced

6 cups Homemade Chicken Stock (page 70)

¼ cup dry sherry

2 tablespoons thin soy sauce

1 tablespoon dark sesame oil

¼ teaspoon white pepper

¼ cup unsalted butter

½ pound store-bought puff pastry

1 tablespoon cornstarch

• advance preparation

Rinse the wild rice. Bring 6 cups water to a vigorous boil, then stir in ½ teaspoon salt and the wild rice. Bring to a low boil, then reduce the heat to low and simmer the wild rice until most of the grains have opened, about 45 minutes. Transfer the wild rice to a colander, rinse under cold water, and drain thoroughly. Set aside.

Wipe all of the mushrooms with a damp cloth. Cut the button mushrooms into ⅛-inch-thin slices. Discard the shiitake stems and cut the caps into ¼-inch-wide strips. Cut the chanterelle mushrooms into ⅛-inch-thin bite-sized pieces.

Snap off and discard the asparagus ends, then cut the asparagus on a diagonal into 1-inch-long pieces. Separate the chicken meat from the bones. Cut the meat into bite-sized pieces. Set aside the chives. Combine the garlic and shallots and set aside.

In a large bowl, combine the chicken stock, sherry, soy sauce, sesame oil, and white pepper.

Place a large sauté pan over medium heat. Add the butter, garlic, and shallots, and sauté until the garlic sizzles. Add the mushrooms and sauté until the mushrooms lose about half their volume and become densely textured, about 15 minutes.

Add the chicken stock mixture to the sauté pan and bring to a

simmer. The soup can be completed to this point up to a day in advance.

• last-minute cooking

Preheat the oven to 350°F. Cut the puff pastry into 4 decorative shapes (such as stars, triangles, circles, or hearts) that are slightly smaller than each soup bowl. Place the puff pastry on a baking sheet in the preheated oven and bake until golden and puffed, about 15 minutes.

Bring the soup to a simmer. Stir in the wild rice and smoked chicken. Combine the cornstarch with an equal amount of cold water and stir into the soup. Stir in the chives and asparagus. Taste and adjust the seasonings, adding about 2 teaspoons salt.

Ladle the soup into 4 large heated soup bowls. Top each one with a puff pastry tent and serve at once.

• menu ideas

For a summer feast: Begin the evening with Creole Salmon Dumplings, followed by Wild Mushroom Soup, then Watermelon and Sweet Red Onion Salad, and, for dessert, Valrhona Cocoa Truffles and sliced fresh peaches.

note: For variation, omit the puff pastry crown, or omit the smoked chicken and stir into the soup just prior to serving ⅓ pound each bay scallops, shelled and deveined shrimp, and thinly sliced raw salmon filet. Or create a masterpiece by stir-frying at the last moment wild or domesticated duck meat, then centering these tender, rich-tasting morsels in the middle of each soup bowl.

Marco Polo Soup

Leftover stews and curries rescued from the depth of the refrigerator are perfect starting points for creating quick main-dish soups. For example, one night we took the leftover tomato, leek, and fresh herb sauce from Braised Chicken East and West, added chicken stock, stirred in more fresh herbs, and intensified the flavors with a judicious addition of salt. Then we rubbed lamb chop meat with Secret Asian Barbecue Sauce, seared the meat in a very hot oven, cut the meat into bite-sized pieces, and mounded it in the center of our 2 soup bowls. Here is a version of that soup.

- Moderate
- Serves 4 as a main entrée.

1 pound meat from leg of lamb
⅓ cup hoisin sauce
¼ cup plum sauce
2 tablespoons heavy soy sauce
1 tablespoon honey
1 to 1½ teaspoons Asian chile sauce
1 small leek, white part only
6 cloves garlic, finely minced
1 small yellow onion, peeled and
  chopped
1 pound button mushrooms, thinly sliced
2 red bell peppers, seeded and chopped
1½ pounds vine-ripened tomatoes,
  seeded and chopped

¼ cup fresh tarragon leaves
4 large sprigs fresh rosemary
6 cups Homemade Chicken Stock
  (page 70)
1 cup white wine
2 tablespoons oyster sauce
1 tablespoon grated or finely minced
  lemon zest (colored part of skin)
1 bunch chives
¼ cup light-grade olive oil
Salt and freshly ground black pepper, to
  taste.

• advance preparation

Trim the fat from the lamb. Cut the lamb into long strips, about 1 inch thick. In a bowl, combine the hoisin sauce, plum sauce, soy sauce, honey, and 1 teaspoon of the chile sauce. Add the lamb, mix well, and marinate at least 1 hour.

Split the leek in half lengthwise, separate and wash each layer, then cut crosswise into ⅛-inch-thin slices. Combine the leek, garlic, onion, and mushrooms.

Combine the bell peppers and tomatoes and set aside. In a large bowl, combine the tarragon, rosemary, chicken stock, wine, oyster sauce, lemon zest, and, if desired, the remaining ½ teaspoon chile sauce.

Place the olive oil in a deep sauté pan or large saucepan over medium heat. When the oil is hot, add the leeks, garlic, onion, and mushrooms, and sauté until the mushrooms expel all their moisture and become very densely textured, about 15 minutes. Add the bell peppers and tomatoes. Bring to a rapid boil, then add the chicken stock mixture. Bring

to a simmer, turn the heat to low, and cook for 30 minutes. If not serving the soup immediately, cool to room temperature and refrigerate. Chop the chives and set aside. The recipe to this point can be completed up to 8 hours in advance of last-minute cooking.

• last-minute cooking

Preheat the oven to 400°F. Line a baking sheet with foil and spray with nonstick cooking spray. Lay the lamb on the baking sheet and cook approximately 15 minutes; the meat should still be very pink in the center. Let cool 5 minutes, then cut crosswise into ⅛-inch-thin slices.

While the meat is cooking, bring the soup to a simmer. Remove the rosemary sprigs. Taste and adjust the seasonings, adding about 2 teaspoons salt.

Spoon the soup into 4 heated soup bowls. Place the lamb in the center of each bowl, garnish with chives, and serve at once.

• menu ideas

For a simple and hearty meal, accompany this soup with Santa Fe Corn Bread and Tropical Salad with Citrus-Herb Dressing; then, for dessert, serve a premium store-bought chocolate ice cream topped with fresh fruit.

Oxtail Soup with Mushrooms and Thyme

Hail to the lowly oxtail, beloved by knowledgeable home cooks who appreciate the rich, intense flavor of the meat, unmatched by any other cut of beef. In this recipe, developed to glorify that special taste, oxtails are first broiled until deep golden, next combined with mushrooms that have been sautéed until shrunken and densely textured, then simmered for hours in an herb-infused broth until the meat becomes succulent. Finally, the soup, with its deep, low-note flavor, is crowned with dollops of sour cream or crème fraîche, the perfect creamy, sour, high-note match to the main ingredients.

- Challenging
- Serves 4 as a main entrée.

3 to 4 pounds oxtails, cut into 2-inch lengths

3 tablespoons white flour

4 ounces bacon or pancetta

4 cloves garlic, finely minced

1 yellow onion, chopped

2 pounds medium-sized button mushrooms, cut in half

8 cups Homemade Chicken Stock (page 70)

2 cups red wine

2 tablespoons heavy soy sauce

½ teaspoon Asian chile sauce

1 tablespoon tomato paste

2 bunches fresh thyme (tied together in a bundle with string)

1 bay leaf

2 bunches baby carrots

1 bunch chives, chopped

Salt and freshly ground black pepper, to taste

½ cup sour cream or crème fraîche

• advance preparation

Place the oxtails in a cast-iron frying pan. Turn the oven setting to broil, place the oxtails in the oven 4 inches from heat, and broil on both ends until golden, about 15 minutes. If using an electric oven, leave the oven door slightly open. Remove the pan from the oven, sprinkle the flour over the oxtails, and broil another 4 minutes.

Meanwhile, place a large heavy stew pot over medium heat. Cut the bacon crosswise into ⅛-inch-thin slices. Add the bacon or pancetta and cook until crisp. Add the garlic, onion, and mushrooms, and sauté until the onions turn brown and the mushrooms become dark and acquire a dense texture, about 20 minutes.

Transfer the oxtails to the stew pot, then place the frying pan used for browning the oxtails on the stove. Turn the heat to high, add 4 cups of the chicken stock and bring to a rapid boil. Scrape the drippings away from the surface of the pan, then pour the stock into the stew pot.

To the stew pot, add the remaining chicken stock, the red wine, soy sauce, chile sauce, tomato paste, thyme, and bay leaf. Bring to a low boil, then cover the pot, reduce the heat to very low, and simmer until the meat is tender, about 3 to 4 hours. If necessary, add water to maintain the original amount of liquid in pot. The recipe to this point can be completed up to a day in advance of serving.

Lightly peel the carrots, trim off the ends, then cut each carrot in half on a diagonal. If prepared more than 1 hour in advance of serving the soup, cover the carrots with cold water and refrigerate. Set aside the chives.

• last-minute cooking

Bring the soup to a simmer. Remove and discard the thyme. Taste and adjust seasonings, adding about 2 teaspoons salt. Add the carrots and simmer in the soup until tender, about 15 minutes.

Place the soup in 4 large heated soup dishes. Add a dollop of sour cream to the center of each dish, sprinkle on the chopped chives, and serve at once.

• menu ideas

Dinner for 8 on a winter night in front of a roaring fire: Bruschetta East and West, Oxtail Soup with Mushrooms and Thyme (double recipe) served with baguettes, Cal-Asian Salad with Red Sweet Ginger Dressing (double recipe), and, for dessert, Kahlúa Passion Tiles.

note: For variation, stir into the soup just before serving 1½ cups cooked wild rice and 2 cups asparagus cut on a diagonal into 1-inch lengths. Simmer until the asparagus turn bright green, about 4 minutes.

Tropical Isle Bouillabaisse

young chefs pull ingredients diverse cultures to create their culinary statements. The following recipe, a bouillabaisse with cal ingredients as coconut , mint, and lemongrass, is the creation of John Barrett, chef at Cafe Nola in Philadelphia. When John cooks this dish at the restaurant, he splits a live lobster in half, sautés it in a heavy skillet, then flames it with brandy before transferring it into the rich soup. While the following recipe omits the lobster, if you love drama in the kitchen, drop a live 1½-pound lobster into 2 inches of rapidly boiling water, cover the pot, and steam for 6 minutes. Remove the lobster from the water and let it cool for 5 minutes, then split in half lengthwise, cut each half into 4 pieces, and transfer the pieces to the soup.

The complex tastes of this soup need only the simplest accompanying dishes, such as Baby Greens with Blue Cheese-Pecan Dressing and, for dessert, Ginger Banana Cream Tart Lined with Chocolate.

- Challenging
- Serves 4 as a main entrée.

3 small lemongrass stems, minced
4 cloves garlic, minced
1 medium-sized red onion, chopped
1 small leek, white part only, chopped
2 small carrots, chopped
10 medium-sized button mushrooms, thinly sliced
1 bunch fresh tarragon, chopped
1 bay leaf
1 teaspoon Asian chile sauce
½ teaspoon salt
1 cup white wine
Large pinch saffron
3 cups Homemade Chicken Stock (page 70)
3 cups coconut milk
½ cup whipping cream
2 vine-ripened tomatoes, seeded and finely chopped
6 tablespoons light-grade olive oil
16 steamer clams
16 small black mussels
16 large raw shrimp, shelled and deveined
½ pound fresh white-fleshed fish, such as sole, halibut, or swordfish
½ pound fresh bay scallops
¼ cup mixed minced fresh cilantro, basil, and mint
¼ cup cognac
Salt and pepper, to taste

• advance preparation

Place together in a bowl the lemongrass, garlic, onion, leek, carrots, and mushrooms. In a small bowl, combine the tarragon, bay leaf, chile sauce, salt, and white wine. In a separate bowl, combine the saffron, chicken stock, coconut milk, cream, and tomatoes.

Place an 8-quart heavy pot over medium-high heat. Add 4 tablespoons of the olive oil and the lemongrass mixture and sauté until the onion begins to turn light golden and the carrots soften, about 10 minutes. Add the wine mixture, bring to a boil, and cook until almost no liquid remains, about 10 minutes. Add the chicken stock mixture, bring to a simmer, turn the heat to low, and simmer 15 minutes. The recipe to this point can be completed up to 8 hours in advance of serving. Cool and refrigerate until ready to continue.

• last-minute cooking

Scrub the clams and mussels, pulling away the beard from each mussel. Split the shrimp in half lengthwise. Cut the fish into ⅛-inch-thin bite-sized rectangular slices.

Bring the soup to a low simmer. Place a 14-inch sauté pan over highest heat and add the remaining 2 tablespoons olive oil. When hot, add the clams and mussels. Cover the pan tightly, shake the pan briefly, and cook until the clams and mussels just begin to open, about 3 minutes.

Using a slotted spoon, transfer the clams and mussels to the soup. Using a fine-meshed sieve, strain all the liquid from the sauté pan into the soup. Stir the remaining seafood into the soup. Stir in the minced herbs and cognac. Taste and adjust the salt and pepper. Fill 4 large heated soup bowls. Serve at once.

Szechwan Noodle Soup with Chicken

The recipe for this soup, which I created for the Big Bowl Restaurant in Chicago, involves stirring strips of grilled chicken into a complex-flavored noodle broth. The secret ingredient is the rich-tasting chicken marinade that gets its depth of flavor from the low notes of hoisin sauce, soy sauce, and dark sesame oil, the high notes of cilantro, green onions, garlic, ginger, and chile sauce, and the rich, roundness of honey. The marinade works wonders as a marinade/barbecue sauce for all meat and seafood, and lasts indefinitely in the refrigerator as long as the cilantro and green onions are left out until the day it is to be used.

- Easy
- Serves 4 as a main entrée.

• marinade

2 whole green onions, trimmed and minced

¼ cup fresh cilantro sprigs, chopped

4 cloves garlic, finely minced

1 tablespoon very finely minced fresh ginger

6 tablespoons dry sherry

¼ cup hoisin sauce

¼ cup thin soy sauce

3 tablespoons red wine vinegar

2 tablespoons dark sesame oil

2 tablespoons honey

1½ tablespoons Asian chile sauce

•

3 whole chicken breasts, boned but not skinned

½ pound dried thin noodles

2 tablespoons cooking oil

1 large carrot

½ pound medium-sized button mushrooms

¼ pound small snow peas

1 bunch chives, chopped

2 tablespoons cornstarch

8 cups Homemade Chicken Stock (page 70)

Salt, to taste

• advance preparation

In a bowl, combine all of the marinade ingredients and stir to combine; then set aside ½ cup to use for seasoning the soup. Rinse the chicken breasts with cold water, then pat dry. Add the chicken breasts to the marinade and marinate in the refrigerator for at least 1 hour and no longer than 8 hours.

In a large stockpot over highest heat, bring 6 quarts water to a vigorous boil. Add the noodles and cook until they soften but are still firm, about 5 minutes. Immediately tip the noodles into a colander, rinse with cold water, and drain thoroughly. Add the cooking oil to the noodles, then transfer to a bowl, cover, and refrigerate.

Peel the carrot. Cut on a sharp diagonal into ⅛-inch-thin slices; then overlap the slices and cut into ⅛-inch slivers. Cut the mushrooms into ⅛-inch-thin slices. Snap the ends off the snow peas and remove the fiber running along the edge. Set aside the chives. The recipe to this point can be completed up to 8 hours in advance of last-minute cooking.

• last-minute cooking

If using a gas barbecue or indoor grill, preheat to medium (350°F.). If using charcoal or wood, prepare a fire. When the coals or wood are ash-covered or the gas barbecue or indoor grill is preheated, brush the grill with oil and place the chicken on it. Cook about 4 minutes on each side, brushing on more of the marinade, until the chicken feels firm to the touch and has just lost its raw color in the center. Remove the chicken and allow to cool for 5 minutes.

Meanwhile, combine the cornstarch with an equal amount of cold water and set aside. Bring the stock to a boil in a 4-quart saucepan, then add the noodles, vegetables, and the ½ cup of reserved marinade. When the soup comes to a low boil, stir in the cornstarch mixture. Taste and adjust the seasonings in the soup, adding about 2 teaspoons salt. Cut the chicken breasts into halves, then cut each half into ¼-inch-thin strips. Stir half the strips into the soup. Ladle the soup into 4 large heated soup bowls, then scatter the remaining strips of chicken on top. Sprinkle with the chives and serve at once.

• menu ideas

Dinner for 4: Szechwan Noodle Soup with Chicken, a big garden salad, hot rolls, and a premium store-bought ice cream topped with fresh fruit.

New Wave Soups for Main Entrées

Chilled Tomato and Crab Soup with Avocado Crown

This is a spicy Asian gazpacho, made with chopped vine-ripened tomatoes, sweet raw corn kernels, floral-tasting papaya, nutty avocado, and intensely herbaceous fresh cilantro and mint. Rising from the center of each soup bowl, a crown of creamy guacamole adds a silky texture, rich taste, and dramatic color contrast.

- Moderate
- Serves 4 as a main entrée.

• guacamole

½ large ripe avocado
2 tablespoons minced green onion
1 tablespoon chopped fresh cilantro
½ teaspoon Asian chile sauce
2 teaspoons freshly squeezed lemon juice
¼ teaspoon salt

• chilled tomato soup

¾ pound fresh crab meat
3 pounds vine-ripened tomatoes
2 ears white corn
1 ripe avocado
1 small firm papaya
¼ cup chopped fresh cilantro
¼ cup chopped fresh mint leaves
3 cloves garlic, very finely minced
3 shallots, very finely minced
3 tablespoons extra-virgin olive oil
1 cup Homemade Chicken Stock (page 70)
2 tablespoons fish sauce
1 teaspoon Asian chile sauce
Salt, to taste
1 lime
¼ cup sour cream

• advance preparation

Make the guacamole: Place the avocado flesh, green onion, cilantro, chile sauce, lemon juice, and salt in a food processor fitted with a chopping blade and purée; then taste and adjust seasonings. Transfer the guacamole to a small bowl, press plastic wrap over the surface, and refrigerate. Use within 8 hours.

Pick through the crab meat to remove all shell and cartilage, then set the meat aside. Cut 1½ pounds of the tomatoes into quarters, place in the food processor, and purée. Chill the liquid.

Remove the seeds from the remaining tomatoes and coarsely chop the tomatoes. Stand the corn on end and cut off all of the kernels. Cut around the avocado seed. Twist the avocado to separate into 2 halves, remove the seed, and scoop out the flesh and cut into ¼-inch-thin bite-sized rectangles. Using a vegetable peeler, remove the skin from the papaya; split the papaya in half, scrape away the seeds, and cut into ¼-inch-thin bite-sized rectangles. Set aside the cilantro, mint, garlic, and shallots.

Place a 10-inch sauté pan over medium heat. Add the olive oil, garlic, and shallots, and sauté a few seconds until the garlic sizzles. Add the chicken stock and bring to a low boil, then remove the sauté pan from the heat. Cool the stock to room temperature.

Add the tomato purée, chopped tomatoes, raw corn, avocado, papaya, cilantro, mint, fish sauce, and chile sauce to the room-temperature stock. Taste and adjust the seasonings, adding about 2 teaspoons salt and, for a more tart-tasting soup, a squeeze of lime juice. Chill the soup for at least 2 hours. The recipe to this point can be completed up to 8 hours in advance of serving.

• serving

To serve, stir in the crab meat. Ladle the soup into 4 chilled wide-lipped bowls. Place a scoop of guacamole in the center of each bowl. Garnish with sour cream and serve at once.

• menu ideas

This is a perfect main entrée for a hot summer night, accompanied by Southwest Caesar Salad with Chile Croutons, Any Kind of Bread Rolls, and, for dessert, Fantastic Raspberry Ice Cream with Velvet Chocolate Sauce.

note: Sometimes vine-ripened tomatoes have very tough skin. If this is the case, plunge the tomatoes in boiling water for 15 seconds; then cool the tomatoes and slip off the skin. Or, if you are purchasing supermarket tomatoes, which invariably have no taste, cut the tomatoes into quarters and roast in a 400°F. oven for 20 minutes, until they look shriveled. Another way to create a more complex tomato taste is to barbecue thickly sliced tomatoes, or to smoke tomatoes in one of the small portable smokers sold by most hardware stores.

Mussel Soup with Cilantro and Serrano Chiles

Here is one of the "wow" dishes from Robert Del Grande's Cafe Annie Restaurant in Houston. Mussels are steamed open, then removed from the shell and returned to a soup made from the steaming liquid, cilantro, chiles, and cream. The pièce de résistance is Ancho Chile Jam mounded in a mussel shell positioned in the center of each soup bowl. Swirls of this fruity, sweet, and mildly spicy condiment infuse the soup and serve as the perfect balance to the rich herb and mussel taste of the broth.

- Moderate
- Serves 4 as a main entrée.

40 black mussels, about 3 pounds
3 cups Homemade Chicken Stock
   (page 70)
2 large bunches fresh cilantro, large
   stems removed
1 bunch chives
2 whole green onions, trimmed and
   chopped
4 cloves garlic, chopped
2 to 4 serrano chiles, stemmed and
   seeded
1 tablespoon finely minced fresh ginger
2 cups whipping cream

• ancho chile jam

½ pound dried ancho chiles
6 tablespoons red currant jelly
¼ cup honey
2 tablespoons white distilled vinegar
½ teaspoon salt
2 cloves garlic, peeled
1 small shallot, peeled

• advance preparation

Using a stiff brush, scrub the mussels under cold water. Pull away and discard the little seaweed "beard" that clings between the shells. Place the chicken stock in a saucepan large enough to hold the mussels and bring the stock to a vigorous boil over high heat. Add the mussels, cover the pot, and steam until the shells just open, about 4 minutes. Immediately remove the mussels from the pot with a slotted spoon and let cool. Remove the mussels from their shells, place in a small bowl, then cover and refrigerate. Save 4 mussel shell halves.

Strain the mussel broth through a fine-meshed sieve, then set aside and let cool. Set aside a few sprigs of cilantro for garnish. Chop the remaining cilantro along with the chives, green onions, garlic, serrano chiles, and ginger, then place in a blender with the mussel broth and purée until smooth. Transfer to a large bowl, add the cream, and refrigerate.

Make the Ancho Chile Jam: Stem and seed the ancho chiles, then soak in hot water until very soft, about 30 minutes. Drain off and discard the water. Place the softened chiles in a food processor fitted with a chopping blade, add the jelly, honey, vinegar, salt, garlic, and shallot, and blend until very smooth and thick. Transfer the Ancho Chile Jam to a glass jar, cover, and refrigerate. (Makes 2¾ cups. Lasts indefinitely in the refrigerator.)

Fill the 4 reserved mussel shells with Ancho Chile Jam and set aside. The recipe to this point can be made up to 8 hours in advance.

• last-minute cooking

Add the mussel-cilantro broth to a 2½-quart saucepan and bring to a simmer. Turn the heat to very low, then taste the soup and adjust the seasonings, especially for salt. Divide the mussels among 4 heated soup bowls. Ladle the hot soup over the mussels. Place a mussel shell filled with Ancho Chile Jam in the center of each soup bowl. Garnish with the reserved sprigs of cilantro and serve at once.

• menu ideas

For an elegant dinner, begin with Asian Barbecued Quail, then serve the soup with hot sourdough rolls, Papaya and Avocado Salad, and, for dessert, Chocolate Ginger Mousse with Raspberry Essence.

note: This soup is also delicious with little steamer clams, fresh bay scallops, or fresh lump crab meat. Since Ancho Chile Jam keeps indefinitely in the refrigerator, make use of it as a seasoning resource. Add it to mayonnaise, brush it across a pork loin roasting in the oven, or sandwich it underneath squab and chicken skin prior to barbecuing the birds.

Leaping
Fresh
from
the Sea,
Lakes,
and
Rivers

Grilled Mahi Mahi Tacos with Tropical Fruit Salsa

We like to involve our dinner guests in as many activities as possible, such as folding dumplings, sprinkling toppings over pizza, shelling barbecued jumbo prawns at the table, picking up the whole romaine leaves in a traditional Caesar salad, or as in the following recipe, assembling their own tacos by wrapping barbecued mahi mahi and a tropical fruit salsa in hot tortillas. The next time you entertain, try this hands-on Southwestern-Caribbean style dinner: Asian Pot Stickers with Southwest Ketchup (early arrivals help fold the dumplings), Watermelon and Sweet Red Onion Salad served with Grilled Mahi Mahi Tacos with Tropical Fruit Salsa, and, for dessert, Ginger Banana Cream Tart Lined with Chocolate. Cook to the steel band sounds of Bob Marley, begin dinner with daiquiris, and have everyone dress in white or tropical cottons.

- Easy
- Serves 4 as a main entrée.

½ fresh pineapple
1 ripe mango
2 whole green onions, minced
¼ cup chopped fresh cilantro
1 tablespoon finely minced fresh ginger
3 tablespoons freshly squeezed orange juice
2 tablespoons light brown sugar
2 tablespoons fish sauce
1 teaspoon Asian or Caribbean chile sauce

•

2 pounds fresh mahi mahi
¼ cup dry vermouth or dry sherry
¼ cup thin soy sauce
2 tablespoons oyster sauce
2 tablespoons dark sesame oil
¼ cup finely minced fresh ginger
1 teaspoon Asian or Caribbean chile sauce
12 flour or corn tortillas, 6-inch diameter (optional)

•advance preparation

Cut the top and bottom off the pineapple. Cut the pineapple in half lengthwise. Cut off and discard the fibrous center core. Remove the pineapple flesh and chop coarsely. Peel the mango, cut away the flesh, and chop coarsely. In a medium bowl, combine the pineapple, mango, green onions, cilantro, ginger, orange juice, sugar, fish sauce, and chile sauce. This salsa must be used the day it is made. Keep refrigerated.

Cut the mahi mahi into 4 serving pieces. In a shallow bowl, combine the vermouth or dry sherry, soy sauce, oyster sauce, sesame oil, ginger, and chile sauce, then add the fish. Marinate the mahi mahi for at least 15 minutes but for no longer than 2 hours.

•last-minute cooking

Bring the salsa to room temperature. Wrap the tortillas with foil so that they are completely sealed. If using a gas barbecue or indoor grill, preheat to medium (350°F.). If using charcoal or wood, prepare a fire. When the coals or wood are ash-covered or the gas barbecue or indoor grill is preheated, brush the grill with oil, then grill the mahi mahi about 6 minutes on each side, brushing on more of the marinade during cooking. The mahi mahi is done when it just begins to pull apart when prodded with a fork or it just loses its raw color in the center. (Alternatively, preheat the oven to 500°F. Then turn the oven setting to broil and broil the fish 4 inches from the heat for about 10 minutes. If using an electric oven, leave the oven door ajar.)

Warm the tortillas on the grill while cooking the fish. Or warm in the oven for about 6 minutes.

Transfer the fish to 4 heated dinner plates. Spoon the salsa widthwise across each piece of fish. Or, if using the tortillas, place 3 tortillas, a piece of fish, and a fourth of the salsa on each dinner plate and let each person assemble his or her own fish tacos. Serve at once.

Leaping Fresh from the Sea, Lakes, and Rivers

Swordfish with Thai Butter Sauce

We are always amazed by how easy it is to modify flavors by simply substituting herbs and spices. For example, Thai Butter Sauce is one of the easiest, most versatile, and most elegant sauces to spoon across barbecued, broiled or steamed fish. We start with what the French call a beurre blanc, then veer from tradition by adding such Thai seasonings as lemongrass, kaffir lime leaf, basil, mint, and chile sauce. To change the flavor profile, substitute lemon or vinegar for the lime juice, replace the garlic with 2 tablespoons finely minced fresh ginger, omit the sometimes difficult to find lemongrass and kaffir lime leaf in favor of a bay leaf or capers, lessen the heat by substituting green peppercorns for the Asian chile sauce, or rely on other fresh herbs, such as tarragon, thyme, oregano, and cilantro, in place of the basil or mint.

- Easy
- Serves 4 as a main entrée.

• thai butter sauce

⅓ cup freshly squeezed lime juice
¼ cup white wine
2 teaspoons light brown sugar
1 shallot, finely minced
3 cloves garlic, finely minced
1 stalk lemongrass (optional)
1 kaffir lime leaf (optional)
½ cup unsalted butter, softened
½ teaspoon Asian chile sauce
¼ cup chopped fresh basil leaves
¼ cup chopped fresh mint leaves

•

4 fresh swordfish steaks, ½ pound each
¼ cup white wine
¼ cup fish sauce
¼ cup cooking oil
2 teaspoons Asian chile sauce
4 cloves garlic, finely minced

• advance preparation

Start the butter sauce: Place the lime juice, wine, sugar, shallot, and garlic in a small non-corrosive saucepan. Very finely mince 2 tablespoons of the lemongrass. Add the lemongrass and whole lime leaf to the saucepan, bring the mixture to a rapid boil over high heat, and boil until only ¼ cup liquid remains. If not using right away, cool to room temperature and refrigerate for up to 8 hours.

Place the fish in a nonmetal dish. Combine the white wine, fish sauce, cooking oil, 2 teaspoons chile sauce, and the garlic. Pour the marinade over the fish and marinate for at least 15 minutes but for no longer than 2 hours.

• last-minute cooking

If using a gas barbecue or indoor grill, preheat to medium (350°F.). If using charcoal or wood, prepare a fire. When the coals or wood are ash-covered or the gas barbecue or indoor grill is preheated, brush the grill with oil, then grill the swordfish about 5 minutes on each side, brushing on more of the marinade during cooking. The swordfish is done when it just begins to pull apart when prodded with a fork or when the center just loses its raw color. (Alternatively, preheat the oven to 500°F., turn the oven setting to broil, and broil the fish 4 inches from the heat for about 10 minutes. If using an electric oven, leave the oven door ajar.) Transfer the swordfish to 4 heated dinner plates.

Cut the softened butter into small pieces. Set aside the ½ teaspoon chile sauce, the basil, and mint. Bring the sauce to a fast boil over medium heat. Add the butter, all at the same time, and beat vigorously with a whisk. After about 30 seconds, while a few pieces of butter remain unincorporated, remove the saucepan from the heat. Stir in the chile sauce, basil, and mint. Taste and adjust seasonings, especially for chile. Add salt to taste.

Spoon the Thai Butter Sauce over the fish and serve at once.

• menu ideas

Easy dinner for 4 or more guests: Swordfish with Thai Butter Sauce accompanied by Wild Rice with Currants, Pine Nuts, and Port, a mixed green salad with one of the salad dressings from Chapter 3, and a store-bought premium-quality ice cream accented with Caramel Sauce.

Barbecued Lobster with Herb Butter-Lime Sauce

Long gone are the days when, after severe Atlantic storms, farmers collected lobsters lying on New England beaches and used them for fertilizer. Now commercial fishermen venture miles offshore along the North Atlantic coast to capture the ever-dwindling supply of these magnificent crustaceans. Another type of lobster, called spiny lobster, is captured along the coast from California to Chile, in Florida, throughout the South Pacific, and in the Mediterranean. These lobsters, sometimes derisively called ocean crawfish, lack the magnificent front claws packed with succulent meat, as well as the tenderness and ocean flavor of their New England cousins.

If possible, make a point to buy lobsters that have just been pulled from the ocean, for their special flavor gradually dissipates when they are kept in a holding tank. Live lobsters can be placed in a shallow pan, covered with a wet kitchen towel, and refrigerated for up to 24 hours prior to cooking. If you don't have the courage to split the live lobsters in half (you will need a very heavy and sharp knife), drop them head first into a very large pot of rapidly boiling water for 3 minutes, then proceed with splitting and barbecuing as instructed in the recipe.

• Challenging
• Serves 4 as a main entrée.

1 cup unsalted butter
2 teaspoons Asian chile sauce
1 teaspoon ground Szechwan pepper
12 cloves garlic, very finely minced
2 tablespoons grated or finely minced lime zest (colored part of skin)
½ cup freshly squeezed lime juice
2 bunches chives, minced
⅔ cup minced fresh cilantro
4 2-pound live lobsters

• preparation and last-minute cooking

Place the butter, chile sauce, pepper, garlic, and lime zest in a small saucepan over low heat. Melt the butter until it bubbles around the edges. Remove from the heat and stir in the lime juice, chives, and cilantro. Set aside half the butter sauce to use as a dipping sauce.

If using a gas barbecue or indoor grill, preheat to medium (350°F.). If using charcoal or wood, prepare the fire. When the coals or wood are ash-covered or the gas barbecue or indoor grill is preheated, using a heavy knife and beginning at the head, split the lobsters in half lengthwise. The lobster innards do not need to be removed.

Brush the grill with oil. Brush the lobster meat with the remaining butter mixture and place, meat side down, on the grill.

Grill the lobsters about 6 minutes, then turn over, brush the meat with more of the butter mixture, and cook another 5 minutes. When the lobster shells turns bright red and the meat becomes white, serve immediately on 4 heated dinner plates, accompanied by the butter dipping sauce.

• menu ideas

An elegant dinner for 4: Marinated Goat Cheese with Pepper Berries, Garlic, and Mint, Barbecued Lobster with Herb Butter-Lime Sauce, Jade Rice, Baby Greens with Blue Cheese-Pecan Dressing, and Kahlúa Passion Tiles.

Caribbean Shrimp with Allspice, Curry, and Pineapple

We are always on the lookout for ways to expand favorite recipes to serve larger groups. However, following this recipe exactly, you are limited to doubling the yield, and this requires using two sauté pans simultaneously. Trying to use a much larger pan when home stoves create so little heat even at the highest setting, or cooking more than a single layer of shrimp in the sauté pan, cause the shrimp to steam and lose their sweet interior liquid. As an alternative, use a 24-inch wok placed over an outdoor portable wok burner so that the high heat and very large surface area properly sear the shrimp. Another alternative is to marinate and "velvet" the shrimp in oil (see page 97), make the sauce separately, then spoon the sauce across the shrimp.

- Moderate
- Serves 4 as a main entrée.

1½ pounds large raw shrimp
4 cloves garlic, finely minced
2 shallots, minced
1 tablespoon finely minced fresh ginger
1 Scotch Bonnet chile or 4 fresh serrano chiles, minced (including seeds)
1 green bell pepper, stemmed, seeded, and chopped
1 large vine-ripened tomato, seeded and chopped
2 teaspoons curry powder
½ teaspoon whole allspice berries, finely crushed
½ cup Homemade Chicken Stock (page 70)
¼ cup dry sherry
2 tablespoons thin soy sauce
2 teaspoons cornstarch
⅓ cup plus 1 tablespoon brown sugar
3 tablespoons light-grade olive oil or cooking oil
½ fresh pineapple
Salt, to taste

• advance preparation

Shell, devein, and cut the shrimp deeply lengthwise. Combine the garlic, shallots, ginger, and chile(s). In a medium bowl, combine the bell pepper, tomato, curry powder, allspice, chicken stock, dry sherry, soy sauce, cornstarch, and 1 tablespoon of the brown sugar.

Place a 10-inch sauté pan over medium-high heat. Add 1 tablespoon of the oil along with the garlic, shallots, ginger, and chile(s). Sauté for 15 seconds, then add the sauce. Bring the sauce to a boil and cook until it thickens enough to lightly coat a spoon, about 2 minutes. Transfer to a bowl, cool, cover, and refrigerate.

Cut the top and bottom off the pineapple. Cut the pineapple in half lengthwise. Cut off and discard the fibrous center core. Remove the pineapple flesh, cut into ½-inch-thin slices, and set aside. The recipe to this point can be completed up to 8 hours in advance of last-minute cooking.

• last-minute cooking

Coat the pineapple with the remaining ⅓ cup brown sugar. Turn the oven setting to broil or prepare a barbecue. If using a gas barbecue or indoor grill, preheat to medium (350°F.). If using charcoal or wood, prepare a fire. When the coals or wood are ash-covered or the gas barbecue or indoor grill is preheated, brush the grill with oil and grill the pineapple slices until they become slightly soft and golden, about 2 minutes; then turn the pineapple over and grill on the other side. If broiling, place the pineapple on a baking sheet lined with aluminum foil and broil 4 inches from the heat until golden. Then turn the pineapple over and cook on the other side until golden.

Meanwhile, place a 12-inch sauté pan over highest heat. When hot, add the remaining 2 tablespoons cooking oil. When the oil becomes very hot and just gives off a wisp of smoke, add the shrimp. Stir and toss until the outsides of the shrimp turn white, about 2 minutes.

Add the curry-tomato sauce ingredients and bring to a low boil. Stir in the barbecued pineapple. Taste and adjust the seasonings. Transfer to 4 heated dinner plates and serve at once.

•menu ideas

A party for 12: Magical Chicken Wings (double recipe), Papaya and Avocado Salad (triple recipe), Caribbean Shrimp with Allspice, Curry, and Pineapple (triple recipe; prepare using one of the alternative techniques explained in the introduction to the recipe) accompanied by hot flour tortillas, and, for dessert, Chocolate Ginger Mousse with Raspberry Essence.

Spicy Southwestern Scallops

This recipe is another good example of the great flavor revolution we are now experiencing. Fresh bay scallops, not traditionally available in the Southwest, are combined with a Southwestern-style salsa of sweet vine-ripened tomatoes, crunchy jicama, intensely flavored cilantro, and fiery serrano chiles enriched with fresh ginger and nutty sesame oil. The sparkling range of high-note flavors in this dish makes it an ideal choice to serve either on hot summer nights or in the depth of winter in front of a crackling fire. To capture every speck of sauce, accompany Spicy Southwestern Scallops with rice pilaf, steamed rice, grilled polenta, noodles, or bread.

• Easy
• Serves 4 as a main entrée.

•salsa

1½ pounds vine-ripened tomatoes, seeded and chopped
½ cup chopped green onions
½ cup chopped fresh cilantro
½ cup chopped jicama
4 serrano chiles, stemmed and finely minced (including seeds)
4 cloves garlic, finely minced
1 tablespoon finely minced fresh ginger
3 tablespoons red wine vinegar
1 tablespoon dark sesame oil
1 tablespoon vegetable oil
1½ teaspoons sugar
½ teaspoon salt

•

2 tablespoons light-grade olive oil or cooking oil
1½ pounds fresh bay scallops

•advance preparation

Make the salsa: Cut the tomatoes in half, squeeze each half to remove the seeds, then chop enough tomatoes to fill 2 cups. Combine the tomatoes, green onions, cilantro, jicama, chiles, garlic, ginger, vinegar, sesame and vegetable oils, sugar, and salt. Complete this step the same day the dish is to be cooked; store the salsa at room temperature.

•last-minute cooking

Place a 12-inch sauté pan over highest heat. When hot, add the olive oil and roll it around the sides of the pan. When the oil just begins to smoke, add the scallops and sauté until they just begin to feel firm, about 2 minutes. Add the tomato salsa and bring to a rapid boil. Taste and adjust seasonings. Serve at once on 4 heated dinner plates.

•menu ideas

Southwestern dinner for 8: Pork and Corn Dumplings in Cilantro Cream, Southwest Caesar Salad with Chile Croutons, Spicy Southwestern Scallops served with Santa Fe Corn Bread, and, for dessert, Kahlúa Passion Tiles.

Soft-Shell Crabs with Roasted Red Pepper and Eggplant Sauce

There are few gastronomic treats as wondrous and as easy to cook as the entirely edible soft-shell crab. Harvested in the Gulf of Mexico and along the East Coast from April to September, soft-shell crabs are small blue crabs that slip out of their exterior shells, then during the next few days, before their new shells harden, are prey to all types of hungry creatures, including human beings. Soft-shell crabs are highly perishable, so always check to make sure they are alive. Have the crabs cleaned at the market, then cook them the same day. In this recipe, the soft-shell crabs are sautéed in a little seasoned butter and served with a red pepper-eggplant sauce. We have also enjoyed brushing the crabs with salad dressings from Chapter 3 and barbecuing them.

- Moderate
- Serves 4 as a main entrée.

3 Japanese eggplants

3 red bell peppers, seeded and stemmed

¼ cup cooking oil

¼ cup thin soy sauce

¼ cup unseasoned Japanese rice vinegar

3 tablespoons freshly squeezed lime juice

2 tablespoons brown sugar

2 tablespoons fish sauce

1 teaspoon Asian chile sauce

2 tablespoons minced green onion

1 tablespoon chopped fresh cilantro, plus extra for garnish

1 tablespoon very finely minced fresh ginger

4 cloves garlic, finely minced

¼ cup unsalted butter

8 soft-shell crabs, cleaned

Approximately ½ cup white wine

Salt and freshly ground black pepper, to taste

• advance preparation

Trim the ends off the eggplants, then cut each eggplant lengthwise into 3 pieces. Cut the bell peppers into 1-inch-wide strips. In a rectangular dish, combine 2 tablespoons of the cooking oil, the soy sauce, and vinegar, then add the eggplant and peppers. Marinate for 1 hour, turning the vegetables every 15 minutes.

If using a gas barbecue or indoor grill, preheat to medium (350°F.). If using charcoal or wood, prepare a fire. When the coals or wood are ash-covered or the gas barbecue or indoor grill is preheated, brush the grill with oil, then grill the eggplant and bell peppers about 4 minutes on each side, until both soften slightly. (Alternatively, place the vegetables on a baking sheet and broil 4 inches below the heat source.) Coarsely chop the eggplant and peppers. In a small bowl, combine the eggplant, peppers, remaining 2 tablespoons cooking oil, lime juice, sugar, fish sauce, chile sauce, green onion, chopped cilantro, ginger, and half the minced garlic. Set aside at room temperature. Set aside the remaining garlic in a small container. The recipe to this point can be prepared up to 8 hours prior to last-minute cooking.

• last-minute cooking

Place two 12-inch sauté pans over highest heat. Add half the butter to each pan. When the butter melts, add the reserved garlic. When the garlic begins to sizzle, add the soft-shell crabs. Cook the crabs on each side until they turn red, about 2 minutes per side. If the crabs begin to scorch during cooking, add about ¼ cup white wine to each pan. Season the crabs with salt and pepper. Place the crabs on 4 heated dinner plates. Spoon some of the sauce across each crab. Garnish with cilantro and serve at once.

• menu ideas

Accompany this dish with Southwest Caesar Salad with Chile Croutons, Wild Rice with Currants, Pine Nuts, and Port, and Chocolate Nut Tart.

Braised Catfish in Hot Garlic Sauce

This recipe combines a favorite fish of the Chinese with a rich, complex-tasting sauce traditionally used on noodle dishes in Northern China. Its creation was a result of improvisation during a cooking class I was giving several years ago in Hong Kong. Winding through the outdoor market, the class bought freshwater chestnuts, bean sprouts with ends snapped off, bundles of Chinese garlic chives, and a large thrashing catfish pulled fresh from a tank. After completing the preparation, we sautéed minced garlic and ginger in a wok for a few seconds, added the catfish steaks, poured in a sauce featuring bean sauce, hoisin sauce, oyster sauce, and dry sherry, covered the wok, and steam-cooked the fish. A few minutes later we savored a dish that juxtaposed the sweet, very tender catfish with an earthy, low note sauce and the searing aftertaste of chiles.

- Easy
- Serves 4 as a main entrée.

4 large or 8 small fresh catfish, salmon, or halibut steaks, about 2 pounds total
¼ pound ground pork
2 whole green onions, trimmed and chopped
1½ teaspoons finely minced garlic
1 tablespoon finely minced fresh ginger
1 cup Homemade Chicken Stock (page 70)
¼ cup dry sherry
3 tablespoons hoisin sauce
2 tablespoons oyster sauce
1 tablespoon bean sauce
1 tablespoon dark sesame oil
1 tablespoon red wine vinegar
1 tablespoon Asian chile sauce
1 teaspoon sugar
¼ teaspoon freshly ground Szechwan pepper
2 tablespoons cornstarch
2 tablespoons cooking oil

•advance preparation

In separate containers, set aside the catfish, pork, and green onions. Combine the garlic and ginger. In a small bowl, combine the chicken stock, sherry, hoisin sauce, oyster sauce, bean sauce, sesame oil, vinegar, chile sauce, sugar, and Szechwan pepper. The recipe to this point can be completed up to 8 hours in advance of cooking.

•last-minute cooking

Mix the cornstarch with an equal amount of cold water. Place a large wok or a 12-inch sauté pan over highest heat. When hot, add the cooking oil and coat the surface of the pan. When the oil is hot, add the garlic-ginger mixture. Sauté a few seconds, then add the pork. Using the back of a spoon, press the pork against the pan to break the meat into individual grounds. As soon as the pork loses all its raw color, add the sauce. Bring the sauce to a low boil, gently add the fish steaks, sprinkle on the green onions, and cover the pan.

Turn the heat to low and simmer the catfish until it just begins to flake when prodded with a fork, about 8 minutes. Be sure the sauce simmers but does not boil. When the catfish is done, transfer it to 4 heated dinner plates.

Turn the heat under the pan to high and stir in a little of the cornstarch mixture to lightly thicken the sauce. Taste and adjust the seasonings. Spoon the sauce over the catfish. Serve at once.

•menu ideas

Asian dinner party for 8: Start with Curried Lamb Coins, then serve Cal-Asian Salad with Red Sweet Ginger Dressing (double recipe); follow with Braised Catfish in Hot Garlic Sauce (double recipe) accompanied by Thai Rice Pilaf with Lemongrass, Basil, and Mint (cooked several hours ahead and reheated). Conclude with Chocolate Meltdown Cookies with a premium store-bought ice cream.

note: Utilize this sauce the same way you might a marinara sauce. Make it in a sauté pan and add it to stir-fried shrimp, spoon it over broiled fish, or toss it with ½ pound freshly cooked penne.

Leaping Fresh from the Sea, Lakes, and Rivers

Velvet Shrimp with Watercress Sauce

Chinese chefs marinate shrimp with egg white, then poach the shrimp in oil. This marinating technique and very gentle cooking, called "velveting," produces extraordinarily tender shrimp without any trace of oiliness. Some home cooks are reluctant to try the velveting technique because it involves poaching the shrimp in a large amount of oil. But if you position a colander in a heat-proof bowl next to the stove, it is a simple matter to drain the shrimp, then finish the sauce in the already preheated wok. However, if you prefer a low-oil cooking approach, just sauté the shrimp as described in the recipe for Caribbean Shrimp with Allspice, Curry, and Pineapple.

- Moderate
- Serves 4 as a main entrée.

• velvet marinade

2 egg whites
3 tablespoons cornstarch
3 tablespoons cooking oil
1 tablespoon dry sherry
½ teaspoon salt
•
1½ pounds large raw shrimp
½ red bell pepper, stemmed and seeded
3 cups cooking oil

• watercress sauce

1 cup tender watercress ends
1 bunch chives
½ cup loosely packed, tender spinach leaves
½ cup fresh cilantro sprigs
⅓ cup fresh basil leaves
1 tablespoon finely minced ginger
2 shallots, chopped
¾ cup whipping cream
¼ cup Homemade Chicken Stock (page 70)
2 teaspoons Dijon mustard
½ teaspoon salt
¼ teaspoon Asian chile sauce
¼ teaspoon sugar

• advance preparation

Make the Velvet Marinade: In a small bowl, beat the egg whites just until they become slightly frothy, then stir in the cornstarch, cooking oil, sherry, and salt. Shell the shrimp, then split the shrimp deeply along the top ridge, rinse away the vein, and pat dry. Add the shrimp to the velvet marinade and mix thoroughly using your fingers. Refrigerate the shrimp for a minimum of 1 hour and as long as 8 hours. Alternatively, do not marinate the shrimp; instead, follow the low-oil cooking instructions for shrimp described on page 92.

Cut the pepper into very fine shreds and set aside.

In an electric blender, combine all of the sauce ingredients and blend into a liquid. Transfer to a small bowl and refrigerate. The recipe to this point can be completed up to 8 hours in advance of cooking.

• last-minute cooking

Transfer the sauce to a small saucepan, bring to a low boil, and cook until thickened enough to lightly coat a spoon, about 1 minute. Taste and adjust the seasonings. Keep warm.

Place a wok over highest heat. When hot, add the cooking oil and heat until a thin slice of ginger skips across the surface (at about 350°F.). Stir the shrimp, then add to the oil. Cook the shrimp, stirring constantly, until the moment they turn white, about 2 minutes, then tip them into a large sieve or colander placed over a heatproof container.

Drain the shrimp of all oil. Place the watercress sauce across the surface of 4 heated dinner plates. Position the shrimp on top of the watercress sauce. Garnish with the red bell pepper and serve at once.

• menu ideas

Dinner party for 8: Bruschetta East and West as an appetizer, followed by Velvet Shrimp with Watercress Sauce accompanied by Popovers Scented with Garlic (omit the cilantro and chile) as a main course, then Candied Walnut Salad with Goat Cheese, and, for dessert, Black and White Bread Pudding.

Sizzling Shrimp in Tarragon Wine Sauce

Unfortunately, the quality of shrimp available to most consumers is poor. Until much sweeter fresh shrimp become available, we recommend buying large, frozen, freshwater, headless shrimp (often called tiger prawns) in 2-kilo or 5-pound boxes. To use, transfer the block of shrimp from the freezer to an empty sink, run cold water over one end to quickly defrost, then rewrap and return the remaining frozen shrimp to the freezer.

- Challenging
- Serves 4 as a main entrée.

1½ pounds large raw shrimp
Velvet Marinade (page 97)
½ pound medium-sized button
   mushrooms or 3 ounces enoki
   mushrooms
1 bunch baby carrots
5 whole green onions, trimmed
4 cloves garlic, finely minced
3 shallots, minced
1 tablespoon very finely minced fresh
   ginger
1 bunch chives, chopped

• tarragon wine sauce

1 tablespoon finely minced fresh
   tarragon
1 cup white wine
½ cup heavy cream
⅓ cup tomato sauce
2 tablespoons cognac
½ teaspoon Asian chile sauce
½ teaspoon salt
2 teaspoons cornstarch
•
3 cups plus 2 tablespoons cooking oil
2 ounces rice sticks (optional)
2 tablespoons unsalted butter

• advance preparation

Shell the shrimp. Split the shrimp deeply along the top ridge, rinse away the vein, and pat dry.

Make the Velvet Marinade and mix thoroughly with shrimp, then refrigerate at least 1 hour. Alternatively, do not marinate; instead, follow low-oil cooking instructions for shrimp described on page 92.

Cut the button mushrooms into quarter, or if using enoki mushrooms, cut off and discard roots, then separate the enoki threadlike stems. Scrape the carrots. Cut the carrots in half on a sharp diagonal. Cut the green onions on a sharp diagonal into 2-inch lengths. Set aside the vegetables. In a small bowl, combine the garlic, shallots, and ginger. In a separate container, set aside the chives. In a medium bowl, combine the tarragon, wine, heavy cream, tomato sauce, cognac, chile sauce, and salt.

Place 2 tablespoons of the oil and the garlic mixture in a 10-inch sauté pan over high heat. When the garlic sizzles, add the tarragon cream sauce. Bring to a rapid boil and cook until only 1½ cups remain. Transfer the sauce to a small bowl, cool to room temperature, stir in the cornstarch, and refrigerate.

Cook the rice sticks: Add 2 cups of the cooking oil to a 10-inch skillet set over medium-high heat and heat until the end of a rice stick expands within 2 seconds when placed in the oil. Cook a few rice sticks at a time.

As soon as they expand, turn the rice sticks over and push back into the hot oil to cook 5 more seconds. Drain on paper towels. Store at room temperature. Strain and reserve the oil. The recipe to this point can be completed up to 5 hours prior to last-minute cooking.

• last-minute cooking

Break the rice sticks into small pieces and place in an even layer on 4 heated dinner plates. Place a wok over highest heat. When hot, add the oil leftover from cooking the rice sticks plus the remaining 1 cup fresh oil. Heat until a thin slice of ginger skips across the surface. Stir the shrimp, then add the shrimp to the oil. Cook the shrimp, stirring continually, until the moment they turn white, about 2 minutes. Tip the shrimp into a large sieve or colander placed over a heat-proof container.

Immediately return the wok to highest heat. Add the butter. When the butter melts, add the button mushrooms, carrots, and green onions, and stir-fry until the mushrooms soften slightly, about 2 minutes, adding a splash of water or white wine to speed the cooking process.

Add the tarragon sauce, chives, shrimp, and enoki mushrooms, if using, to the wok. Stir and toss the ingredients over high heat until well combined. Taste and adjust the seasonings. Spoon the shrimp onto the rice sticks and serve at once.

Leaping Fresh from the Sea, Lakes, and Rivers

Tiger Prawns with Thai Green Curry Sauce

Thai green curry paste is a multipurpose flavoring resource. As versatile as New World Pesto, a few spoonfuls perk up pasta sauces, add intriguing flavor to American stews and to curries, and are great rubbed underneath chicken skin prior to barbecuing. Always take the extra time to make your Thai curry paste from scratch because it tastes far superior to the very salty commercial curry pastes sold at Asian markets. Similar to Italian pesto, Thai curry pastes that are stored in the refrigerator for more than a few days or are frozen lose the high-note flavor of basil and turn an unappetizing blackish color. The designation "optional" appears next to many of the seasonings in this recipe because we have found that even when we have omitted one or two of them, the essential green curry flavor of the paste hasn't faded.

• Moderate
• Serves 4 as a main entrée.

1½ pounds medium-sized button mushrooms
4 whole green onions
1½ pounds large raw shrimp (prawns)
1 cup coconut milk
¼ cup dry sherry
2 tablespoons fish sauce
2 teaspoons cornstarch
5 tablespoons cooking oil

• thai green curry paste

10 cloves garlic
2 shallots
12 whole serrano chiles
1½ cups fresh basil leaves
1 teaspoon salt
½ cup cooking oil
4 whole cloves (optional)
12 black peppercorns (optional)
2 teaspoons coriander seeds (optional)
1 teaspoon caraway seeds (optional)
1 teaspoon cumin seeds (optional)
1 teaspoon shrimp paste (optional)

• advance preparation

Cut the mushrooms into quarters. Trim the green onions, then cut on a diagonal into 1-inch pieces. Shell, devein, and split each shrimp in half lengthwise into 2 separate pieces.

Combine the coconut milk, sherry, fish sauce, and cornstarch.

Make the green curry paste: Set aside the garlic and shallots. Stem the chiles. Set aside in separate containers the basil leaves, salt, and cooking oil. Place the cloves, peppercorns, and coriander, caraway, and cumin seeds in a small, ungreased frying pan. Place the pan over medium heat and cook the spices until they just begin to smoke, about 3 minutes. Grind the spices into a powder using a mortar and pestle or an electric spice grinder. Set aside the shrimp paste. Place the chopping blade in the food processor. With the machine on, drop down the feed tube, a few at a time, the garlic, shallots, and chiles. Remove the processor top, add the basil and salt, then mince very finely. Add all of the optional ingredients, including the shrimp paste, and mince again. With the machine running, slowly pour ½ cup cooking oil down the feed tube and process until a paste is formed. Set aside ⅓ cup green curry paste for this recipe. Pack the remainder in a glass jar, cover with a film of cooking oil, seal tightly, and refrigerate for up to a month. Alternatively, store indefinitely in ¼ cup quantities in the freezer, though be aware that the flavor will gradually deteriorate.

• last-minute cooking

Place a wok or 12-inch sauté pan over highest heat. When the pan becomes very hot, add 3 tablespoons of the cooking oil. When the oil becomes hot and just begins to smoke slightly, add the mushrooms. Stir and toss, adding a few tablespoons of dry sherry, chicken stock, wine, or water, and cook the mushrooms until they become very densely textured and reduce in volume by approximately half, about 10 minutes. Temporarily transfer the mushrooms to a plate.

Return the sauté pan to highest heat. Add the remaining 2 tablespoons cooking oil. When the oil becomes very hot and just begins to smoke, carefully slide in the shrimp. Stir and toss the shrimp until they lose nearly all of their raw outside color, about 2 minutes. Add ⅓ cup green curry paste. Stir and toss the shrimp. When the shrimp lose all of their raw outside color, add the green onions, coconut milk mixture, and mushrooms. Stir and toss to evenly combine all the ingredients.

Taste and adjust the sauce. If you want more flavor, add more green curry paste. Transfer to 4 heated dinner plates. Serve at once.

•menu ideas

Dinner for 4: Tiger Prawns with Thai Green Curry Sauce, Polenta Madness, a big garden salad, and a premium store-bought ice cream.

Thai Broiled Sole with Mint and Chiles

Those whose palates have not been set ablaze by the sweet, sour, spicy, and herbaceous flavors of Thai food are often surprised to discover that there exists a greater difference between Thai and Chinese food than between the foods of England and France. Whereas Chinese cuisine derives many of its flavors from fermented sauces and condiments such as soy sauce, bean sauce, hoisin sauce, plum sauce, and dark sesame oil, Thai cooking gains its unique tastes from ingredients rarely, if ever used by the Chinese, including fresh basil, mint, cilantro, lemongrass, lime, coconut milk, palm sugar, tamarind paste, and fish sauce.

• Easy
• Serves 4 as a main entrée.

1½ pounds filet of sole
1 tablespoon fish sauce
2 tablespoons dry sherry
1 tablespoon dark sesame oil
¼ pound small button mushrooms
2 cloves garlic, finely minced
1 tablespoon finely minced fresh ginger
1 serrano chile, finely minced
¼ cup chopped fresh mint leaves
¼ cup chopped chives
½ teaspoon grated or finely minced tangerine or orange zest (colored part of skin)
½ cup freshly squeezed tangerine or orange juice
¼ cup dry sherry or rice wine
2 tablespoons fish sauce
2 teaspoons cornstarch
1 tablespoon cooking oil

•advance preparation

Trim all ragged edges from the sole. Combine the fish sauce, sherry, and sesame oil; rub the marinade over the fish and marinate for at least 15 minutes but for no longer than 1 hour.

Very thinly slice the mushrooms. Combine the garlic, ginger, and serrano chile. Combine the mint and chives. In a small bowl, combine citrus zest and juice, dry sherry, fish sauce, and cornstarch.

•last-minute cooking

Preheat the oven to 550°F., then turn the oven setting to broil. Place the sole on a baking sheet sprayed with nonstick cooking oil. Place the sole about 4 inches below the heat source and cook without turning until the fish turns white and just begins to flake when prodded with a fork, about 4 minutes. Immediately transfer to 4 heated dinner plates.

Meanwhile, place a 12-inch sauté pan over highest heat. Add the cooking oil, garlic, ginger, and serrano chile. Sauté until the garlic begins to sizzle, then add the mushrooms and sauté until the mushrooms begin to soften, about 2 minutes. Add the sauce and bring to a vigorous boil. Taste and adjust the seasonings. Spoon the sauce over the sole, sprinkle on the chives, and serve at once.

•menu ideas

Accompany Thai Broiled Sole with such mild dishes as Jasmine Steamed Rice and Candied Walnut Salad with Goat Cheese so that you do not create a flavor "overload."

note: For delicious variation, spoon the sauce across pieces of barbecued chicken, or toss it with ½ pound of cooked dried pasta.

Barbecued Salmon
in New World Pesto Sauce

New World Pesto Sauce uses mint and cilantro in addition to the traditional basil, and overlaps the fresh herb taste with a hint of Asian chile sauce. Since this recipe yields more pesto than you need for the salmon, and its flavor only lasts for a week in the refrigerator (and deteriorates greatly in the freezer), go on a pesto cooking—and eating—frenzy and use the New World Pesto in the following ways: for packing under chicken skin before cooking, stirring into stews, fitting between jumbo shrimp and their shells before barbecuing, brushing across vegetables for grilling, adding to extra-virgin olive oil to make a seasoned oil for bread-dipping, adding to mashed potatoes, spreading across French bread for pesto garlic bread, seasoning salad dressings, rubbing over fish before barbecuing or broiling, tossing with pasta, mixing into veal meat loaf, and stir-frying with very thinly sliced meat in a searing hot wok. This will be a pesto passion week!

• Easy
• Serves 4 as a main entrée.

new world pesto sauce

8 cloves garlic

2 shallots

1 cup fresh basil leaves

¾ cup fresh mint leaves

½ cup fresh cilantro sprigs, packed

½ cup roasted cashews (see page 222)

½ cup extra-virgin olive oil

½ teaspoon salt

1 teaspoon Asian chile sauce

½ cup freshly grated imported
  Parmesan cheese

•

2 pound fresh whole salmon filet, skin
  on, or 4 ½-pound pieces

6 tablespoons freshly squeezed lemon
  juice

¼ cup light-grade olive oil

½ cup white wine

½ teaspoon freshly ground black pepper

½ cup whipping cream

1 cup freshly grated imported Parmesan
  cheese

advance preparation

Make the pesto sauce: Measure all of the ingredients for the pesto sauce. Place the chopping blade in a food processor and, with the motor running, drop the garlic down the feed tube followed by the shallots. Add the basil, mint, and cilantro, and mince finely. Add the nuts and mince finely. With the motor running, add the oil in a slow, steady stream. Add the salt and chile sauce and process for 10 seconds. Shut the motor off, then add the cheese and process briefly to combine. Scrape the pesto into a bowl, cover, and refrigerate. The pesto can be made up to a week in advance. Makes approximately 3 cups. Set aside ½ cup for this recipe.

Remove any bones from the salmon filet. If you plan to grill the salmon in a wire fish basket, remove the salmon skin. Combine the lemon juice, olive oil, ¼ cup of the wine, and the black pepper. Marinate the salmon for at least 15 minutes but for no longer than 2 hours. Combine the cream and the remaining ¼ cup wine. Set aside the Parmesan.

last-minute cooking

If using a gas barbecue, preheat to medium (350°F.). If using charcoal or wood, prepare the fire. When the coals or wood are ash-covered or the barbecue is preheated, lay the salmon, skin side down, on top. Immediately cover and cook the salmon until it just begins to flake when prodded with a fork, about 12 minutes. (If the barbecue cannot be covered, place the salmon in a wire fish basket and turn once during cooking). Carefully slide a spatula under the filet. If the salmon is whole, transfer to a heated serving platter; if in individual pieces, transfer to 4 heated dinner plates. The salmon skin should remain on the grill. (Alternatively, preheat the oven to 500°F. Then turn the oven setting to broil and broil the fish 4 inches from the heat until the salmon begins to flake, about 10 minutes. If using an electric oven, leave the door ajar. Or, cook the salmon on an indoor grill or grill pan over medium heat for about 4 minutes on each side.)

Bring the cream and wine to a rapid boil in a 10-inch skillet. Add ½ cup New Wave Pesto Sauce. Taste and adjust seasonings, especially for salt. Spoon the sauce over the fish. Serve at once, accompanied by the freshly grated Parmesan cheese.

menu ideas

Salmon Feast for 8: Scallop and Avocado Tostadas, Barbecued Salmon in New World Pesto Sauce (double recipe), Polenta Madness, Candied Walnut Salad with Goat Cheese (double recipe), and, for dessert, White Chocolate Mousse with Tropical Fruits.

Whole Rainbow Steamed Fish

"**R**ainbow" in this recipe name refers to the colorful combination of herbs and seasonings that are fitted into deep slashes made along each side of a whole fish that is then cooked in a 16-inch Chinese steamer. Although Asian seasonings are featured here, other aromatics, such as Ancho Chile Jam, New World Pesto, or any of the barbecue sauces from this book, produce equally delicious results. As the fish gently cooks, the flavors permeate to the bone, and the condensation of steam plus the marinade serves as the foundation for a sauce. If you do not have a steamer, lay the fish on heavy-duty foil placed on a barbecue, then cook the fish with the barbecue tightly covered. If you substitute fish filets or steaks, just rub the fish with seasonings, marinate 30 minutes, then steam until the flesh just begins to flake when prodded with a fork.

• Moderate
• Serves 4 as a main entrée.

1 whole fresh rock cod or snapper, about 4 pounds
¼ cup dry sherry
¼ cup oyster sauce
¼ cup light-grade olive oil
1 tablespoon Asian chile sauce
1 tablespoon grated or finely minced lemon zest (colored part of skin)
6 cloves garlic, very finely minced
2 tablespoons very finely minced fresh ginger
2 tablespoons salted fermented black beans, rinsed and minced (optional)
¼ cup chopped fresh basil leaves
½ cup minced green onion
1 red bell pepper, stemmed, seeded, and slivered
1 cup fresh cilantro sprigs, for garnish
2 tablespoons cornstarch

• advance preparation

With a sharp knife, scrape the fish to remove all of the remaining scales. With the knife angled toward the head, cut diagonally from the back fin to the belly, making 4 deep cuts to the bone on each side of the fish.

Combine the sherry, oyster sauce, olive oil, chile sauce, lemon zest, garlic, ginger, black beans, basil, and green onion. Rub this seasoning mix inside the slashes in the fish. Fit the slivered red pepper and cilantro into each slash. Refrigerate for up to 5 hours.

• last-minute cooking

Combine the cornstarch with an equal amount of cold water. Over highest heat, bring 4 inches water to a rapid boil in a Chinese steamer. Place a double layer of foil in the steamer tray, making sure there is plenty of room around the edges to allow the steam to circulate. Turn the edges of the foil up to help trap accumulated juices. Rub the foil with a little cooking oil, then lay the fish on the foil. Pour any extra marinade over the fish, then cover the steamer with the lid.

Steam the fish until the flesh becomes white and a chopstick easily sinks into the meat, about 15 to 20 minutes. When the fish is done, lift the foil out of the steamer and slide the fish onto a heated serving platter. Transfer all of the accumulated juices to a small saucepan, bring to a boil, and stir in a little of the cornstarch mixture to lightly thicken. Taste and adjust seasonings. Pour the sauce over the fish and serve at once.

• menu ideas

Dinner party for 4: Marinated Goat Cheese with Pepper Berries, Garlic, and Mint, Whole Rainbow Steamed Fish served with Jade Rice, lettuce greens tossed with one of the salad dressings from Chapter 3, and Fantastic Raspberry Ice Cream.

Sautéed Filet of Sole
with Champagne Herb Sauce

One of the most important goals when creating a new dish is achieving a balance of flavor: No seasoning, spice, or herb should overwhelm the other ingredients. In the following recipe, sautéed sole is topped with a sauce made with champagne, oyster sauce, shiitake mushrooms, fresh herbs, and pine nuts. With each bite you can distinguish the delicate flavor of the sole and a slight crispness from its browned exterior, the yeasty flavor from the champagne, low notes from the oyster sauce and mushrooms, and high notes from the herbs. All the flavors and textures harmonize.

- Easy
- Serves 4 as a main entrée.

8 pieces fresh filet of sole, about 1½
   pounds total
2 tablespoons dried herbes de provence
1 teaspoon salt
½ teaspoon freshly ground black pepper
1 cup white flour

• champagne herb sauce

3 cups dry champagne
1 tablespoon oyster sauce
2 teaspoons dark sesame oil
¼ teaspoon sugar
2 teaspoons cornstarch
•
2 cloves garlic, finely minced
1 red bell pepper, stemmed and seeded
¼ pound fresh shiitake mushrooms
¼ cup pine nuts
2 tablespoons slivered fresh basil leaves
2 tablespoons chopped fresh cilantro
⅓ cup cooking oil

• advance preparation

Preheat the oven to 325°F. Trim the sole of any ragged edges. In a small bowl, combine the herbes de provence, salt, and pepper. Set aside the flour. In a small saucepan, combine the champagne, oyster sauce, sesame oil, sugar, and cornstarch, and place over high heat. Bring the sauce to a boil, then continue to boil until only 1 cup remains. Cool and refrigerate the sauce. Set aside the minced garlic. Cut the bell pepper into 1-inch-long slivers. Discard the mushroom stems. Overlap the caps and cut into ⅛-inch-thin slices. Toast the pine nuts on a baking sheet in the preheated oven until golden, about 8 minutes. The recipe to this point can be completed up to 8 hours in advance of last-minute cooking.

• last-minute cooking

Set aside the basil and cilantro. Place a layer of newspaper or wax paper on the counter. Add the sole and sprinkle with the dry herb mixture. Dust each filet with flour, then shake off all of the excess.

Place two 12-inch sauté pans on 2 burners over high heat. When the sauté pans become hot, add 2 tablespoons of the cooking oil to each one. Roll the oil around the bottom of the pans, then add the sole. Sauté about 1 minute until golden on underside, then carefully turn

over and cook about 1 minute more. The sole is done when it just begins to flake when prodded with a fork. Transfer the sole to 4 heated dinner plates.

Return 1 of the sauté pans to high heat. Add the remaining oil, garlic, bell pepper, and mushrooms. Sauté 15 seconds, then add the champagne sauce. Bring the sauce to a rapid boil and cook until the mushrooms soften, about 20 seconds. Stir in the basil, cilantro, and pine nuts. Spoon the sauce over the filets and serve at once.

• menu ideas

Easy weeknight dinner for 4: Sautéed Filet of Sole with Champagne Herb Sauce, spinach salad with one of the salad dressings from Chapter 3, hot sourdough rolls, and fresh fruit.

note: It is impractical to serve this dish to more than 4 people unless you want to stand in front of the stove panfrying the fish in relays while your friends eat their portions in the dining room. For large amounts, rub the filets with a little thin soy sauce and dry sherry, then broil the sole, make the sauce separately in a small sauté pan, and spoon this over the cooked fish.

Creole Sea Scallops with Crab and Asparagus

"Food people" are usually planning their next dining adventure before the current meal has even been served. Thus, on our first visit to New Orleans, having heard of a talented young chef named Susan Spicer, and feeling afraid we were about to miss the lunch hour, we went directly from the airport to the little restaurant next to the Maison De Ville Hotel where she was "chefing." The complex tastes of her food fired our imaginations as we planned our culinary conquest of the finest restaurants in New Orleans in between Jazz Festival events. Although in this recipe, which is based on flavor memories from her restaurant, the scallops simmer in a rich sauce, the sauce is also excellent cooked separately in a sauté pan, then spooned over barbecued or broiled fish. The only divergence from orthodox Creole cooking is the use of Chinese oyster sauce, which adds depth of flavor.

- Easy
- Serves 4 as a main entrée.

1½ pounds large fresh sea scallops, about 12
½ pound fresh crab meat
1 bunch pencil-thin asparagus
5 cloves garlic, finely minced
2 shallots, peeled and minced
1 bay leaf
¼ cup fresh thyme sprigs
¼ cup chopped fresh oregano leaves
1 medium-sized vine-ripened tomato, seeded and chopped
1 cup whipping cream
½ cup dry vermouth
1 tablespoon oyster sauce
¼ teaspoon ground cayenne pepper or Asian chile sauce
¼ teaspoon sweet paprika
¼ cup light-grade olive oil or cooking oil
Salt, to taste

• advance preparation

Remove and discard the little secondary muscle from the side of each scallop. Pick over the crab meat to remove any shells. Snap off and discard the tough ends from the asparagus, then cut the asparagus on a diagonal into 2-inch-long pieces.

Set aside the garlic and shallots. In a small bowl, combine the bay leaf, thyme, oregano, tomato, cream, vermouth, oyster sauce, cayenne pepper, and paprika. Place a 10-inch sauté pan over medium-high heat. Add 2 tablespoons of the oil and the minced garlic and shallots. Sauté for 10 seconds, then add the sauce.

Bring to a rapid boil and cook the sauce until it thickens enough to lightly coat a spoon, about 3 minutes. Transfer the sauce to a small bowl, cool, cover, and refrigerate. The recipe to this point can be completed up to 8 hours in advance of last-minute cooking.

• last-minute cooking

Place a 12-inch sauté pan over highest heat. When hot, add the remaining 2 tablespoons oil. When the oil becomes hot, add the scallops in a single layer and sauté on both sides until lightly browned, about 2 minutes total.

Add the sauce, scatter on the crab and asparagus, and cover the pan. Reduce the heat to medium and steam the scallops about 1 minute more. Scallops are done when they just begin to feel firm to the touch and are slightly undercooked in the center. Transfer scallops to 4 heated dinner plates. If the asparagus are not fully cooked, cover the pan and steam-cook them for a few more seconds. Taste the sauce and adjust the seasonings, then spoon the asparagus, crab, and sauce over the scallops and serve at once.

• menu ideas

An elegant dinner for 4: Crunchy Wild Rice Salad, Creole Sea Scallops with Crab and Asparagus accompanied by Garlic Mashed Potatoes with Mascarpone, and, for dessert, Chocolate Sorbet with Mangoes.

Szechwan Chile Clams

The smaller the clam, the more tender it is. That is why we are not fond of littleneck and cherrystone clams, and prefer the smaller steamer clams. When purchasing, ask the vendor to pick out only clams that are tightly closed. Storing clams in a sealed container causes them to suffocate, so if you don't plan to use them until the following day, place the clams in a bowl and cover loosely with a wet kitchen towel. (During refrigeration some of the clams will open.) When ready to cook the clams, remove them from the refrigerator, cover with cold water for 5 minutes, and discard any that do not close. While this recipe tosses clams in a spicy chile-garlic sauce, clams also taste wonderful matched with the sauces from the following recipes: Tiger Prawns with Thai Green Curry Sauce, Spicy South-western Scallops, or Thai Broiled Sole with Mint and Chiles.

- Easy
- Serves 4 as a main entrée.

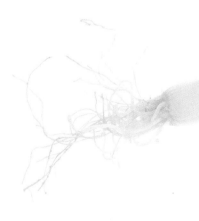

4 pounds steamer clams or small black mussels
1 small green bell pepper, stemmed and seeded
1 small red bell pepper, stemmed and seeded
2 whole green onions
1 small bunch fresh cilantro
¼ pound ground pork
6 cloves garlic, finely minced
2 tablespoons very finely minced fresh ginger
2 tablespoons dry sherry
1 tablespoon heavy soy sauce
1 tablespoon dark sesame oil
1 tablespoon Asian chile sauce
2 teaspoons red wine vinegar
½ teaspoon sugar
2 tablespoons cornstarch
2 tablespoons cooking oil

• advance preparation

Using a stiff-bristled brush, scrub the clams under cold water, then place in a bowl and refrigerate. Cut the bell peppers into ¼-inch-wide strips, then cut crosswise into ¼-inch cubes. Cut the green onions on a sharp diagonal into 1-inch lengths and set aside with the bell peppers. Coarsely chop the cilantro and set aside. Combine the pork, garlic, and ginger. In a small bowl, combine the sherry, soy sauce, sesame oil, chile sauce, vinegar, and sugar. The recipe to this point can be completed up to 8 hours prior to last-minute cooking.

• last-minute cooking

Combine the cornstarch with an equal amount of cold water. In a large pot, over highest heat, bring 4 cups water to a vigorous boil. Add all the clams, cover the pot, and steam the clams just until they open, about 5 minutes. Immediately tip the clams into a colander lined with cheesecloth placed over a large bowl (you will need 1 cup of the steaming liquid for the sauce).

Place a wok over highest heat, and when the wok becomes very hot, add the cooking oil. When the oil becomes hot, add the pork mixture. Stir-fry the pork, pressing it against the sides of the pan, until it loses all raw color and breaks apart into little pieces, about 4 minutes.

Add the bell peppers and green onions and stir-fry until the peppers brighten, about 2 minutes. Add the sauce plus 1 cup of the steaming liquid. Bring to a rapid boil, then stir in enough of the cornstarch mixture to lightly thicken the sauce. Taste and adjust the seasonings. Stir in the cilantro. Add the clams and toss to coat evenly with the sauce. Transfer to 4 heated dinner plates and serve at once.

• menu ideas

A chile festival dinner for 8: Spicy Gravlax with Mango Salsa, Grilled Vegetable Salad with Tortilla Threads, Szechwan Chile Clams served with Thai Rice Pilaf with Lemongrass, Basil, and Mint, and White Chocolate Mousse with Tropical Fruits.

Leaping Fresh from the Sea, Lakes, and Rivers

Barbecued Shrimp Brushed with Creole Butter

Here is one of the best ways to cook shrimp. Leaving the shell intact, cut along the top ridge, rinse out the vein, then pack seasoned butter, a flavored oil, fresh herbs, or Asian seasonings between the shell and shrimp body. When the shrimp are cooked, the flavors permeate the body while the exterior armor preserves an intense shrimp taste and keeps the bodies moist. Always purchase large or jumbo shrimp in order to make it easy to work the seasonings underneath the shell. If desired, complete the process hours in advance, keep the shrimp refrigerated, then lay them on the barbecue, pop them into the oven for broiling, or panfry in a heavy ungreased sauté pan. Note that this recipe will yield extra Creole Butter. Use it as a spread for "new wave" garlic bread, place small pieces across fish filets about to go under the broiler, or add to a pan before sautéing scallops or vegetables.

• Easy
• Serves 4 as a main entrée or 6 to 10 as an appetizer.

1½ pounds large raw shrimp, shells on
8 cloves garlic
4 shallots
¼ cup chopped fresh oregano leaves
2 tablespoons fresh thyme leaves
½ pound unsalted butter, softened
1 tablespoon Worcestershire sauce
½ teaspoon salt
½ teaspoon freshly ground black pepper
½ teaspoon freshly ground white pepper
1 teaspoon ground cayenne powder
2 lemons, cut into wedges

• advance preparation

Using small, sharp scissors, snip along the top ridge of each shrimp shell. Using a small knife, cut into the top surface of the shrimp to reveal the vein, then rinse it away.

In a food processor fitted with a chopping blade, mince the garlic, shallots, oregano, and thyme. Add the butter, Worcestershire sauce, salt, black and white peppers, and cayenne powder, and process until thoroughly blended. Fit the Creole Butter between the shell and shrimp and refrigerate. Set aside the lemon wedges. The recipe to this point can be completed up to 8 hours in advance of cooking.

• last-minute cooking

If using a gas barbecue or indoor grill, preheat to medium (350°F.). If using charcoal or wood, prepare a fire. When the coals or wood are ash-covered or the gas barbecue or indoor grill is preheated, brush the grill with oil, then place the shrimp on the grill. When the shells turn pink on the underside, turn the shrimp over. Cut into a shrimp to test for doneness. The shrimp are done when the shells turn pink and the shrimp meat has just lost its raw inside color, after about 6 minutes. (Alternatively, preheat the oven to 500°F. Then turn the oven setting to broil and broil the shrimp 4 inches from the heat for about 6 minutes. If using an electric oven, leave the oven door ajar.)

Serve the shrimp immediately on 4 heated dinner plates accompanied by lemon wedges and plenty of napkins.

• menu ideas

Outdoor summer dinner party: Barbecued Shrimp Brushed with Creole Butter, Cajun Asian Dirty Rice, Asian Stir-fried Asparagus with Tangerine and Pine Nuts, and Chocolate Nut Tart.

Cross-
Cultural
Cooking
with
Poultry
and
Game

Barbecued Chicken Breasts Caribbean

PRECEDING PAGE
Southwestern Fried Chicken
with Spicy Apricot Sauce

The cuisines of the world have been intermingling since Columbus unknowingly inaugurated the first great wave in the evolution of fusion food. Interestingly, nowhere did the Columbus discovery have a more immediate impact on a cuisine than in the Caribbean itself. Settlers from all over Europe followed Columbus, bringing with them food-stuffs as well as African slaves and then indentured servants from China and India. The cuisines of these diverse people fused with the cui-sine of the islands' indigenous popu-lation to become an entirely new style of cooking.

In the following recipe, such New World flavors as allspice, chiles, and rum are matched with chicken and olive oil (introduced into the Caribbean by the Spanish) as well as Asian ginger and soy sauce.

• Easy
• Serves 4 as a main entrée.

• **caribbean barbecue sauce**

¼ **cup chopped fresh cilantro**
2 **tablespoons finely minced fresh ginger**
¼ **cup freshly squeezed lime juice**
¼ **cup light-grade olive oil**
¼ **cup rum**
¼ **cup light brown sugar**
¼ **cup thin soy sauce**
2 **teaspoons Asian chile sauce**
1 **teaspoon freshly grated nutmeg**
½ **teaspoon ground allspice**
½ **teaspoon ground cinnamon**
¼ **teaspoon salt**
•
4 **whole boneless chicken breasts, skin on**
2 **cups sliced nectarine, mango, or papaya, for garnish**

• **advance preparation**

In a medium bowl, combine all of the barbecue sauce ingredients and stir well. The barbecue sauce can be made up to 24 hours in advance and refrigerated.

• **last-minute cooking**

Wash and pat dry the chicken breasts. Trim any excess fat from around the edges.

Combine two thirds of the barbecue sauce with the chicken and mari-nate for at least 15 minutes but for no longer than 1 hour. Set aside the remaining sauce to be spooned over the chicken after it has finished cooking.

If using a gas barbecue or indoor grill, preheat to medium (350°F.). If using charcoal or wood, prepare a fire. When the coals or wood are ash-covered or the gas barbecue or indoor grill is preheated, brush the grill with oil, then grill the chicken, skin side down, for about 6 minutes. Brush the chicken with more of the marinade that the chicken breasts soaked in, then turn the chicken over and cook about 6 minutes more. The chicken is done as soon as the breasts feel firm to the touch and the meat has just lost any pink tinge in the center.

Place the chicken on 4 heated dinner plates. Spoon over the reserved barbecue sauce (do not use the barbecue sauce that the chicken was soaked in) and garnish with sliced fruit. Serve at once.

• **menu ideas**

Summer dinner party for 8: Barbe-cued Chicken Breasts Caribbean, Panfried Potatoes with Rosemary, Candied Walnut Salad with Goat Cheese, and White Chocolate Mousse with Tropical Fruits.

note: In place of chicken breasts, substitute a frying chicken cut into pieces or quarters. Or substitute veal or pork chops, or firm-fleshed fish suitable for barbecuing, such as mahi mahi, swordfish, sea bass, or shark. As for the marinade, easy flavor variations include the substi-tution of lemon juice and its grated zest for the lime juice, honey or pineapple for the brown sugar, or mint for the cilantro.

Chicken Simmered in Cajun Tomato Sauce

Understanding the possibilities for varying recipes opens up the exciting, spontaneous world of culinary adventure. For example, in the following recipe, substitute a spicy sausage for the Cajun andouille sausage, replace thyme with cilantro, or stir roasted bell peppers into the sauce to enrich its flavors. Use the Cajun Tomato Sauce as you would an Italian tomato sauce. Make it in advance and refrigerate for 1 week or freeze for no longer than 3 months. Reheat, then generously spoon onto dinner plates with barbecued veal chops or broiled sole, or toss with 2 pounds boiled ravioli or tortellini.

• Moderate
• Serves 4 as a main entrée.

1 andouille sausage or other spicy sausage, about ½ pound
1 yellow onion, chopped
4 shallots, chopped
6 cloves garlic, finely minced
Grated zest (colored part of skin) from 1 lemon
¼ cup chopped fresh oregano leaves
¼ cup fresh thyme sprigs
1 green bell pepper, seeded and chopped
2 pounds vine-ripened tomatoes, seeded and chopped, about 3 cups
1 cup white wine or Homemade Chicken Stock (page 70)
2 tablespoons thin soy sauce
1 tablespoon Asian chile sauce
1 teaspoon gumbo filé (see note)
1 teaspoon cumin seeds, crushed
1 teaspoon salt
¼ teaspoon allspice
•

6 tablespoons light-grade olive oil or cooking oil
2 bunches chives, chopped
1 4-pound chicken, cut into pieces, or 8 breast halves, bone and skin on
Salt and freshly ground black pepper, to taste
1 cup unbleached white flour

• advance preparation

Cut the sausage into ⅛-inch slices. Set aside together the onion, shallots, and garlic. In a large bowl, combine the grated lemon zest, oregano, thyme, green bell pepper, chopped tomatoes, wine or stock, soy sauce, chile sauce, gumbo filé, cumin, salt, and allspice.

Place a 12-inch frying pan over medium heat. Add 2 tablespoons of the olive oil. When the oil is hot but not smoking, add the sausage, onion, shallots, and garlic, and sauté until the onion turns a deep golden, about 15 minutes. Add the sauce ingredients. Bring to a boil, then reduce the heat to low and simmer, uncovered, for 30 minutes, stirring occasionally. The sauce can be made up to a week in advance. If proceeding directly to the next step, temporarily transfer the sauce to a bowl, wipe out the frying pan, and return the frying pan to the stove.

Set aside the chives.

• last-minute cooking

Rinse and pat dry the chicken. If using chicken breasts, cut off the rib bone edge. Place the chicken on a baking sheet or layer of newspaper and sprinkle with salt and freshly ground black pepper. Coat the chicken with flour, shaking off all of the excess flour. Place a 12-inch frying pan over medium-high heat. Add the remaining ¼ cup olive oil. When the oil becomes hot but is not yet smoking, add the chicken. Brown the chicken until golden on each side, about 8 minutes total cooking time.

Transfer the chicken to a layer of paper towels. Tip out and discard all of the oil from the frying pan. Add the Cajun Tomato Sauce to the pan, bring to a boil, and scrape the bottom of the pan to incorporate the chicken drippings into the sauce. Add the chicken, skin side down, reduce the heat to low, cover the pan, and simmer until a meat thermometer registers 160°F. when inserted deeply into the meat or the chicken feels firm to the touch, about 15 minutes.

Transfer the chicken to 4 heated dinner plates. Remove all visible fat from the surface of the sauce using strips of paper toweling. Taste and adjust seasonings, then spoon the sauce over the chicken. Sprinkle with chopped chives and serve at once.

• **menu ideas**

For a simple dinner, serve Chicken Simmered in Cajun Tomato Sauce with Two-Way Pasta and a garden salad tossed with one of the salad dressings from Chapter 3.

note: The special ingredient in the sauce is gumbo filé, a mixture of ground young sassafras leaves. Gumbo filé is available at fine markets and gourmet shops.

Chinese Barbecued Chicken with Ginger, Cinnamon, and Chiles

A favorite Chinese method of cooking chicken is to submerge it in a large amount of simmering water or flavored stock, then cover the pot, turn off the heat, and leave the chicken submerged for 1 hour. During the slow cooling process, the chicken finishes cooking, the flavor notes permeate right to the bone, and the meat remains extraordinarily tender. Start the cooking process just an hour or two before you plan to serve dinner, then, veering from Chinese culinary practice, finish the chicken on a barbecue in order to crisp the skin and add to its depth of flavor.

• Easy
• Serves 4 as a main entrée.

Red-Cooked Sauce (page 142)
2 frying chickens, cut into pieces
Mango Salsa (page 27)

• **advance preparation**

One to two hours prior to serving the dish, wash and pat dry the chicken pieces. Using a heavy saucepan that will be large enough to hold the chicken pieces, make the Red Sauce and simmer 1 hour. Add the chicken pieces. If the liquid does not cover the chicken, add enough boiling water to barely cover the chicken. Bring the sauce back to a simmer, cover the pot, and cook the chicken 5 minutes. Then turn the heat off and let the chicken cool in the pot for 1 to 2 hours.

Prepare the salsa.

• **last-minute cooking**

If using a gas barbecue or indoor grill, preheat to medium (350°F.). If using charcoal or wood, prepare a fire. When the coals or wood are ash-covered or the gas barbecue or

indoor grill is preheated, brush the grill with oil, then grill the chicken about 5 minutes on each side, until the meat is thoroughly heated through and the skin is crisp.

Divide the barbecued chicken among 4 dinner plates. Spoon the salsa next to the chicken. Serve at once. Refrigerate the leftover Red Sauce for up to 1 month or freeze indefinitely.

• **menu ideas**

Dinner party for 4: Chinese Barbecued Chicken with Ginger, Cinnamon, and Chiles served with Any Kind of Bread Rolls, Baby Greens with Blue Cheese-Pecan Dressing, and, for dessert, fresh strawberries with Valrhona Cocoa Truffles.

Stir-Fried Coconut Curry Chicken with Bok Choy and Basil

The Chinese have perfected blow torch cooking with restaurant wok burners that produce 150,000 BTUs of heat! To duplicate this intensity, strictly on a hobby level, purchase a portable outdoor wok burner, available at Chinese restaurant supply stores in large cities, or buy a very large wok and position it over your gas or charcoal barbecue. No more soggy vegetables, rubbery meat, or blaring fire alarms—just crowds of spectators watching your new outdoor sport.

- Moderate
- Serves 4 as a main entrée.

2 whole chicken breasts, boned and skinned, about 1¼ pounds
2 tablespoons dry sherry
1 tablespoon hoisin sauce
1 tablespoon dark sesame oil
1 small bunch bok choy
1 red bell pepper
5 whole green onions
4 cloves garlic, finely minced
1 tablespoon very finely minced fresh ginger
3 tablespoons cooking oil

• stir-fry sauce

¼ cup chopped fresh basil leaves
⅓ cup dry sherry
⅓ cup coconut milk
1 tablespoon oyster sauce
1 tablespoon hoisin sauce
1 tablespoon dark sesame oil
1 tablespoon red wine vinegar
1 teaspoon cornstarch
1 teaspoon sugar
1 teaspoon store-bought Indian curry paste or 1 tablespoon curry powder

• advance preparation

Cut the chicken lengthwise into 1-inch-wide strips. With your knife, working on a sharp bias, cut each strip into ⅛-inch-thin rectangular pieces. Place the chicken in a bowl, add the sherry, hoisin sauce, and sesame oil, and mix thoroughly with your fingers. Marinate at least 15 minutes but no longer than 8 hours.

Separate the bok choy stalks. Cut each stalk on a sharp diagonal into 1-inch lengths, turning the stalk over half a turn after each cut. Set aside 4 cups bok choy. Stem and seed the red bell pepper, then cut into ¼-inch-by-1-inch rectangles. Cut the green onions on a sharp diagonal into ½-inch lengths. Combine the garlic and ginger. In a small bowl, combine all of the ingredients for the stir-fry sauce. The recipe to this point can be completed up to 8 hours in advance of cooking.

• last-minute cooking

Place a wok over highest heat. When the wok becomes very hot, add 2 tablespoons of the cooking oil to the center. Tilt the wok to coat the sides with oil. When the oil just begins to smoke, add the chicken and stir-fry just until it loses its raw outside color, about 1 minute. Transfer to a platter.

Immediately return the wok to highest heat. Add the remaining 1 tablespoon cooking oil to the center, then add the garlic mixture. Sauté the garlic for a few seconds, then add the vegetables and stir-fry until they brighten, about 2 minutes.

Return the chicken to the wok and pour in the sauce. When the sauce comes to a low boil, taste and adjust the seasonings. Transfer to 4 heated dinner plates. Serve at once.

• menu ideas

Asian dinner party for 8: Scallop Dumplings in Coconut-Basil Sauce (ask the guests to help fold the dumplings), Cal-Asian Salad with Red Sweet Ginger Dressing, Stir-Fried Coconut Curry Chicken with Bok Choy and Basil served with Jasmine Steamed Rice, and Fantastic Raspberry Ice Cream with Velvet Chocolate Sauce.

Southwestern Fried Chicken with Spicy Apricot Sauce

Amidst the anti-salt, anti-cholesterol movement that plagues our country, this battering and frying technique may be a culinary dinosaur. Yet there are few eating sensations as delectable as biting through a crunchy batter into juicy chicken.

This recipe requires a little advance planning on the part of the cook. First the chicken is soaked for a minimum of 8 hours in a chile, cilantro, and buttermilk mixture that flavors and tenderizes the meat. Then the chicken is dusted with seasoned flour and air-dried for at least 45 minutes, which ensures that the batter will remain fixed in place throughout the frying process and creates a crisp coating. Everything except the last-minute cooking can be completed hours in advance.

• Moderate
• Serves 4 as a main entrée.

2 cups buttermilk
1 cup chopped fresh cilantro
6 cloves garlic, finely minced
2 shallots, minced
1 tablespoon crushed chile flakes
1 tablespoon salt
2 small frying chickens, cut into pieces
3 cups unbleached white flour
Salt and freshly ground black pepper, to taste
2 cups cooking oil

• spicy apricot sauce

12 dried apricots
12 ounces apricot nectar
¾ cup sugar
½ cup white distilled vinegar
½ cup water
1 tablespoon finely minced fresh ginger
1 teaspoon Asian chile sauce

• advance preparation

In a bowl large enough to hold the chicken, combine the buttermilk, cilantro, garlic, shallots, chile flakes, and salt. Stir well. Rinse the chicken pieces and pat dry. Add the chicken to the buttermilk mixture and marinate in the refrigerator for at least 8 hours or overnight.

After the chicken has marinated, place the flour in a large bowl and season with a sprinkling of salt and freshly ground black pepper. Dip the chicken pieces, one at a time, into the flour, then shake off all excess flour and place the chicken on a wire rack set over a baking sheet. Repeat this operation with the remaining chicken. Refrigerate the chicken, uncovered, on the wire rack for at least 45 minutes and for as long as 4 hours.

Make the Spicy Apricot Sauce: In a 2-quart saucepan, combine all of the sauce ingredients and bring to a low boil. Reduce the heat to low, cover the saucepan, and simmer 20 minutes. Then cool the sauce to room temperature. Place the sauce in an electric blender and blend until completely liquefied. Spicy Apricot Sauce will last indefinitely if stored in a tightly sealed jar in the refrigerator.

• last-minute cooking

Preheat the oven to 180°F. Warm the apricot sauce. Place the cooking oil in a 14-inch skillet and heat to 365°F. (at this temperature, bubbles will form around the end of a wooden spoon when it is dipped into the oil). Place half the chicken, skin side down, in the hot oil. Reduce the heat to medium and fry the chicken until golden on one side, about 10 minutes. Turn the chicken pieces and cook until golden on the other side, about 10 more minutes. Turn the pieces once more and cook about 5 minutes. During the cooking, adjust the heat so the oil is always bubbling around the pieces but is never smoking. The chicken is done when a meat thermometer registers 160°F. when inserted deeply into the meat and when the juices run clear when the chicken is pierced deeply with a fork. Drain the chicken on a wire rack, then transfer to heated dinner plates and keep warm in the oven while cooking the remainder. Serve at once accompanied by the Spicy Apricot Sauce.

Braised Chicken Breasts with Saffron Ginger Sauce

Unlike braised beef, lamb, and pork, which improve in flavor if made a day or two in advance, braised chicken, lacking the necessary marbling of fat, becomes tough once it is cooked and refrigerated no matter how carefully it is reheated. Because of this, begin the braising process just before guests arrive, and when the chicken becomes tender, set the pot aside and gently reheat a short time later. Braising more than a double portion of chicken is impractical. Instead, when you need to make very large quantities, marinate and barbecue the chicken and while it sizzles on the outdoor grill, make the sauce in a sauté pan. Transfer the barbecued chicken to heated dinner plates and spoon the sauce across the top of the chicken.

• Moderate
• Serves 4 as a main entrée.

4 whole chicken breasts, keel bone removed and breasts split in half
1 cup unbleached white flour
1½ teaspoons salt
½ teaspoon freshly ground black pepper
1 bunch chives, chopped
1 medium carrot
½ cup pine nuts
2 tablespoons finely minced fresh ginger
1 cup whipping cream
½ cup white wine
1 tablespoon oyster sauce
1 tablespoon honey
½ teaspoon Asian chile sauce
Large pinch saffron threads
⅓ cup cooking oil

• advance preparation

Preheat the oven to 325°F. Wash and pat dry the chicken breasts. With a heavy knife or poultry shears, cut off the rib bone edge. Set aside separately the flour, 1 teaspoon of the salt, the pepper, and chives. Peel the carrot and cut on a sharp diagonal into ⅛-inch slices; then overlap the slices and cut into ⅛-inch-thin matchsticks. Toast the pine nuts in the preheated oven until golden, about 8 minutes. Combine the ginger, cream, wine, oyster sauce, honey, chile sauce, remaining ½ teaspoon salt, and saffron. The recipe to this point can be completed up to 8 hours in advance of cooking.

• last-minute cooking

Place a 12- or 14-inch sauté pan over medium-high heat. Place the chicken on a baking sheet or layer of news-paper. Sprinkle the chicken with salt and freshly ground pepper. Coat the chicken with flour, then shake each piece to remove all excess flour. Add the oil to the sauté pan and when the oil just begins to give off a wisp of smoke, add the chicken. Cook until the chicken turns golden, about 4 minutes, then turn the chicken over and cook until golden on the other side, about 4 more minutes. Regulate the heat so that the oil is always sizzling but never smoking.

When the chicken becomes golden, temporarily remove from the pan. Discard all of the oil from the pan and return the chicken, skin side up, to the pan. Add the sauce. Bring the sauce to a low simmer, cover the pan, reduce the heat to low, and simmer until a meat thermometer inserted deeply into the chicken registers 160°F. or the chicken feels firm to the touch, about 15 minutes. Transfer the chicken to 4 heated dinner plates. Remove all visible fat from the surface of the sauce using strips of paper toweling. Bring the sauce to a rapid boil, cook until the sauce thickens enough to lightly coat a spoon, then add the carrots. Taste and adjust sauce for salt and pepper. Spoon the sauce over the chicken. Sprinkle on the chives and pine nuts. Serve at once.

• menu ideas:

Since this recipe requires last-minute attention, choose a do-ahead side dish, such as Jade Rice, Polenta Madness, or Santa Fe Corn Bread.

Braised Chicken Breasts with Exotic Mushrooms

This recipe is a good example of how to combine flavor ideas from around the world to achieve new tastes. Exotic mushrooms and oyster sauce are used to achieve low, deep flavors while fresh oregano and chives provide fresh high notes. You can expand the flavor profile by adding 1 teaspoon Asian chile sauce to the sauce and sprinkling 1 tablespoon grated lemon and orange zest over the chicken just before serving. This braised chicken dish is also very good made with the lowly button mushroom rather than the "exotic" mushrooms now sold in supermarkets nationwide.

- Moderate
- Serves 4 as a main entrée.

2 shallots, minced

3 cloves garlic, finely minced

1 pound exotic fresh mushrooms (such as morels, portabellos, chanterelles, or shiitakes)

1 cup Homemade Chicken Stock (page 70)

½ cup whipping cream

1 tablespoon oyster sauce

¼ teaspoon freshly ground black pepper

¼ cup fresh oregano leaves

1 bunch fresh chives, chopped

3 whole chicken breasts, split in half

½ cup light-grade olive oil or cooking oil

¼ cup dried herbes de provence

Salt and freshly ground black pepper, to taste

1 cup unbleached white flour

• advance preparation

Set aside the shallots and garlic. Wipe the mushrooms with a damp towel, then cut into ¼-inch slices. In a small bowl, combine the chicken stock, cream, oyster sauce, pepper, and oregano. Set aside the chives.

Wash and pat dry the chicken. Trim the excess fat from the edges of the chicken. With a heavy knife or poultry shears, cut off the rib bone edge. The recipe to this point can be completed up to 8 hours in advance of cooking.

• last-minute cooking

Warm the oven to 180°F. Place a 12-inch sauté pan over high heat. Add ¼ cup of the oil, the shallots, and garlic. When the garlic begins to sizzle, add the mushrooms. Stir and toss the mushrooms until they begin to soften, about 5 minutes. Temporarily remove the mushrooms from the sauté pan and set aside at room temperature.

Return the sauté pan to high heat and add the remaining ¼ cup oil. Place the chicken breasts on a baking sheet or layer of newspaper and sprinkle with the dried herbs and salt and pepper on both sides. Dust the chicken with a thin layer of flour, shaking off all of the excess.

When the oil becomes hot, add the chicken, bone side down, and cook until the underside of the breasts becomes golden, about 4 minutes. Turn the chicken over and brown until the breast skin becomes golden, about 4 more minutes.

Sprinkle the mushrooms over the chicken; then add the chicken stock mixture. Bring to a low boil, then cover, reduce the heat to low, and simmer until a meat thermometer registers 160°F. when inserted deeply into the meat or the chicken feels firm, about 15 minutes.

Transfer the chicken to 4 heated dinner plates and keep warm in the oven. Remove all visible fat from the surface of the sauce using strips of paper toweling. Bring the sauce to a vigorous boil and cook until it thickens enough to lightly coat a spoon. Spoon the sauce over the chicken, sprinkle with the chives, and serve at once.

• menu ideas

Dinner party for 8: Tuna Carpaccio with Capers, Chiles, and Ginger, then Tropical Salad with Citrus-Herb Dressing (make the dressing a day ahead) followed by Braised Chicken Breasts with Exotic Mushrooms served with hot Any Kind of Rolls (kept stockpiled in the freezer for just such occasions). Conclude with Kahlúa Passion Tiles made a week prior to the dinner.

Braised Chicken East and West

To go through life recipe-bound, repeating the measurements of ingredients with dreary exactitude, is to ignore the infinite creative possibilities present in every dish. In this recipe, for example, you can substitute veal shanks for the chicken, replace the leek with a fistful of shallots, or cast out fresh tarragon in favor of aromatic fresh cilantro. Or you can leave out the sauce and simply season the chicken and panfry as described in the recipe. Once the exterior of the chicken turns a wonderful golden, reduce the heat to low, cover the pan, and cook about 15 minutes more, until the internal temperature reaches 160°F. Panfried chicken, sheathed with its crisp, herb-flecked skin, is excellent served with lemon wedges, Creole Mayonnaise, or with any of the salsas from this book.

- Moderate
- Serves 4 as a main entrée.

1 small leek, white section only
6 cloves garlic, finely minced
1 small yellow onion, chopped
½ pound button mushrooms, thinly sliced
1 red bell pepper, seeded and chopped
1½ pounds vine-ripened tomatoes, seeded and chopped
1 cup white wine
¼ cup fresh tarragon leaves
2 tablespoons oyster sauce
½ teaspoon Asian chile sauce (optional)
2 tablespoons grated or finely minced lemon zest (colored part of skin)
1 tablespoon grated or finely minced orange zest (colored part of skin)

2 3-pound frying chickens, cut into pieces
¼ cup dried herbes de provence
Salt and freshly ground black pepper, to taste
2 cups unbleached white flour
½ cup light-grade olive oil or cooking oil

• advance preparation

Split the white end of the leek in half lengthwise, separate and wash each layer, then cut crosswise into ⅛-inch-thin slices. Combine the leeks, garlic, and onion.

Combine the mushrooms and bell pepper. Combine the tomatoes, wine, tarragon, oyster sauce, chile sauce, and 1 tablespoon of the lemon zest. In a separate small dish, set aside the remaining lemon zest and the orange zest.

Wash and pat dry the chicken. If the breasts are whole, then split them in half; cut off and discard the rib bone edge. Trim the excess fat from the edges of the chicken pieces. The recipe to this point can be completed up to 8 hours in advance of cooking.

• last-minute cooking

Place a 14-inch sauté pan or very large frying pan over high heat. Place the chicken pieces on a baking sheet or layer of newspaper and sprinkle the chicken with the dried herbs, salt, and freshly ground black pepper. Dust the chicken with a thin layer of flour, shaking off all of the excess.

When the pan becomes very hot, add the olive oil. When the oil becomes hot, add the chicken, skin side down. Cook the chicken until golden, then turn the pieces over and cook the other side until golden, about 8 minutes total cooking time. While browning the chicken, regulate the heat so that the oil always sizzles but never smokes. Temporarily remove the chicken from the pan.

Tip out all but ¼ cup of the oil from the sauté pan. Return the pan to high heat and add the leeks, garlic, and onion. Sauté 2 minutes, then add the mushrooms and pepper. Sauté 1 minute, then add the wine sauce. Return the chicken to the pan, skin side up, and spoon the sauce over the chicken. Bring the sauce to a boil, cover the pan, reduce the heat to very low, and simmer the chicken 15 minutes, or until a meat thermometer registers 160°F. when inserted deeply into the meat.

Transfer the chicken to 4 heated dinner plates. Remove all visible fat from the surface of the sauce using strips of paper toweling. Bring the sauce to a vigorous boil. Taste and adjust the seasonings, especially for salt. Spoon the sauce over the chicken pieces, sprinkle on the grated lemon and orange skin, and serve at once.

• menu ideas

An easy menu for 8: Marinated Goat Cheese with Pepper Berries, Garlic, and Mint, a garden salad with the dressing from Southwest Caesar Salad, Braised Chicken East and West with Jasmine Steamed Rice, and, for dessert, a premium ice cream topped with Caramel Butter Sauce.

Cross-Cultural Cooking with Poultry and Game

Wok-Seared Duck with Shrimp, Pine Nuts, and Tangerine Zest

Tired of ending up with mushy textures, watery sauces, and rubbery meats when cooking in a wok? Then follow these simple guidelines. Unless you have a commercial stove-top or wok jet burner, never stir-fry more than 1 pound of meat or seafood or more than 4 cups of vegetables at one time in the wok. Cut ingredients into very thin slices in order to speed the cooking process. Line up all of the ingredients next to the stove in the order they are going into the wok and toss away the recipe directions. Cooking in a wok and reading are incompatible activities. Preheat the wok over highest heat until it is blistering hot. Then proceed with the stir-frying without ever reducing the heat. The moment an ingredient changes color, it's cooked; proceed with the next step in the stir-fry process. If you deviate from these rules during the minute or so it takes to stir-fry a dish, it will be time to start reviewing takeout menus from nearby Chinese restaurants.

• Moderate
• Serves 4 as a main entrée.

1 large boneless duck breast, about 1¼ pounds, or the meat from 1 whole duck, boned by your butcher
2 tablespoons hoisin sauce
2 tablespoons dry sherry
2 tablespoons dark sesame oil
½ pound raw medium shrimp
2 medium zucchini
2 red bell peppers
4 whole green onions
½ cup pine nuts
4 cloves garlic, finely minced
1 tablespoon very finely minced fresh ginger
½ cup pomegranate seeds (optional)
¼ cup cooking oil

• sauce

¼ cup dry sherry
2 tablespoons tomato sauce
2 tablespoons oyster sauce
1 tablespoon hoisin sauce
1 tablespoon dark sesame oil
2 teaspoons white wine vinegar
2 teaspoons Asian chile sauce
2 teaspoons cornstarch
1 teaspoon grated tangerine zest plus the juice from 1 tangerine
¼ cup chopped fresh cilantro

• advance preparation

Remove and discard all of the duck skin. Cut the duck into ⅛-inch-thin slices, then cut the slices into 1-inch lengths. Place the duck in a bowl, add the hoisin sauce, sherry, and sesame oil, then mix thoroughly and refrigerate for at least 15 minutes but no longer than 8 hours. Shell

and devein the shrimp, then split in half lengthwise and refrigerate. Cut the zucchini into ⅛-inch-thin disks. Stem and seed the bell peppers, then cut into 1-by-¼-inch rectangles. Cut the green onions on a sharp diagonal into 1-inch lengths, then combine with the zucchini and bell peppers.

Preheat the oven to 325°F. Place the pine nuts on a baking sheet, place in the preheated oven, and toast until golden, about 8 minutes. Set aside the garlic and ginger together. Set aside the pomegranate seeds. In a small bowl, combine all of the sauce ingredients. The recipe to this point can be completed up to 8 hours in advance of cooking.

• last-minute cooking

Place a wok over highest heat. When the wok becomes very hot, add 2 tablespoons of the oil to the center and roll the oil around the sides. When the oil just begins to smoke, add the duck and stir-fry until it just loses its raw outside color, about 2 minutes. Transfer the duck to a plate. Immediately return the wok to highest heat. Add 1 tablespoon cooking oil and roll it around the sides of the wok. When the oil gives off a wisp of smoke, add the shrimp. Stir and toss until the shrimp turn white and pink, then slide the shrimp from the wok onto the plate holding the duck.

Immediately return the wok to highest heat. Add the remaining 1 tablespoon cooking oil to the center, then add the garlic and ginger. Sauté a few seconds, then add the vegetables and stir-fry until they brighten, about 2 minutes.

Return the duck and shrimp to the wok, then pour in the sauce. Bring the sauce to a low boil, then stir in the pine nuts and pomegranate seeds. Taste and adjust seasonings. Spoon onto a heated platter or individual dinner plates. Serve at once.

•menu ideas

Chinese party for 8: Crisp Salmon Spring Rolls, Cal-Asian Salad with Red Sweet Ginger Dressing, Wok-Seared Duck with Shrimp, Pine Nuts, and Tangerine Zest served with Jade Rice, and, for dessert, Black and White Bread Pudding.

Thai Red Curry Duck Santa Fe Style

Let roast duck remain in the province of restaurant cooking. Eliminate grease-splattered ovens and, if you are a duck addict as we are, always braise or barbecue duck. Ask the butcher to cut the duck into pieces. Trim away all excess fat around the edges of each piece, then using a sharp knife, score the duck skin in a crisscross pattern. To braise duck, first brown it in a heavy, non-oiled skillet until all the fat is rendered and the skin glistens in a deep golden hue. Then transfer the duck to a simmering sauce such as the one used for Braised Lamb Shanks East and West or Creole Osso Buco and simmer only 15 minutes to complete the cooking. To barbecue duck, first marinate the duck pieces with their skin scored, then barbecue the pieces until the skin becomes crisp while the meat is still pink.

In the following recipe, the barbecued duck is placed on a Thai Red Curry Sauce and garnished with avocado fans, a sprinkling of tender raw white corn kernels, and chopped cilantro. Serve this duck with do-ahead dishes such as Southwest Caesar Salad with Chile Croutons, Garlic Mashed Potatoes with Mascarpone Cheese, and Chocolate Nut Tart.

• Challenging
• Serves 4 as a main entree.

• red curry sauce

2 dried ancho chiles
2 medium-sized vine-ripened tomatoes
2 shallots
4 cloves garlic
¼ cup white wine vinegar
2 tablespoons sugar
2 tablespoons fish sauce
1 teaspoon coriander seeds, finely ground
1 teaspoon cornstarch

•

2 whole fresh ducks, each cut into pieces
¼ cup hoisin sauce
¼ cup dry sherry
2 large limes
3 ears white corn
1 large ripe avocado
½ cup chopped fresh cilantro or mint
1 tablespoon light-grade olive oil or cooking oil

• advance preparation

Make the Red Curry Sauce: Stem and seed the dried chiles. Place the chiles in a saucepan, cover with water, bring to a simmer, and remove from the heat. Cover and let rest for 25 minutes. Seed and coarsely chop the tomatoes. Peel the shallots and garlic. Place the chiles, tomatoes, shallots, garlic, vinegar, sugar, fish sauce, coriander, and cornstarch in an electric blender. Blend until completely smooth. Transfer to a glass jar, seal tightly, and refrigerate for up to 1 month.

Cut off and discard all excess fat from the duck. Using a sharp knife, score the skin in a crisscross pattern. In a bowl, combine the hoisin sauce, sherry, and grated or finely minced zest (colored part of skin) from 2

limes as well as the lime juice and pulp. Marinate the duck for 1 hour.

Remove the husks from the corn. Stand the corn on its end, cut off the kernels, and set aside.

• last-minute cooking

Cut around the avocado seed, twist the avocado to separate into 2 halves, then remove the seed, and with a large spoon, scoop out the flesh. Cut the avocado into thin slices and sprinkle with lime juice, lemon juice, or a little wine vinegar to prevent discoloration. Set aside the herbs.

If using a gas barbecue, preheat to medium (350°F.). If using charcoal or wood, prepare a fire. When the gas barbecue is preheated or the coals or wood are ash-covered, brush the grill with oil, then grill the duck, skin side down, about 10 minutes, until the skin turns deep golden. Brush the duck with more marinade, turn the pieces over, and barbecue about 10 more minutes, until the meat is still slightly pink in the center, and a meat thermometer registers 145°F. when inserted deeply into the duck.

Meanwhile, place a 10-inch sauté pan over medium heat. Add the olive oil and Red Curry Sauce, and bring to a low boil. Taste and adjust seasonings, especially for salt. Place the sauce on 4 heated dinner plates, then position duck pieces on top of the sauce. Place a little fan of avocado on each plate, and sprinkle raw corn and cilantro over the duck. Serve at once.

Thai Barbecued Squab with Banana Salsa

Our first exposure to Thai barbecued chicken occurred late one morning when we left the northern Thai city of Chiang Mai, motored through fields studded with rice paddies, and, making a series of hairpin turns, climbed high into the mountains to visit the famous Doi Suthep temple. Joining bus tours, peasants, and European trekking groups, we fortified ourselves with sticks of barbecued chicken cooked by vendors on small portable barbecues, then began our ascent up 290 broad steps flanked on each side by huge undulating ceramic dragon tails serving as railings to steady weary travelers.

The following barbecue sauce duplicates the marvelous balance of sour, spice, and richness we tasted in that Thai barbecued chicken. It is equally good with other barbecued meats, firm fish, and jumbo shrimp barbecued with their shells on. Because the flavor of fresh lime juice deteriorates quickly, make the barbecue sauce the day you plan to use it.

• Easy
• Serves 4 as a main entrée.

• thai barbecue sauce

Grated zest (colored part of skin), juice, and pulp from 3 large limes
1 cup hoisin sauce
⅓ cup oyster sauce
¼ cup fish sauce
¼ cup dry sherry
¼ cup honey
¼ cup Thai chile sauce
¼ cup finely minced fresh ginger
10 cloves garlic, finely minced
2 shallots, minced
½ cup mixture of chopped fresh cilantro, basil, or mint

•
4 fresh squab

• banana salsa

2 medium-sized firm bananas, peeled and chopped
1 red bell pepper, stemmed, seeded, and chopped
1 small ripe avocado, seeded, skinned, and diced
1 whole green onion, minced
¼ cup chopped fresh cilantro
2 tablespoons very finely minced fresh ginger
2 tablespoons freshly squeezed orange juice
2 tablespoons freshly squeezed lime juice
2 tablespoons brown sugar
2 tablespoons fish sauce
2 teaspoons Thai chile sauce

• advance preparation

Combine all of the ingredients for the Thai Barbecue Sauce and stir well. Using poultry shears or a heavy knife, split the squab in half. Within 1 hour of cooking, combine the barbecue sauce and the squab.

In a separate bowl, within 2 hours of serving, combine all of the ingredients for the banana salsa. Taste and adjust seasonings.

• last-minute cooking

If using a gas barbecue or indoor grill, preheat to medium (350°F.). If using charcoal or wood, prepare a fire. When the coals or wood are ash-covered or the gas barbecue or indoor grill is preheated, brush the grill with oil, then grill the squab, bone side down, for about 8 minutes. Brush with more sauce, turn the squab over, brush with sauce again, and cook for about 8 more minutes. Squab are done when the internal temperature on a meat thermometer reaches 145°F. for pink meat, and 155°F. for well-done meat. If roasting the squab, preheat the oven to 400°F. Place the squab on a wire rack over a shallow baking pan and roast approximately 20 minutes. Transfer the squab to 4 heated dinner plates, garnish with banana salsa, and serve at once.

• menu ideas

Dinner for 4: A green salad with one of the salad dressings from Chapter 3, Thai Barbecued Squab with Banana Salsa served with hot flour tortillas, and, for dessert, Chocolate Sorbet with Mangoes.

Quail Stuffed with Cèpes, Goat Cheese, and Sun-Dried Tomatoes

While local supermarkets routinely sell fresh Chilean sea bass, farm-raised salmon flown in from Norway, and an ever-expanding selection of fruits from the tropics, this passion for fresh, rare ingredients has yet to extend to commercially raised game birds such as squab and quail. If fresh quail are not available by special-order, rather than buying them frozen, substitute 4 bone-in, fresh game hens (and follow the recipe as written), or 4 whole boned but not skinned chicken breasts and proceed as follows: Lay the chicken breasts on a work surface, meat side up, spread the stuffing in the center, roll each breast into a cylinder, and tie closed using kitchen string. Season the chicken breasts with salt and freshly ground black pepper, dust with flour, and brown in ¼ cup light-grade olive oil until the skin is golden. Then follow the roasting instructions given in the recipe.

- Moderate
- Serves 4 as a main entrée.

½ ounce dried cèpes or porcini
    mushrooms
10 sun-dried tomatoes
4 cloves garlic, finely minced
½ yellow onion, minced
¼ pound button mushrooms, very thinly
    sliced
1 tablespoon fresh thyme leaves
¼ cup unsalted butter
2 tablespoons cognac
½ teaspoon each salt and freshly
    ground black pepper
4 ounces goat cheese

8 fresh quail, preferably with breast
    bone removed
¼ cup light-grade olive oil
¼ cup thin soy sauce
2 tablespoons honey

• **sauce**

⅓ cup Ancho Chile Jam (page 84)
1 cup whipping cream
Salt, to taste
¼ cup chopped fresh cilantro

• **advance preparation**

Place the dried mushrooms and tomatoes in a bowl and cover with 2 cups boiling water. After 30 minutes, remove the mushrooms and tomatoes and chop finely. Strain the water through a fine-meshed sieve and set aside.

In a medium bowl, combine the garlic, onion, fresh mushrooms, thyme, and the dried mushrooms and sun-dried tomatoes. Place a 12-inch sauté pan over high heat and add the butter. When the butter melts, add the mushroom mixture and sauté until the mushrooms soften. Add the water that the dried mushrooms and sun-dried tomatoes soaked in and the cognac and cook over high heat until all the liquid disappears, about 15 minutes. Add the salt and black pepper. Transfer the stuffing mixture from the sauté pan to a bowl and cool to room temperature. Then add the goat cheese and, using your fingers, combine until all of the ingredients are thoroughly mixed.

Wash and pat dry the quail. Stuff the quail, and if you wish, truss the openings closed. Refrigerate until ready to roast. In a small bowl, combine the olive oil, soy sauce, and honey.

In a small bowl, combine the Ancho Chile Jam and cream. The recipe to this point can be completed up to 8 hours in advance of cooking.

• **last-minute cooking**

Preheat the oven to 350°F. Set aside the cilantro. Place an elevated rack in a shallow roasting pan and position the quail on the rack. Brush the quail with the olive oil basting sauce, sprinkle with salt, and bake in the preheated oven 30 minutes, basting the quail every 10 minutes. Quail are done when the skin is golden but the meat is still slightly pink.

Place the quail on 4 heated dinner plates. Place the roasting pan on the stove-top over high heat. Add the ancho chile sauce and bring to a rapid boil. Scrape up all of the pan drippings and incorporate into the sauce. Taste and adjust the seasonings. Spoon the sauce around the quail. Sprinkle on the chopped cilantro and serve at once.

Rabbit Potpie with Roasted Vegetables

The following rabbit potpie recipe was inspired by Executive Chef Steven Kantrowitz at Tumblebrook Country Club in Connecticut. Roasted vegetables contribute rich low-note tastes, and a puff pastry garnish lessens the scorched-tongue syndrome common among chicken and rabbit potpie enthusiasts. Although these directions call for stir-frying the meat from a boned rabbit and assembling the "pies" at the last moment, the recipe can easily be modified so that everything is done in advance. Just complete the entire recipe but undercook the rabbit. To serve, gently reheat, then taste and adjust the seasonings and crown with the puff pastry decoration. Simplify the preparation by asking your butcher to bone the rabbit for you.

- Challenging
- Serves 4 as a main entrée.

2 ribs celery

3 medium carrots

½ pound small button mushrooms

1 small red onion

6 tablespoons light-grade olive oil or cooking oil

Salt and freshly ground black pepper, to taste

2 cups loosely packed spinach leaves, stems removed

1 rabbit, boned, or 1¼ pounds boned and skinned chicken thigh meat

1 tablespoon hoisin sauce

1 tablespoon thin soy sauce

6 tablespoons dry sherry

1 tablespoon dark sesame oil

½ teaspoon Asian chile sauce

4 cloves garlic, finely minced

1 tablespoon finely minced fresh ginger

⅔ cup whipping cream

½ cup Homemade Chicken Stock (page 70)

1 tablespoon cornstarch

2 tablespoons coarsely chopped fresh basil leaves

¼ cup coarsely chopped fresh oregano leaves

1 bunch chives, chopped

1 puff pastry sheet, 6 inches square

•advance preparation

Preheat the oven to 400°F. Cut the celery into ½-inch lengths. Cut the carrots into ⅛-inch-thin rounds. Discard the mushroom stems. Peel the onion and cut into ½-inch cubes. Place the celery, carrots, mushrooms, and onion in a bowl, toss with ¼ cup of the olive oil, and sprinkle with salt and black pepper. Spread the vegetables over a shallow roasting pan and roast in the oven until slightly brown and golden, about 20 minutes. Set aside the spinach leaves.

Cut the rabbit meat into ⅛-inch-thin bite-sized pieces. Place the rabbit in a bowl, add the hoisin sauce, soy sauce, 2 tablespoons of the sherry, the sesame oil, chile sauce, garlic, and ginger, and mix well. Marinate for at least 30 minutes and up to 8 hours.

In a small bowl, combine the cream, chicken stock, the remaining 4 tablespoons sherry, the cornstarch, basil, oregano, and chives. The recipe to this point can be completed up to 8 hours in advance of serving.

•last-minute cooking

Preheat the oven to 400°F. Cut the puff pastry into four 3-inch squares, triangles, circles, or rectangles. Place on a baking sheet and bake in the oven until golden and puffed, about 6 to 10 minutes.

Place the chicken stock mixture in a 12-inch sauté pan and bring to a low simmer. Add the roasted vegetables. Bring the sauce to a low boil, then turn the heat to the lowest setting.

Place a wok over highest heat. When the wok becomes very hot, add the remaining 2 tablespoons olive oil. When the oil becomes very hot, add the rabbit and stir and toss until it loses all raw outside color. Transfer the rabbit to the sauté pan holding the sauce.

Stir the spinach leaves into the sauce. Taste and adjust the seasonings, especially for salt and pepper. Ladle the rabbit onto 4 large heated dinner plates or large wide-lipped soup plates. Position a piece of puff pastry in the center of each plate. Serve at once.

•menu ideas

Hearty dinner for 4 on a cold winter evening: Rabbit Potpie with Roasted Vegetables accompanied by a simple green salad tossed with one of the dressings from Chapter 3, Polenta Madness, and, for dessert, wine glasses filled with White Chocolate Mousse and topped with fresh berries.

Spicy Barbecued Rabbit with Rosemary, Chiles, and Hoisin Sauce

Rabbit has no protective skin, which affects the way it should be cooked. For braising, dust the rabbit pieces with seasoned flour, lightly brown in a little fat, then simmer in a braising liquid for about 40 minutes, until the legs become tender. If roasting or barbecuing rabbit, cook it over medium-low heat, basting and turning the pieces frequently in order to keep the meat moist. Since the loin cooks more quickly than the legs, remove the loin and keep it warm in an oven while the legs finish cooking. As for stir-frying, rabbit makes a wonderful substitute for chicken, pork, and shrimp. Just ask your butcher to bone the rabbit for you, then proceed with the stir-fry directions as usual.

- Easy
- Serves 4 as a main entrée.

1 rabbit, cut into pieces for barbecuing
½ cup hoisin sauce
½ cup plum sauce
½ cup red wine
¼ cup Dijon mustard
¼ cup freshly squeezed lemon juice
6 cloves garlic, finely minced
4 serrano chiles, stemmed and finely minced (including seeds)
⅓ cup fresh rosemary sprigs
¼ cup chopped fresh sage

• advance preparation and last-minute cooking

Wash and pat dry the rabbit. In a bowl large enough to hold the rabbit pieces, combine all of the remaining ingredients and mix well. The recipe to this point can be completed up to a day ahead of cooking.

Add the rabbit to the marinade, combine evenly, and marinate for at least 30 minutes but for no longer than 2 hours.

If using a gas barbecue or indoor grill, preheat to medium (350°F.). If using charcoal or wood, prepare a fire. When the coals or wood are ash-covered or the gas barbecue or indoor grill is preheated, brush the grill with oil, add the rabbit, cover the barbecue, and reduce the heat to medium-low. Barbecue the rabbit until a meat thermometer registers 160°F. when inserted deeply into the meat, about 20 minutes. About every 6 minutes, remove the barbecue top, brush the rabbit with more of the marinade, and turn the pieces over. Because the loin cooks about 5 minutes more quickly than the legs, remove the loin first while continuing to cook the legs. (Alternatively, if roasting the rabbit, preheat the oven to 350°F. Place the rabbit on a wire rack and roast approximately 30 minutes, rotating the pieces and brushing on more marinade every 10 minutes.) Transfer the rabbit to 4 heated dinner plates and serve at once.

• menu ideas

Spicy Barbecued Rabbit with Rosemary, Chiles, and Hoisin Sauce, Garlic Mashed Potatoes with Mascarpone, baby lettuce greens with a salad dressing from Chapter 3, and Ginger Banana Cream Tart Lined with Chocolate.

Game Hens with Tamarind Glaze

In this recipe, rainbows of flavor, with new levels of taste blossoming after each bite, create a dynamic, intriguing eating experience. The garlic, soy sauce, and browned game hen skin contribute low, deep notes. Tamarind juice, Szechwan pepper, star anise, and fresh basil add high notes. By boiling down the sauce so that it nearly caramelizes, every flavor becomes magnified and hidden flavor nuances come to the surface.

• Moderate
• Serves 4 as a main entrée.

• tamarind sauce

1 cup freshly squeezed orange juice
1 cup Homemade Chicken Stock
  (page 70)
⅓ cup tamarind liquid (page 225)
¼ cup sugar
¼ cup dry sherry
1 tablespoon thin soy sauce
¼ teaspoon crushed Szechwan peppercorns
½ teaspoon salt
¼ star anise
2 cloves garlic, finely minced
1 tablespoon very finely minced fresh
  ginger
•

⅓ cup slivered fresh basil leaves
4 game hens, split in half
Salt and freshly ground black pepper, to
  taste
1 cup unbleached white flour
¼ to ½ cup cooking oil

• advance preparation and last-minute cooking

In a medium bowl, combine all of the ingredients for the Tamarind Sauce and stir well. The recipe to this point can be completed up to 8 hours in advance of cooking.

Set aside the basil leaves. Warm the oven to 180°F. Wash and pat dry the game hens. Place the game hens on a baking sheet or layer of newspaper and sprinkle with a little salt and black pepper. Dust the pieces with flour on all sides, then shake off all of the excess.

Place a deep, 14-inch skillet over high heat. When hot, add ¼ cup of the cooking oil. When the cooking oil becomes hot and just gives off a wisp of smoke, add the game hens in a single layer, bone side down. Sauté until they turn light golden, then turn the pieces over and continue cooking until golden, about 8 minutes total cooking. Regulate the heat so the oil is always sizzling but never smoking. Remove the game hens temporarily, and if the pan was not big enough to complete the browning of the game hens in one batch, brown the remaining game hens, adding additional oil if necessary, and remove from the pan.

Tip all the cooking oil from the pan. Add the sauce. Return the game hens, bone side down, to the pan, then bring the sauce to a low boil and cover the pot. Reduce the heat to very low and simmer until the meat feels firm or a meat thermometer registers 160°F. when inserted deeply into the meat, about 15 minutes.

Transfer the game hens from the pan to 4 heated dinner plates and place in the warm oven. Remove all visible fat from the surface of the sauce using strips of paper toweling. Turn the heat under the sauce to high and boil the sauce furiously, until it has reduced to ¾ cup and becomes golden, about 8 minutes. Stir in the basil. Remove and discard the star anise. Taste and adjust seasonings, then spoon the sauce over the game hens.

• menu ideas

As a special dinner for 4: Accompany the game hens with Wild Rice with Currants, Pine Nuts, and Port, Cajun Asian Ratatouille, and a premium store-bought ice cream topped with fresh berries.

Roast Turkey Breast MediterAsian

It takes a sense of style, imagination, and boldness to keep the menu simple when entertaining. All too often one falls victim to "menu of the month" hoaxes highlighting a succession of elaborate courses served in settings of unattainable splendor. Here is an example of a realistic menu plan for an evening of fun with 12 friends.

Begin by serving Creole Salmon Dumplings (double recipe, make the filling in the morning in the food processor, and ask dinner guests to help fold the dumplings), then serve Roast Turkey Breast MediterAsian (barbecue 2 turkey breasts, make the Mediterranean-Asian sauce earlier in a sauté pan, then reheat the sauce before spooning it on the turkey slices). Accompany this with Polenta Madness (make a double portion of the recipe in the morning, then cut it into wedges and simply reheat under the broiler) followed by a salad course of mixed torn lettuce greens flavored with one of the salad dressings from Chapter 3 (make a double portion of the dressing a day ahead). Conclude with fresh seasonal fruit and a single recipe of Chocolate Meltdown Cookies (make the batter up to 4 days in advance and bake the cookies the day of the party).

• Easy
• Serves 4 as a main entrée.

• marinade

¼ cup white wine
1 tablespoon grated or finely minced lemon zest (colored part of skin)
¼ cup freshly squeezed lemon juice
¼ cup extra-virgin olive oil
3 tablespoons oyster sauce
2 tablespoons Dijon mustard
1 teaspoon Asian chile sauce (optional)
½ teaspoon sugar
3 tablespoons capers
6 cloves garlic, finely minced
2 shallots, finely minced
½ cup chopped fresh, tender rosemary ends or basil

•

2¼ pound turkey breast or 2 small frying chickens, cut into pieces
¼ pound button or shiitake mushrooms
3 whole green onions, chopped
2 vine-ripened tomatoes, seeded and chopped
½ cup freshly grated imported Parmesan cheese
¼ cup unsalted butter
½ cup white wine
Salt and freshly ground black pepper, to taste

• advance preparation

Combine all of the marinade ingredients and stir well. Wash and pat dry the turkey or chicken pieces. Rub the marinade over the turkey or chicken pieces and marinate for 1 to 8 hours in the refrigerator.

Cut the mushrooms into ⅛-inch-thin slices. In a medium bowl, combine the mushrooms and green onion. Set aside the tomatoes. Set aside the grated cheese. The recipe to this point can be completed up to 8 hours in advance of cooking.

• last-minute cooking

Preheat the oven to 425°F. Place the turkey or chicken pieces in a very shallow, heavy pan. Place in the oven and roast the turkey approximately 1 hour, the chicken approximately 30 minutes, brushing on additional marinade midway through cooking. The turkey and chicken are done when a meat thermometer registers 160°F. when inserted deeply into the meat. Save all remaining marinade.

Remove the meat temporarily from the pan. Place the pan over highest heat, add the butter, and when the butter melts, add the mushrooms, green onions, and tomatoes. Bring to a furious boil. When the mushrooms soften (after about 3 minutes), add the white wine and the reserved marinade. Bring to a furious boil. Taste and adjust the flavors, especially for salt and black pepper.

If serving turkey, cut the meat into thin slices, place on dinner plates, and spoon the sauce over the meat. If serving chicken, return the chicken to the pan and rotate the pieces to glaze with the sauce; then transfer to dinner plates. Sprinkle the turkey or chicken with grated Parmesan. Serve at once.

Red Meats for Winter Nights and Summer Barbecues

Chinois Butterflied Leg of Lamb

A butterflied leg of lamb is one of the easiest and most impressive party dishes to prepare and cook, and the slightly uneven thickness of the lamb ensures that you can satisfy everyone with slices of meat cooked to their preference.

Even if you did not graduate at the top of your class at Butcher's College USA, and have just acquired your first set of kitchen knives, why not have a culinary adventure and butterfly the lamb yourself rather than having a butcher do it for you. Work alone to protect trade surgical secrets. Give your boning knife a few swipes on a sharpening steel and have ready a glass of red wine to steady your hand. Since there is no precise place to make the initial incision, just cut along the length of the bone beginning at the bottom shin. As you cut, loosen the meat in one large piece. After removing the bone, cut the thicker sections of the meat lengthwise so that the leg lays open, or is "butterflied." Remove the little thumb-sized fat gland laying in the heart of the meat; then trim all the excess fat from the outside of the lamb.

This is an open-book test. If there was something wrong with the lamb and it is not in one beautifully boned piece, cut the meat into cubes, thread it on skewers, and brush with the marinade. No one needs to know that Chinois Lamb Kebabs were meant to be Chinois Butterflied Leg of Lamb.

• Easy
• Serves 6 to 8 as a main entrée.

1 leg of lamb, boned and butterflied
1¼ cups hoisin sauce
¾ cup red wine
½ cup light-grade olive oil
½ cup Dijon mustard
3 tablespoons heavy soy sauce
1 tablespoon Asian chile sauce
12 cloves garlic, finely minced
⅔ cup tender fresh rosemary ends

• advance preparation

Trim off and discard as much fat as possible from the lamb. In a large bowl, combine all of the remaining ingredients. Add the lamb and marinate for 1 hour at room temperature.

• last-minute cooking

If using a gas barbecue or indoor grill, preheat to medium (350°F.). If using charcoal or wood, prepare the fire. When the coals or wood are ash-covered or the gas barbecue or indoor grill is preheated, brush the grill with cooking oil and lay the lamb on the grill. Turn the lamb over every 7 minutes, for a total cooking time of approximately 28 minutes, brushing the lamb with the marinade throughout the cooking process. For medium-rare, the internal temperature should be 140°F. when the meat is prodded deeply with a meat thermometer. (Alternatively, preheat the oven to 425°F., place the lamb on an elevated wire rack over a shallow baking pan, and cook 30 to 40 minutes.) Remove the lamb from the barbecue or oven and let "rest" for 5 minutes before cutting and serving.

• menu ideas

Summer barbecue for 8: Scallop and Avocado Tostadas, Chinois Butterflied Leg of Lamb (make sauce 1 week in advance) served with Thai Rice Pilaf with Lemongrass, Basil, and Mint (make in the afternoon and reheat in the oven before serving), Shiitake Mushroom Salad with White Corn and Crisp Rice Sticks (make dressing a day in advance), and Chocolate Sorbet with Mangoes (make the sorbet 3 days in advance).

PRECEDING PAGE

Soft Asian Beef Tacos
with Exotic Mushrooms

Grilled Lamb Chops with Tequila, Chiles, and Goat Cheese

Sauces that can be created at the last moment and spooned over barbecued, roasted, or broiled meats and seafood contribute a complex flavor and a look of elegance. In this recipe, little lamb chops, called "French-cut," are barbecued or broiled and topped with a sauce made from homemade chicken stock, a little oyster sauce to lend depth of flavor, finely minced fresh chiles for spice, and crumbled goat cheese to contribute a creamy texture. Complete the menu with Any Kind of Bread Rolls (made ahead and stockpiled in the freezer), Braised Baby Onions, Mushrooms, and Carrots (made earlier that day), and, for dessert, fresh berries and Valrhona Cocoa Truffles.

- Easy
- Serves 4 as a main entrée.

8 French-cut lamb chops
½ cup tequila
¼ cup Dijon mustard
¼ cup thin soy sauce
2 teaspoons juniper berries, crushed
1 tablespoon dried herbes de provence
½ teaspoon freshly ground black pepper
6 cloves garlic, finely minced
2 medium shallots
4 fresh serrano chiles
2 tablespoons unsalted butter
2 cups Homemade Chicken Stock
  (page 70)
1 tablespoon oyster sauce
2 teaspoons cornstarch
1 teaspoon heavy soy sauce
2 ounces goat cheese
¼ cup chopped fresh oregano leaves

• advance preparation

Trim away the excess fat from the sides of the chops. In a small bowl, combine ¼ cup of the tequila, the mustard, soy sauce, juniper berries, herbes de provence, pepper, and half the minced garlic. Stir well, then rub over the lamb chops. Marinate for at least 30 minutes but for no longer than 2 hours.

Mince the shallots. Discard the stems from the chiles, then very finely mince the chiles and their seeds. Combine the remaining garlic with the shallots, chiles, and butter. Place the chicken stock in a small saucepan over high heat and boil furiously until reduced to 1 cup. Cool the chicken stock to room temperature, then stir in the oyster sauce, cornstarch, and soy sauce and refrigerate. Crumble the goat cheese and set aside.

• last-minute cooking

Set aside the oregano leaves. Set aside the remaining ¼ cup tequila. If using a gas barbecue or indoor grill, preheat to medium (350°F.). If using charcoal or wood, prepare a fire. When the coals or wood are ash-covered, or the gas barbecue or indoor grill is preheated, spray the rack with nonstick cooking spray, place the chops on the rack, and cover the barbecue. Barbecue approximately 5 minutes on each side, brushing on more marinade

when turning the chops over, until the chops are cooked through but still feel slightly soft when pressed with the end of your finger and are still pink in the center. (Alternatively, turn the oven to broil. Place a wire rack on a shallow roasting pan, spray with nonstick cooking spray, and lay the chops on the rack. Place the chops 4 inches under the broiler heat and broil about 4 minutes on each side.) Transfer the chops to 4 heated dinner plates.

Meanwhile, place a 10-inch sauté pan over medium-high heat. Add the butter mixture. Sauté until the garlic sizzles, then add the chicken stock. Bring to a low boil, taste and add salt to taste, then remove from the heat. Stir in the oregano, the remaining tequila, and the goat cheese. Before the goat cheese melts entirely, spoon the sauce over the chops and serve at once.

Stir-Fried Spicy Lamb
with Eggplant and Onion

The assertive flavor of lamb demands aggressive seasonings, which in European cooking means such ingredients as garlic, shallots, juniper berries, mustard, rosemary, oregano, sage, and homemade stocks boiled into glazes to achieve concentrated flavor. For this recipe, however, we looked to China for inspiration, and after several culinary experiments, chose a blend of bean, hoisin, and oyster sauces as well as dark sesame oil to contribute low earthy notes to complement the lamb. The balancing high note elements of stir-fried crisp onion, garlic, a dash of vinegar, and Asian chile sauce both heighten the deep, robust flavors and add a sparkling contrast.

• Moderate
• Serves 4 as a main entrée.

1¼ pounds lean lamb leg meat
1 tablespoon bean sauce
1 tablespoon dark sesame oil
1 tablespoon honey
4 small Japanese or Chinese eggplants
2 medium-sized yellow onions
8 cloves garlic, finely minced

• stir-fry sauce

⅓ cup Homemade Chicken Stock (page 70)
2 tablespoons dry sherry
1 tablespoon bean sauce
1 tablespoon oyster sauce
1 tablespoon hoisin sauce
1 tablespoon dark sesame oil
1 tablespoon red wine vinegar
2 teaspoons cornstarch
2 teaspoons sugar
2 teaspoons Asian chile sauce
½ teaspoon ground Szechwan pepper (optional)
•
3 tablespoons cooking oil
¼ cup water, white wine, or sherry

• advance preparation

Trim all of the fat from the lamb meat. Cut the lamb into ⅛-inch-thin slices, then cut the slices into ½-inch-by-1-inch rectangular pieces. Place the lamb in a bowl and add the bean sauce, sesame oil, and honey. Mix thoroughly using your fingers. Marinate for at least 15 minutes at room temperature or up to 8 hours in the refrigerator.

Discard the eggplant stems. Cut the eggplants in half lengthwise, then cut crosswise into ⅛-inch-thin pieces. Trim the ends off the onions, then peel and cut into ¼-inch-thin wedges. Set aside the garlic. In a small bowl, combine all of the ingredients for the stir-fry sauce. The recipe to this point can be completed up to 8 hours in advance of cooking.

• last-minute cooking

Place the wok over highest heat. When the wok is very hot, add 2 tablespoons of the cooking oil to the center. Tilt the wok to coat the sides with oil. When the oil just begins to smoke, add the lamb and stir-fry until it just loses its raw outside color, about 1 minute. Temporarily transfer to a platter.

Immediately return the wok to highest heat. Add the remaining 1 tablespoon cooking oil to the center, then add the garlic. Sauté for a few seconds, then add the vegetables. Stir-fry the vegetables briefly, then add ¼ cup water, white wine, or sherry. Cover the wok and steam-cook the vegetables until the eggplant softens, about 4 minutes. Periodically remove the top to stir and toss the vegetables; if they appear dry but still are not fully cooked, add a splash more liquid before covering the wok again.

Return the lamb to the wok and pour in the sauce. When the sauce comes to a low boil, taste and adjust the seasonings. Transfer to a heated platter or 4 heated dinner plates. Serve at once.

• menu ideas

An informal dinner for 4: Stir-Fried Spicy Lamb with Eggplant and Onion accompanied by hot flour tortillas in which to roll the lamb, a side dish of Watermelon and Sweet Red Onion Salad, and, for dessert, Chocolate Nut Tart served with fresh peach slices.

Braised Lamb Shanks East and West

Large dinner parties can become nightmarish unless the menu remains simple and includes several do-ahead dishes. Here's a good example to follow when serving 12 people: Start with Scallop Dumplings in Coconut-Basil Sauce (double the recipe; make the filling in the food processor; and have your guests help fold the dumplings). Then serve Cal-Asian Salad with Red Sweet Ginger Dressing (triple the recipe; make the salad dressing a day in advance). Follow this course with a triple batch of Braised Lamb Shanks East and West (made earlier in the day and reheated) accompanied by Polenta Madness (double the recipe) simply brushed with olive oil and cooked under the broiler until golden. Conclude the dinner with White Chocolate Mousse (double the recipe and make several days in advance) served in wine glasses and decorated with fresh berries, bittersweet chocolate curls, and mint sprigs. By dessert, you are sure to be voted a dinner party hero by your guests—and you won't be too exhausted by the preparations to enjoy the honor.

- Easy
- Serves 4 as a main entrée.

8 lamb shanks
¼ cup light-grade olive oil
Salt and freshly ground black pepper
1 cup unbleached white flour
8 cloves garlic, finely minced
1 pound button mushrooms
¼ cup unsalted butter
3 cups red wine
1 cup Homemade Chicken Stock
  (page 70)
1 cup tomato sauce
¼ cup hoisin sauce
2 tablespoons oyster sauce
1 tablespoon Thai chile sauce
½ cup fresh oregano leaves
½ cup chopped flat-leaf Italian parsley

• advance preparation and cooking

Trim off any excess fat from the sides of the lamb shanks. Place a 12-inch sauté pan over medium-high heat. Add the olive oil. Place the lamb shanks on a layer of newspaper, sprinkle with a little salt and pepper, then dust with flour. When the oil becomes hot and just begins to smoke, shake all of the excess flour from the shanks and place the shanks in the sauté pan. Brown the shanks on all sides until golden, about 15 minutes, regulating the heat so that the oil is always sizzling but never smoking. Transfer the shanks to a heavy saucepan or small stew pot that holds the shanks snugly.

While browning the lamb shanks, set aside the garlic. Cut the mushrooms into quarters. Set aside separately the butter and 1 cup of the wine. In a medium bowl, combine the remaining wine with the chicken stock, tomato sauce, hoisin sauce, oyster sauce, chile sauce, oregano, and parsley.

After transferring the shanks to the saucepan, return the sauté pan to the burner and set over medium-high heat. Add the butter and garlic. When the garlic begins to sizzle, add the mushrooms. Sauté the mushrooms about 2 minutes, then add 1 cup red wine. Continue cooking the mushrooms until all of the liquid disappears from the pan and the mushrooms become smaller and densely textured, about 15 minutes.

Transfer the mushrooms to the saucepan holding the shanks. Pour in the sauce. Place over medium-high heat, bring the sauce to a simmer, cover the pot, and reduce the heat to low. Simmer the lamb shanks until tender, about 2½ hours, turning the lamb shanks over every 30 minutes. Once the lamb shanks are tender, remove them from the heat and place on 4 heated dinner plates. Using strips of paper toweling, dab up any fat floating on the surface of the sauce. Then spoon the sauce over the lamb shanks and serve immediately. Or, turn off the heat and leave the lamb shanks in the liquid on the stove-top for up to 2 hours before gently reheating. Or, refrigerate up to a day in advance of serving, then gently reheat over low heat until piping hot.

Red-Cooked Barbecued Lamb Shanks

Fusion food combines ingredients, techniques, and presentations from around the world to achieve new results. Here Chinese "red cooking" is reinvented when red wine and chiles are added to the braising liquid in which lamb shanks simmer until tender. The Chinese would serve the shanks directly from the liquid, but we give the shanks a brief searing on the barbecue to create a richer, more intriguing, earthy taste. You can use the same simmering and barbecuing technique very successfully with veal shanks and pot roasts. Any of these meats accompanied by Southwest Salsa, Garlic Mashed Potatoes with Mascarpone, a simple salad of tossed greens, and a fruit tart from a local pastry shop, would make a wonderful winter dinner.

• Easy
• Serves 4 as a main entrée.

• red-cooked sauce

2 cups red wine
1 cup heavy soy sauce
½ cup brown sugar
2 cinnamon sticks or 1 star anise
20 juniper berries, crushed
10 whole cloves
3 dried red chiles (optional)
6 thin slices fresh ginger
10 cloves garlic, peeled and crushed
1 orange
•
4 large lamb shanks
Southwest Salsa (page 93)

• advance preparation

In a 4-quart saucepan, combine the wine, soy sauce, sugar, cinnamon, juniper berries, cloves, chiles, ginger, and garlic. Using a potato peeler, remove all of the colored outside skin from the orange and add it, plus the juice from the orange, to the saucepan. Add 4 cups water, place over high heat, and bring to a low boil. Cover, reduce the heat to low, and simmer the sauce for 1 hour.

Add the lamb shanks to the saucepan. If the liquid does not cover all the shanks, add enough boiling water to cover the shanks. Cover the saucepan and simmer until the meat tastes tender, about 2½ hours. If serving the lamb within 4 hours, turn off the heat and set the saucepan aside at room temperature. If done further ahead (up to a day in advance of serving), refrigerate the lamb shanks submerged in the sauce. After removing the lamb shanks from the sauce, refrigerate the sauce, including all of the seasonings, for up to 1 month, or freeze indefinitely. (This sauce can be used over and over for years.) Prepare the salsa.

• last-minute cooking

If using a gas barbecue or indoor grill, preheat to medium (350°F.). If using charcoal or wood, prepare a fire. When the coals or wood are ash-covered or the gas barbecue or indoor grill is preheated, brush the grill with oil, then grill the lamb shanks about 5 minutes on each side until thoroughly heated through, brushing on more sauce throughout the cooking process. Transfer the lamb shanks to 4 heated dinner plates. Place some salsa next to the shanks and serve at once.

• menu ideas

Dinner party for 8 on a cold winter night: Red-Cooked Barbecued Lamb Shanks served with Southwest Salsa, Garlic Mashed Potatoes with Mascarpone, Baby Greens with Blue Cheese-Pecan Dressing, and, for dessert, Angels in Heaven.

note: Since the flavor of this sauce improves with each successive use, store it for up to 1 month in the refrigerator or freeze indefinitely. Each time you use the sauce, enrich its taste by adding a splash of soy sauce and a few more aromatics.

Baby Pork Back Ribs
with Secret Asian Barbecue Sauce

Exhausted from a hard day at work? Rub Secret Asian Barbecue Sauce across chicken pieces before roasting them in the oven for a simple dinner. Wondering how to perk up a fresh sea bass filet? Brush the fish with a little of this barbecue sauce before pushing the fish underneath the broiler. Want to impress your neighborhood friends with your culinary prowess? Marinate a butter-flied leg of lamb for an hour with the barbecue sauce and then barbecue the lamb. The sauce lasts for years as long as it is kept refrigerated and the green onions and cilantro are withheld until a day or two before it is to be used.

• Easy
• Serves 4 as a main entrée or 12 to 20 as an appetizer.

4 slabs baby pork back ribs, 8 ribs each

• secret asian barbecue sauce

1 cup hoisin sauce
½ cup plum sauce
⅓ cup oyster sauce
¼ cup red wine vinegar
¼ cup honey
2 tablespoons heavy soy sauce
2 tablespoons dry sherry
1 tablespoon dark sesame oil
1 tablespoon Asian chile sauce
2 teaspoons curry powder (optional)
½ teaspoon five-spice powder (optional)
1 tablespoon grated or finely minced lemon zest (colored part of skin)
1 tablespoon grated or finely minced orange zest (colored part of skin)
10 cloves garlic, very finely minced
¼ cup very finely minced fresh ginger
3 tablespoons white sesame seeds, toasted until golden
½ cup finely minced green onion
½ cup chopped fresh cilantro

• advance preparation

On the underside of the ribs is a tough white membrane; using your fingernail or a sharp, pointed knife, loosen the membrane along the bone at one edge, then, gripping the membrane with a paper towel, pull it away. Set the ribs aside.

In a large bowl, combine all of the barbecue sauce ingredients and mix well. If not using within 2 days, omit the green onions and cilantro. This sauce can be refrigerated indefinitely.

• last-minute cooking

If using a gas barbecue or indoor grill, preheat to medium (350°F.). If using charcoal or wood, prepare a fire. When the coals or wood are ash-covered or the gas barbecue or indoor grill is preheated, brush the ribs with barbecue sauce, spray the rack with nonstick cooking spray, lay the ribs on the rack, and cover the barbecue. Roast the ribs at medium temperature until the meat begins to shrink from the ends of the rib bones, about 45 minutes, brushing the ribs with more barbecue sauce and turning them over every 10 minutes. (Alternatively, preheat the oven to 350°F. Place a rack in a shallow roasting pan, spray the rack with nonstick cooking spray, brush the ribs with barbecue sauce, and lay the ribs, meaty side up, on the rack. Place the ribs in the oven and roast until the meat begins to shrink from the ends of the bones, about 1 hour. Do not turn the ribs over during roasting, but brush them every 20 minutes with more barbecue sauce.)

Serve the ribs hot or at room temperature. If serving as an appetizer, cut the slabs into individual ribs.

• menu ideas

On the Fourth of July serve these ribs with Steamed White Corn with Szechwan Butter Glaze, Any Kind of Bread Rolls with honey butter, Watermelon and Sweet Red Onion Salad, and Fantastic Raspberry Ice Cream with Velvet Chocolate Sauce.

Thai-Style Wok-Seared Pork Tenderloin

Stir-frying a succession of dishes turns a party into a culinary kung-fu event with the host and hostess sprinting from the dining table to the kitchen initiating a cacophony of banging and scraping noises that dampens all dinner conversation among the guests. Limit your stir-frying to get-togethers of no more than 4 people and serve this single stir-fry dish as the main entrée accompanied by rice and a salad tossed with a simple vinaigrette. If you double a stir-fry dish, enlist a volunteer to stir-fry a duplicate portion by copying your actions in another wok. However, if you want to stir-fry even larger amounts, purchase a wok with a 22- to 26-inch diameter and cook over an outdoor gas or charcoal barbecue, or atop a commercial Chinese outdoor wok burner, a cooking medium that generates over 100,000 BTUs of heat and is available at Chinese restaurant supply stores in large cities.

- Moderate
- Serves 4 as a main entrée.

1¼ pounds pork tenderloin
2 tablespoons hoisin sauce
1 tablespoon heavy soy sauce
1 tablespoon dry sherry
5 cloves garlic, finely minced
Zest (colored part of skin) from 1 lime, grated or finely minced
3 whole green onions
1 cup raw shelled, skinless peanuts
1 cup cooking oil

• stir-fry sauce

⅓ cup freshly squeezed orange juice
2 tablespoons fish sauce
1 tablespoon Thai chile sauce
2 teaspoons sugar
2 teaspoons cornstarch
¼ cup chopped fresh mint leaves

• advance preparation

Trim all of the fat from the pork. Cut the pork in half lengthwise, then cut crosswise into ⅛-inch slices. Place the pork in a large bowl and add the hoisin sauce, soy sauce, sherry, garlic, and lime zest. Mix thoroughly using your fingers. Marinate for at least 15 minutes at room temperature or up to 8 hours in the refrigerator.

Cut the green onions on a sharp diagonal into 1-inch pieces. Place the peanuts and cooking oil in a saucepan set over high heat; stir the peanuts steadily, and as soon as they turn a light golden, tip them and the oil through a heatproof sieve placed over another small saucepan. Cool the peanuts to room temperature, then pat dry. Reserve 2 tablespoons of the oil.

In a small bowl, combine all of the ingredients for the stir-fry sauce and mix well. The recipe to this point can be completed up to 8 hours in advance of cooking.

• last-minute cooking

Place the wok over highest heat. When the wok becomes very hot, add the reserved 2 tablespoons cooking oil to the center, then tilt the wok to coat the sides with oil. When the oil just begins to smoke, add the pork and stir-fry until it just loses its raw outside color, about 1 minute.

Stir in the green onions, peanuts, and sauce. When the sauce comes to a boil and thickens enough to coat a spoon, taste and adjust seasonings. Transfer to a heated platter or 4 heated dinner plates. Serve at once.

• menu ideas

This spicy stir-fry pork dish is delicious served with sliced green beans and Jasmine Steamed Rice or rolled inside hot flour tortillas, accompanied by such do-ahead dishes as Candied Walnut Salad with Goat Cheese and Chocolate Sorbet with Mangoes.

Beijing Pork with Fire-Roasted Parsnips and Red Peppers

Ingredients from around the world are fused to create a new balance of flavors in this pork stew. The natural sweetness of pork and its mild middle-note flavor act as perfect foils for the deep low notes of a sauce made with oyster, hoisin, and bean sauces, roasted vegetables with a slight low-note char, and the balancing high notes of chile, vinegar, and ginger. Make the stew a day in advance, then gently reheat and the meat will be even more tender and the flavors more pronounced.

• Moderate
• Serves 4 as a main entrée.

3 red bell peppers
4 parsnips
8 whole green onions
1 tablespoon finely minced garlic
1 tablespoon very finely minced fresh ginger
¾ cup Homemade Chicken Stock (page 70)
¼ cup dry sherry
3 tablespoons hoisin sauce
2 tablespoons oyster sauce
1 tablespoon bean sauce
1 tablespoon white wine vinegar
1 teaspoon Asian chile sauce
1 teaspoon sugar
2½ pounds boneless pork shoulder
¼ cup cooking oil
1 tablespoon cornstarch

• advance preparation

Roast the red bell peppers: Turn the oven setting to broil. Cut off and discard the ends from the peppers. Remove the seeds and ribbing, then flatten. Place the peppers, skin side up, directly on a wire oven rack and place the rack 3 inches from the broiler heat. Roast the peppers until the skin turns black, about 5 minutes. Remove the peppers from the oven and transfer to a plastic bag. After 5 minutes, using your fingers, rub off the blackened skin. Cut the peppers into 1-inch cubes.

Peel the parsnips. Place the parsnips and green onion under the broiler heat and cook until lightly charred on both sides. Cut the parsnips on a sharp diagonal into 1-inch pieces, rolling the parsnips a quarter turn after each cut. Trim the green onions, then cut on a diagonal into 1-inch-long pieces. In a small bowl, combine the garlic, ginger, chicken stock, sherry, hoisin sauce, oyster sauce, bean sauce, vinegar, chile sauce, and sugar.

Cut off and discard all excess fat from the pork, yielding about 2 pounds stew meat. Cut the meat into ½-inch cubes. Place a wok or heavy 12-inch skillet over high heat. When the pan becomes hot, add the cooking oil. When the oil just begins to smoke, add the meat and sauté until it loses its raw outside color, about 6 minutes. Tip out all of the oil from the pan, then add the parsnips and sauce. Bring the sauce to a low boil, reduce the heat to very low, and cover the pot. Simmer the meat until it tastes tender, about 1½ hours. Remove the stew from the stove and stir in the red pepper and green onion. If desired, cool and store in the refrigerator for a day before serving.

• last-minute cooking

Place the stew over low heat and warm until heated through, about 10 minutes. Remove all fat from the surface of the sauce using strips of paper toweling. Combine the cornstarch with an equal amount of cold water, then stir in just enough to lightly thicken the sauce. Taste and adjust the seasonings. Serve at once.

• menu ideas

Serve Beijing Pork with Polenta Madness and a tossed green salad flavored with one of the salad dressings from Chapter 3. Conclude with Chocolate Sorbet with Mangoes.

Herb-Crusted Loin of Pork

Pork, like veal and chicken, is finely textured, lean, and delicate-tasting, and is perfectly matched with a wide spectrum of preparation techniques and sauces. The misconception still lingers that pork is fatty. Yet today's pork is 31 percent leaner, 17 percent lower in calories, and 10 percent lower in cholesterol than the pork available in 1983, and 50 percent leaner than the pork available in 1973. The huge advances in pork production have also virtually eliminated the danger of trichinosis, which is killed when the meat's internal temperature reaches 137°F. All the recipes in this book specify that barbecued, roasted, or broiled pork be removed from the heat when the internal temperature reads 155°F. on a meat thermometer. By allowing the meat to "rest" for 5 minutes before serving, the internal temperature rises to 160°F. The resulting slightly pink, juicy, and tender meat is a great taste sensation, so very different than the dry, unpalatable pork cooked the old-fashioned way to 180°F.

- Easy
- Serves 4 as a main entrée.

• mediterranean barbecue
  sauce

⅓ cup chopped fresh basil, oregano, or thyme
6 cloves garlic, finely minced
1 tablespoon finely minced fresh ginger
2 tablespoons grated or finely minced lemon zest (colored part of skin)
½ cup freshly squeezed lemon juice
⅓ cup white wine
⅓ cup extra-virgin olive oil
¼ cup thin soy sauce
¼ cup Dijon mustard
1 teaspoon freshly ground black pepper
•
2 pounds pork loin
10 long sprigs fresh rosemary
10 long sprigs fresh sage
20 long sprigs fresh thyme
20 long sprigs fresh oregano

• advance preparation

In a small bowl, combine all of the ingredients for the barbecue sauce and stir well. Place the pork loin in a glass bowl or dish, add the barbecue sauce, and marinate for 1 hour.

After 1 hour, remove the pork from the dish, saving the marinade. Using kitchen string, tie the herb sprigs along the entire outside surface of the meat. The meat can be refrigerated for up to 8 hours.

• last-minute cooking

If using a gas barbecue or indoor grill, preheat to medium (350°F.). If using charcoal or wood, prepare a fire. When the coals or wood are ash-covered or the gas barbecue or indoor grill is preheated, brush the grill with oil. Place the pork loin on the grill and cook about 30 to 45 minutes, rotating the meat and brushing on marinade every 10 minutes. The pork is done when its internal temperature registers 155°F on a meat thermometer. (Alternatively, if using the oven, preheat to 350°F., place the pork on an elevated wire rack, set over a shallow baking sheet, and follow the cooking instructions given for the barbecue.)

Remove the pork from the barbecue or oven. Allow to stand 5 minutes before cutting into 1-inch-thick slices. Place on 4 heated dinner plates and serve at once.

• menu ideas

Comfort food for 4: Herb-Crusted Loin of Pork and Garlic Mashed Potatoes with Mascarpone followed by a salad of tossed greens with one of the dressings from Chapter 3, then Kahlúa Passion Tiles.

Smoked Double-Thick Pork Chops Caribbean

Gourmet shops, supermarkets, and hardware stores carry a wide range of wood chips that can be used to impart a smoky flavor to barbecued foods. After soaking the wood chips for an hour, place them in an open pouch of foil and lay directly on the coals or on the gas barbecue rack. Once the wood begins to smoke heavily, place the food on the coals or rack and cover the barbecue securely. This combination barbecue-smoking technique, which we call "hot smoking," adds a smoky exterior flavor. On the other hand, with another smoking technique, called "cold smoking," the heat is maintained at 150°F. to 250°F. so that during the long cooking process the smoky flavor permeates to the center of the food. Although most gas barbecues cannot maintain this low temperature, many hardware stores and home improvement centers sell small, inexpensive portable electric cold smokers. If you have a cold smoker or a gas barbecue capable of maintaining low temperatures, try cold-smoking the marinated chops for 1 hour, or the marinated butterflied leg of lamb from page 136 for 3 hours. Then barbecue the chops or lamb for a final few minutes in order to finish cooking the meat and to impart an additional deep barbecue flavor.

- Easy
- Serves 4 as a main entrée.

4 double-thick pork chops
2 cups wood chips
½ cup chopped fresh cilantro

• southwest barbecue sauce

½ teaspoon whole allspice
½ teaspoon whole cloves
½ teaspoon whole coriander seeds
½ teaspoon ground cinnamon
¼ cup Ancho Chile Jam (page 84)
¼ cup light-grade olive oil
2 tablespoons Worcestershire sauce
2 tablespoons honey
2 tablespoons thin soy sauce
4 cloves garlic, very finely minced
1 shallot, finely minced
3 serrano chiles, stemmed and finely minced (including seeds)
1 teaspoon finely grated lime zest (colored part of skin)
1 teaspoon finely grated orange zest (colored part of skin)

• advance preparation

Trim the excess fat from the sides of the pork chops. Soak the wood chips in cold water for 1 to 2 hours.

Make the barbecue sauce: Place the allspice, cloves, and coriander in a small saucepan over high heat and toast until they just begin to smoke; then grind finely. In a small bowl, combine the ground spices with the remaining barbecue sauce ingredients. Mix well. This sauce can be made 2 days in advance. If not to be used within 2 days, omit the cilantro and refrigerate indefinitely.

Combine the chops and barbecue sauce and marinate for at least 15 minutes but for no longer than 2 hours.

• last-minute cooking

Chop the cilantro. If using a gas barbecue or indoor grill, preheat to medium (350°F.). If using charcoal or wood, prepare a fire. When the coals or wood are ash-covered or the gas barbecue or indoor grill is preheated, drain the wood chips, place on a 6-inch square of foil, and put directly on the coals. When the chips begin to smoke, spray the rack with nonstick cooking spray, lay the chops on the rack, and cover the barbecue. Roast at medium temperature until the internal temperature of the pork registers 155°F. when pierced deeply with a meat thermometer, about 30 minutes, brushing the chops with more barbecue sauce and turning them over every 10 minutes. (Alternatively, preheat the oven to 350°F. Do not use the wood chips. Place a wire rack in a shallow roasting pan, spray the rack with nonstick cooking spray, and lay the chops on the rack. Place the chops in the preheated oven and roast until the internal temperature reaches 155°F., about 40 minutes.) Place the chops on 4 heated dinner plates, sprinkle with chopped cilantro, and serve at once.

Braised Beef with Mushrooms, Thyme, and Asian Accents

In this recipe, a large quantity of mushrooms are sautéed for a long time to give them a very dense texture and deep flavor that perfectly match the tender slices of beef. With the addition of heavy soy sauce, Asian chile sauce, and a bunch of fresh thyme, the complex flavors of this stew linger long after the last bite.

• Easy
• Serves 4 as a main entrée.

4-ounce slab of bacon

1½ pounds beef stew meat (such as cubed chuck meat)

4 cloves garlic, finely minced

1 medium carrot, peeled and thinly sliced

1 yellow onion, chopped

2 pounds medium-sized button mushrooms, cut in half

2 cups good red wine

1 cup Homemade Chicken Stock (page 70)

2 tablespoons heavy soy sauce

1 tablespoon tomato paste

½ teaspoon Asian chile sauce

1 bunch fresh thyme (tied together with kitchen string)

1 bay leaf

2 tablespoons light-grade olive oil

1½ tablespoons unbleached white flour

Salt, to taste

• advance preparation and cooking

Cut the bacon crosswise into ⅛-inch-thin slices. Cut the stew meat against the grain into ¼-inch-thin slices. Combine the garlic, carrot, onion, and mushrooms, and set aside. In a medium bowl, combine the wine, chicken stock, soy sauce, tomato paste, chile sauce, fresh thyme, and bay leaf.

Preheat the oven to 450°F. Place a 12-inch cast-iron skillet or a heavy sauté pan with ovenproof handles over medium heat. Add the bacon and cook until it becomes crisp and all the fat is rendered. Using a slotted spoon, temporarily remove the bacon from the pan. Turn the heat to high, and when the pan is very hot, add the beef. Cook the beef until it loses its raw outside color and becomes lightly browned, about 6 minutes. Temporarily remove the beef from the pan.

Add the olive oil to the pan. When the oil becomes hot, add the vegetables. Turn the heat to medium and sauté the vegetables until the moisture expelled by the mushrooms evaporates and the mushrooms acquire a dense texture, about 15 minutes.

Sprinkle the beef and bacon across the surface of the vegetables, then sprinkle the flour evenly across the surface of the meat. Place the pan in the preheated oven for 6 minutes; then stir the meat and continue cooking in the oven another 6 minutes. Stir in the wine sauce, then reduce the heat to 325°F., cover the pot, and cook the stew until the meat becomes tender, about 1½ hours. Remove all fat from the surface of the sauce using strips of paper toweling. Taste and adjust the seasonings. Transfer to 4 heated dinner plates and serve at once or cool and refrigerate. This stew can be made a day in advance and reheated on the stove-top over low heat.

• menu ideas

Do-ahead dinner for 20: Begin the event with Bruschetta East and West (double recipe) and Marinated Goat Cheese with Pepper Berries, Garlic, and Mint (double recipe); then serve Southwest Caesar Salad with Chile Croutons (quadruple the recipe) followed by Braised Beef with Mushrooms, Thyme, and Asian Accents (quadruple the recipe) accompanied by Polenta Madness (triple the recipe); conclude with Kahlúa Passion Tiles (double the recipe).

Beef Tenderloin
with Shiitake Cream Sauce

Shiitake Cream Sauce is one of the most delicious and versatile sauces in this book. Its rich and multiflavored taste makes it a fine sauce to spoon over barbecued veal chops or thick slices of meat loaf. It also creates magical results when tossed with ravioli or ½ pound cooked dried pasta.

Since the sauce depends on the intense flavor leached from the shiitake mushrooms, as a substitute choose only similarly flavorful mushrooms, such as fresh morels or chanterelles (rather than button or oyster mushrooms).

- Easy
- Serves 4 as a main entrée.

2 pounds beef tenderloin, trimmed of all fat

1 cup Asian (page 143), Mediterranean (page 147), or Southwest (page 149) Barbecue Sauce

¼ cup unsalted butter

1 tablespoon very finely minced fresh ginger

6 ounces fresh shiitake mushrooms

1 cup heavy whipping cream

½ cup dry sherry

2 tablespoons thin soy sauce

1 tablespoon dark sesame oil

½ teaspoon grated orange zest (colored part of skin)

¼ teaspoon Asian chile sauce

Fresh cilantro sprigs, for garnish

• **advance preparation**

Trim all fat from the tenderloin. Rub the barbecue sauce over the meat. Marinate 1 to 2 hours.

Combine the butter with the minced ginger. Cut off and discard the mushroom stems. Overlap the caps and cut into ¼-inch-thin slices. Combine the cream, sherry, soy sauce, sesame oil, orange zest, and chile sauce. Set aside.

• **last-minute cooking**

Set aside the cilantro sprigs. Preheat the oven to 425°F. Place the meat on a wire rack elevated above the edges of a shallow baking sheet. Or, if barbecuing the meat, preheat a gas barbecue or indoor grill to medium (350°F.). If using charcoal or wood, prepare a fire. When the coals or wood are ash-covered or the gas barbecue or indoor grill is preheated, brush the grill with oil and place the meat on the grill. For both roasting and barbecuing, cook the meat until the internal temperature registers 135°F. on a meat thermometer, about 30 minutes, basting the meat with the barbecue sauce at least once. Transfer the meat to a carving board and let rest 5 minutes before cutting into steaks.

While the meat is resting, place a 12-inch sauté pan over highest heat. Add the butter and ginger. When the butter melts, add the mushrooms and sauté until they soften slightly, about 2 minutes. Add the sauce and bring to a furious boil. Boil the sauce until it thickens so that you can see the surface of the pan while stirring, about 5 minutes.

Cut the meat into 4 steaks and place on 4 heated dinner plates. Spoon the sauce around the edges of the meat, garnish with the cilantro, and serve at once.

• **menu ideas**

Dinner for 8: Spicy Gravlax with Mango Salsa, Beef Tenderloin with Shiitake Cream Sauce accompanied by Wild Rice with Currants, Pine Nuts, and Port, and, for dessert, Ginger Banana Cream Tart Lined with Chocolate.

Soft Asian Beef Tacos with Exotic Mushrooms

We first served this dish at our home to the food and beverage directors of a hotel chain. Taking advantage of a supply of fresh flour tortillas and the availability of a wide range of exotic mushrooms, we created a fusion variation of the usual *mu shu* fillings served at Chinese restaurants. The menu for that meal was rounded out with Asian Barbecued Quail, Five-Cheese Pizza with Grilled Peppers, Tropical Salad with Citrus-Herb Dressing, and White Chocolate Mousse.

• Challenging
• Serves 4 as a main entrée or 8 to 10 as an appetizer.

¾ **pound beef tenderloin, trimmed of all fat**
6 **tablespoons dry sherry**
1 **tablespoon hoisin sauce**
1 **tablespoon dark sesame oil**
1 **teaspoon Asian chile sauce**
½ **teaspoon finely grated orange zest (colored part of skin)**
4 **cloves garlic, finely minced**
½ **pound fresh chanterelle mushrooms**
½ **pound portabello mushrooms**
¼ **pound fresh shiitake mushrooms**
5 **whole green onions**
2 **tablespoons oyster sauce**
½ **teaspoon sugar**
2 **teaspoons cornstarch**
12 **fresh 8-inch flour tortillas**
5 **tablespoons cooking oil**
¾ **cup hoisin sauce, for serving**

• **advance preparation**

Cut the beef crosswise into ⅛-inch-thin slices. Overlap the slices and cut into ⅛-inch-thin matchsticks. Transfer to a medium bowl and add 2 tablespoons of the dry sherry, the hoisin sauce, sesame oil, chile sauce, orange zest, and garlic. Mix well. Marinate for at least 15 minutes at room temperature and up to 8 hours in the refrigerator.

Wipe the chanterelles with a damp cloth, or rinse briefly and immediately dry with paper towels. Cut the chanterelles, including the stems, into ⅛-inch-thin bite-sized slices. Cut the portabellos into ⅛-inch-thin bite-sized slices. Discard the shiitake mushroom stems. Cut the caps into quarters or eighths. Set the mushrooms aside together. Cut the green onions on a diagonal into 1-inch-long pieces.

In a small bowl, combine the remaining 4 tablespoons dry sherry, the oyster sauce, and sugar. The recipe to this point can be completed up to 8 hours in advance of cooking.

• **last-minute cooking**

Combine the cornstarch with an equal amount of cold water. Wrap the tortillas in an aluminum foil envelope and warm for 15 minutes in a preheated 325°F. oven.

Place a sauté pan or wok over high heat. Add 3 tablespoons of the cooking oil. When the oil becomes hot, add the mushrooms. Sauté the mushrooms for 2 minutes, then add the sherry-oyster sauce mixture. Cook the mushrooms over high heat until they soften and all the moisture they expel boils away, about 10 minutes. Add the green onions and stir-fry until they brighten, about 2 minutes.

Transfer the mushrooms and green onions to a plate. Immediately return the pan to highest heat. Add the remaining 2 tablespoons cooking oil. When the oil becomes very hot and just begins to smoke, add the beef. Stir and toss the beef until it just loses its outside raw color, about 1 minute. Return the mushrooms and green onions to the pan. If there is any liquid in the pan, stir in a little of the cornstarch mixture. Taste and adjust seasonings.

Transfer the meat mixture to a heated serving platter. Accompany with hot tortillas and a dish of hoisin sauce. Each person spreads a little hoisin sauce across the inside of a tortilla, adds the filling, rolls the filled tortilla into a cylinder, and eats with his or her hands.

Creole Osso Buco

Of all the cuts of veal, it is the succulently sweet veal shank meat in combination with its soft, buttery marrow that creates the most arresting play of flavors. In this recipe, veal shanks are simmered in a rich sauce, then transferred to heated dinner plates while the sauce is left to boil rapidly until it forms a thick essence to be spooned over the meat. Try substituting veal shanks for braised meats in other recipes, such as Braised Lamb Shanks East and West, Braised Beef with Mushrooms, or Beijing Pork with Fire-Roasted Parsnips and Red Peppers. While this recipe can be prepared ahead and refrigerated, the veal shanks are most tender if cooked in the late-afternoon, cooled and kept at room temperature, then gently reheated within the next 2 hours.

- Moderate
- Serves 4 as a main entrée.

1 pound andouille or other spicy sausage

3 heads roasted garlic (page 220)

1 yellow onion

3 fresh serrano chiles

½ cup fresh oregano leaves

1 bunch fresh thyme

2 cups Homemade Chicken Stock (page 70)

1 cup white wine

2 teaspoons Worcestershire sauce

8 milk-fed veal shanks, each 1½ inches thick

Salt and freshly ground black pepper, to taste

1 cup unbleached white flour

¼ cup light-grade olive oil or cooking oil

½ cup chopped fresh parsley

• advance preparation

Cut the sausage crosswise into ¼-inch pieces. Set aside 30 cloves of roasted garlic. Peel and chop the onion. Discard the stems from the chiles, then mince the chiles with their seeds. Set aside the oregano leaves. Tie the thyme together in a bundle with string. In a medium bowl, combine the chicken stock, wine, and Worcestershire sauce.

Preheat the oven to 325°F. Place a 14-inch skillet with ovenproof handles over medium-high heat. Place the veal shanks on a piece of newspaper, season with a sprinkling of salt and black pepper, dust with flour, then shake off all of the excess flour. Place the oil in the pan and, when the oil just begins to smoke, add the veal shanks. Cook the veal shanks on both sides until deep golden, about 5 minutes on each side. During cooking, regulate the heat so that the oil is always sizzling but never smoking. Temporarily remove the shanks from the pan.

Return the pan to medium-high heat. Add the sausage, garlic, onion, and chiles, and sauté until the onion softens, about 8 minutes. Return the veal shanks to the pan, sprinkle on the oregano leaves, add the thyme, and pour in the chicken stock mixture. Bring to a low boil, cover the pot, and place in the preheated oven. Cook until the veal shanks become tender, about 2 to 3 hours.

Turn the veal shanks and spoon sauce over them twice during cooking. When ready, cool the shanks (without removing them from the pan) to room temperature. Remove all fat from the surface of the sauce using strips of paper toweling. If not serving within 1 to 2 hours, refrigerate the shanks in the pan.

• last-minute cooking

Preheat the oven to 325°F. Return the pan with the veal shanks to the oven and reheat until the shanks are very hot, about 20 minutes if the shanks have been refrigerated.

Remove the pan from the oven and place the shanks on 4 heated dinner plates. Discard the bundle of thyme. Place the pan over highest heat and boil the sauce rapidly until it thickens enough to lightly coat a spoon, about 5 minutes. Taste and adjust seasonings, especially for salt. Spoon the sauce over the veal shanks, sprinkle on the parsley, and serve at once.

• menu ideas

For a divine dinner combination, serve Creole Osso Buco accompanied by Panfried Potatoes with Rosemary, Papaya and Avocado Salad, and Valrhona Cocoa Truffles with fresh strawberries.

Barbecued Veal Chops
with Chinese Herb Marinade

In this recipe, sweet-tasting milk-fed veal serves as a stage on which oyster sauce, honey, cilantro, and chile perform their bold flavor play. Always specify milk-fed veal when placing your veal order. Some markets sell western veal, which is not veal at all, but rather baby beef that has neither the fine texture nor delicate taste of veal, nor the flavor of properly raised and aged beef. Although in the past milk-fed veal was the product of calves fed only their mothers' milk until the age of 6 weeks, today this type of veal comes from calves fed soybean milk until the age of 12 weeks. This current technique produces a heavier calf, yet allows the meat to retain its fine-grained texture, delicate taste, and pinkish white color.

• Easy
• Serves 4 as a main entrée.

4 milk-fed veal chops, each 1½ inches thick
½ cup dry sherry
¼ cup oyster sauce
¼ cup honey
1 teaspoon Asian chile sauce
4 cloves garlic, finely minced
2 tablespoons finely minced fresh ginger
½ cup coarsely chopped fresh cilantro

• **advance preparation**

Trim all excess fat from the sides of the veal chops. In a large bowl, combine all of the remaining ingredients. Add the chops and marinate for at least 15 minutes at room temperature or up to 4 hours in the refrigerator.

• **last-minute cooking**

Bring the veal chops to room temperature before cooking. If using a gas barbecue or indoor grill, preheat to medium (350°F.). If using charcoal or wood, prepare a fire. When the coals or wood are ash-covered or the gas barbecue or indoor grill is preheated, brush the grill with oil. Grill the veal chops about 5 to 8 minutes on each side, brushing with the marinade frequently, until the interior of the meat just loses its pink color (about 150°F. on a meat thermometer). Transfer the veal chops to dinner plates and serve at once.

• **menu ideas**

A quick weekday dinner for 4: Barbecued Veal Chops with Chinese Herb Marinade, Garlic Mashed Potatoes, and fresh berries.

Sweetbreads in Asian Pinot Noir Reduction Sauce

On the ladder of gastronomic perfection, veal sweetbreads rank near the top. Their delicacy of taste and slightly resilient texture make them the perfect match for a wide range of sauces, such as this reduction of Pinot Noir, mushrooms, oyster sauce, and a tiny amount of Asian chile sauce. Since sweetbreads, which are the thymus gland of calves, take time to prepare and appeal only to those with the most sophisticated palates, be sure to inquire into the prejudices of your dinner guests before preparing this dish. A day in advance of serving, sweetbreads are given a preliminary blanching to lessen any organ taste and are then pressed under a heavy weight to firm their texture. If you are short of time or fresh veal sweetbreads are not available, spoon this sauce over barbecued beef filet, small lamb loin chops, veal chops, or chicken.

- Challenging
- Serves 4 as a main entrée.

2 pounds fresh veal sweetbreads

1 teaspoon salt

1 tablespoon vinegar

4-ounce slab bacon

4 cloves garlic, finely minced

1 small yellow onion, chopped

1 pound medium-sized button mushrooms

½ pound fresh shiitake or portabello mushrooms

2 cups red wine, such as Pinot Noir

1 cup Homemade Chicken Stock (page 70)

2 tablespoons oyster sauce

1 tablespoon heavy soy sauce

2 teaspoons tomato paste

½ teaspoon Asian chile sauce

½ teaspoon sugar

1 bunch fresh thyme (tied together with kitchen string)

⅓ cup chopped fresh basil leaves

1 bunch chives, chopped

1 tablespoon cornstarch

Salt and freshly ground black pepper, to taste

• advance preparation (starting at least 8 hours prior to serving)

Place the sweetbreads in a deep saucepan and cover with cold water for 1 hour. Then stir in the salt and vinegar. Over medium-low heat, bring the liquid to a low boil, reduce the heat, and simmer the sweetbreads for 10 minutes. Immediately rinse the sweetbreads under cold water and place on a large plate. Cover the plate with plastic wrap; then put a very large pot filled with cold water on top of the sweetbreads to weigh them down. Refrigerate for 8 hours or overnight.

After 8 hours, pull any thick pieces of outer membrane away from the sweetbreads. Separate the sweetbreads into bite-sized nuggets and set aside until ready to cook.

Cut the bacon crosswise into ¼-inch pieces. Combine the garlic and onion. Cut the button mushrooms in half. Discard the stems from the shiitake or portabello mushrooms, then cut the caps into ½-inch-wide strips. In a medium bowl, combine the wine, chicken stock, oyster sauce, soy sauce, tomato paste, chile sauce, sugar, and the bunch of thyme.

Place a 12-inch sauté pan that is not cast iron or aluminum over medium heat. Add the bacon and gently cook until it becomes crisp and all the fat is rendered. Add the garlic and onion and sauté until the onions become golden, about 15 minutes. Then add the mushrooms and cook until they soften, expel all their moisture, and eventually become densely textured, about 15 minutes.

Add the wine sauce, bring to a boil over medium heat, and cook until the mushrooms begin to show above the sauce, about 8 minutes. Remove the thyme. If desired, cool and refrigerate for up to 8 hours.

Set aside the basil and chives. Combine the cornstarch with an equal amount of cold water. Place a 12-inch sauté pan over medium heat. Add the sweetbreads and mushroom-wine sauce. Bring to a low simmer, reduce the heat to low, cover the pan, and simmer for 20 minutes. Then remove the lid and taste the sauce. Adjust seasonings for salt and pepper. Stir in the basil and chives. Stir in enough of the cornstarch mixture so the sauce lightly coats a spoon. Transfer the sweetbreads and sauce to 4 heated dinner plates and serve at once.

• menu ideas

An elegant dinner for 8: Start with Tuna Carpaccio with Capers, Chiles, and Ginger, then serve Sweetbreads in Asian Pinot Noir Reduction Sauce accompanied by Thai Rice Pilaf, then Cal-Asian Salad with Red Sweet Ginger Dressing, and, for dessert, Chocolate Ginger Mousse with Raspberry Essence.

Grilled Calf's Liver Caribbean

On our frequent visits to Napa Valley's famous Mustards Grill, we often order the calf's liver entrée, which is cooked over a wood-burning indoor barbecue and served with homemade ketchup and grilled polenta. Fortunately, this is an easy menu to duplicate at home. In order to ensure the best-quality liver, purchase it from a meat market where the butcher cuts it while you wait. Either barbecue the liver or cook it on a heavy iron grill pan with raised ridges rather than in a flat skillet. Remove the liver from the barbecue or grill pan when it is still pink in the center and serve with Southwest Ketchup, Polenta Madness, and a premium store-bought ice cream topped with Caramel Butter Sauce.

• Easy
• Serves 4 as a main entrée.

• marinade

½ cup chopped fresh cilantro
4 cloves garlic, finely minced
2 tablespoons finely minced fresh ginger
⅓ cup freshly squeezed orange juice
¼ cup light-grade olive oil
¼ cup rum
¼ cup light brown sugar
¼ cup thin soy sauce
2 tablespoons oyster sauce
2 teaspoons Asian chile sauce
1 teaspoon freshly grated nutmeg
½ teaspoon ground allspice
½ teaspoon ground cinnamon
•
1½ pounds fresh calf's liver, cut ¼ inch thick

• advance preparation

In a small bowl, combine all of the marinade ingredients. Stir well. Within 2 hours of cooking, combine the marinade with the liver and refrigerate.

• last-minute cooking

Place a cast-iron, two-burner grill over 2 burners with the heat turned to medium. Allow to heat for 15 minutes. When very hot, add the liver and cook approximately 2 minutes on each side, brushing on more marinade. The liver is done when it is still very pink in the center. Alternatively, barbecue the liver. If using a gas barbecue or indoor grill, preheat to medium (350°F.). If using charcoal or wood, prepare a fire. When the coals or wood are ash-covered or the gas barbecue or indoor grill is preheated, brush the grill with oil, then grill the liver about 2 to 4 minutes on each side. When the liver is still pink in the center, transfer to 4 heated dinner plates. Serve at once.

note: If you are in the market for a heavy iron grill pan with raised edges, be sure to purchase the model that covers 2 burners. Placed directly on top of your gas or electric burner and preheated until sizzling hot, these grills are wonderful for cooking steaks, boneless chicken breasts, firm-fleshed fish, and one of the great gastronomic sensations, calf's liver.

Stars and *Supporting* Roles *with* *Pasta,* Rice, and *Breads*

Jasmine Steamed Rice

Rice is native to Asia, where 90 percent of the world's supply is grown to feed half the world's population. There are over 2,500 different varieties of rice, including ones with red, blue, and black coloration. The Southeast Asians and Chinese primarily use long-grain white rice, while the Japanese and Koreans prefer sticky short-grain varieties. Most supermarkets in North America sell Texas or California long-grain rice, as well as two other types of white rice rapidly increasing in popularity: Indian basmati rice and Thai jasmine rice. Indian basmati rice has a very long grain that gives it a striking visual appeal. During cooking Thai jasmine rice (which we prefer) gives off a magical aroma that is as captivating as the smell of bread baking in the oven. Use Texas and California long-grain white rice, basmati rice, and Thai jasmine rice interchangeably for all the rice recipes in this book. Under no circumstances should you buy partially precooked "converted" rice, or the rice made by that bad Uncle, both of which taste terrible.

Following are two methods that Asians use to judge the amount of water to add to rice. Either place the tip of your index finger on the top surface of the rice and add enough water to rise up to the first knuckle line above the fingertip. Or rest the bottom of your out-stretched palm on the top surface of the rice and add just enough water to cover the top of your hand. Both methods work whether you use a huge or tiny saucepan, or you are as small as Tom Thumb or as tall as Wilt Chamberlain.

- Easy
- Serves 6 to 8 as a side dish.

2 cups jasmine rice (not minute or converted rice)
¼ cup coconut milk (optional)
Salt and freshly ground black pepper (optional)

• last-minute preparation and cooking

Place the rice in a sieve and rinse with cold water, rubbing the rice grains together with your fingers until the rinse water is no longer cloudy. Place the rice in a 2½-quart saucepan. Add the coconut milk and enough cold water to cover the top surface of the rice by exactly 1 inch.

Place the saucepan over high heat and bring the water to a vigorous boil. As soon as the top surface of the rice is no longer covered with liquid, cover the saucepan, turn the heat to the lowest setting, and simmer the rice 15 minutes.

• menu ideas

Serve this rice with stir-fry dishes or with meat entrées that have lots of sauce.

PRECEDING PAGE
Thai Rice Pilaf with Lemongrass, Basil, and Mint

Thai Rice Pilaf
with Lemongrass, Basil, and Mint

Who wants to be in solitary confinement in the kitchen, mashing mounds of potatoes, draining pasta from cauldrons of boiling water, or laboring over a saucepan of molten polenta, while friends relax in the living room and wait for the dinner bell to ring? Slavery was outlawed in 1863, but kitchen servitude is ever-present today. To solve this problem, at dinner parties that don't involve guests in the kitchen chatting or lending a helping hand, plan on serving rice pilaf. Made a few hours or even a day in advance and reheated in the oven, it makes the perfect do-ahead dish to accompany any meat or seafood entrée.

- Easy
- Serves 6 to 8 as a side dish.

1½ cups jasmine rice (not minute or converted rice)

⅓ cup currants

2 cloves garlic, finely minced

2 tablespoons finely minced fresh
  lemongrass stem (optional)

2 cups Homemade Chicken Stock
  (page 70)

½ cup coconut milk

2 tablespoons dry sherry

2 tablespoons fish sauce

1 teaspoon Asian chile sauce

2 teaspoons orange zest (colored part of
  skin), very finely grated

1 kaffir lime leaf (optional)

3 tablespoons cooking oil

1 red bell pepper, stemmed and seeded

½ cup minced green onions

¼ cup minced fresh basil leaves

¼ cup minced fresh mint leaves

¼ cup white sesame seeds

- **advance preparation**

Place the rice in a sieve. Wash the rice under cold water, stirring with your fingers until the water is no longer cloudy, about 2 minutes. Drain thoroughly and set aside with the currants.

Set aside the garlic and lemongrass. In a small bowl, combine the chicken stock, coconut milk, sherry, fish sauce, chile sauce, orange zest, and kaffir lime leaf. Place a 2½-quart saucepan over high heat and add the cooking oil. Add the garlic and lemongrass and sauté 15 seconds. Add the rice and currants and sauté 5 minutes, until well heated. Add the coconut-stock mixture and bring to a low simmer. Cover the pot, reduce the heat to low, and simmer 20 minutes, until all the liquid disappears and the rice tastes tender. If completed up to 2 hours in advance of serving, set aside at room temperature; if completed further ahead, cool to room temperature, then cover and refrigerate.

Within 2 hours of serving the rice, mince the red bell pepper and set aside with the green onions, basil, and mint. Place the sesame seeds in a small ungreased sauté pan, place over high heat, and cook until light golden; then set aside.

- **last-minute cooking**

If reheating the rice, cover the saucepan and warm in a preheated 325°F. oven until piping hot, about 15 minutes. Remove from the oven and stir in the green onions, basil, mint, red pepper, and sesame seeds. Taste and adjust seasonings. Serve at once.

- **menu ideas**

An Asian dinner party for 10: Asian Pot Stickers with Southwest Ketchup, Tropical Salad with Citrus-Herb Dressing, Braised Lamb Shanks East and West, Thai Rice Pilaf with Lemongrass, Basil, and Mint, and Kahlúa Passion Tiles.

Asian Risotto with Shrimp and Smoked Chicken

Americans have become addicted to risotto. It appears on the menu of nearly every trendy restaurant in disguises that would shock cooks from the old country. Yet, whatever the deviations from authentic risottos, the special ingredient in all of them is the pearly, white, oval Arborio rice from the Piedmont region of Italy. No other rice grain duplicates the creamy yet firm texture of Arborio rice that is stirred continually for 30 minutes as small quantities of hot stock are added. To make risotto at home, enlist the efforts of a captive dinner guest to stir the rice while you add the liquid and attend to other preparation tasks.

• Moderate
• Serves 4 as a main entrée.

½ pound fresh shiitake mushrooms
1 red bell pepper, stemmed and seeded
½ cup pine nuts
1 tablespoon fresh ginger, finely minced
2 cloves garlic, finely minced
¼ cup freshly grated imported
   Parmesan cheese
Half a smoked chicken
¾ pound medium-sized raw shrimp
3¼ cups Homemade Chicken Stock
   (page 70)
¼ cup dry sherry
2 tablespoons thin soy sauce
½ teaspoon Asian chile sauce
6 tablespoons unsalted butter
1 cup Arborio rice
½ cup coarsely chopped fresh cilantro

• advance preparation

Preheat the oven to 325°F. Cut off and discard the mushroom stems. Overlap the caps and cut into ¼-inch-wide strips, then set aside. Cut the bell pepper into ¼-inch cubes. Toast the pine nuts on a baking sheet in the preheated oven until golden, about 8 minutes. Combine the ginger and garlic. Set aside the Parmesan.

Separate the chicken meat from the bones. Cut the meat into bite-sized pieces. Shell and devein the shrimp, then split the shrimp in half along the back.

In a small bowl, combine the chicken stock, sherry, soy sauce, and chile sauce. The recipe to this point can be completed up to 8 hours in advance of last-minute cooking.

• last-minute cooking

Place a 2½-quart saucepan over medium-high heat. Add 4 tablespoons of the butter. When the butter melts and begins to sizzle, after about 2 minutes, add the mushrooms and sauté until they begin to wilt, about 5 minutes. Then transfer the mushrooms to a plate.

Return the saucepan to medium-high heat. Add the remaining 2 tablespoons butter. Add the ginger and garlic and sauté a few seconds; then add the rice. Cook over medium-high heat for 3 minutes, stirring slowly.

Reduce the heat to low. Add the broth, one third at a time, stirring slowly, and not adding the next batch of broth until the rice has absorbed nearly all of the previous batch.

When the rice has absorbed almost all the broth and the rice grains are firm but no longer raw-tasting (after about 20 minutes), stir in the mushrooms, red pepper, pine nuts, smoked chicken, and shrimp. Simmer 4 more minutes to complete the cooking of the shrimp. Taste and adjust the seasonings, especially for salt.

Remove the saucepan from the heat and stir in the cheese and cilantro. Serve at once.

• menu ideas

Spicy Gravlax with Mango Salsa, Asian Risotto with Shrimp and Smoked Chicken accompanied by freshly shelled and buttered peas and a green salad tossed with a dressing from Chapter 3, Chocolate Nut Tart, and champagne from the beginning until the end of the festivities!

Cajun Asian Dirty Rice

How can you let a single day escape without improvising your own rice pilaf? After the rice grains are thoroughly rinsed in cold water to remove all of the starch, sauté the rice briefly in oil or butter, which prevents the grains from sticking together during cooking. Then stir in a seasoned stock and let the rice simmer gently until the grains are tender and have absorbed the liquid.

To create your own version of rice pilaf, all you need is good-quality long-grain white rice and twice as much seasoned liquid as rice. Try making rice pilaf with champagne, the water in which dried mushrooms were soaked, or chicken stock flavored with a little sesame oil, grated orange zest, and chile sauce. As you sauté the rice, try adding a fistful of currants, raisins, or dried cranberries. Give the rice a confetti look by stirring in (just prior to serving) any combination of chopped red pepper, green onions, cilantro, chives, parsley, mint, basil, toasted slivered almonds, or pine nuts.

In the rice pilaf presented here, "dirty" describes the brownish tint contributed by chicken livers and heavy soy sauce. Amazingly, the livers lend their color and richness without giving the rice even the slightest hint of "liver" flavor.

• Moderate
• Serves 6 to 8 as a side dish.

4 cloves garlic, finely minced

1 small yellow onion, chopped

1 stalk celery, chopped

¼ cup button mushrooms, chopped

1 green bell pepper, seeded and chopped

¼ cup chopped fresh cilantro

1 tablespoon fresh thyme leaves

1 tablespoon chopped fresh oregano

½ pound fresh chicken livers

2 cups long-grain white rice (not minute or converted rice)

2½ cups Homemade Chicken Stock (page 70)

2 tablespoons heavy soy sauce

2 tablespoons dry sherry

1 teaspoon Asian chile sauce

½ teaspoon salt

¼ cup unsalted butter

Salt and freshly ground black pepper, to taste

•advance preparation

Combine the garlic, onion, celery, mushrooms, pepper, cilantro, thyme, and oregano in one bowl. Chop the livers and set aside. Place the rice in a sieve and rinse under cold water until the rinse water is no longer cloudy, then thoroughly drain. In a small bowl, combine the chicken stock, soy sauce, dry sherry, chile sauce, and salt.

Place a 2½-quart saucepan over medium-high heat. Add the butter and when the butter melts, add the vegetables and sauté until they become very soft, and the onions begin to brown, about 15 minutes.

Add the livers and sauté until they no longer look raw, about 5 minutes. Add the rice. Stir the rice with the vegetables and liver until the rice becomes hot, about 5 minutes. Add the chicken stock mixture. Bring to a low boil, cover the pan, reduce the heat to very low, and simmer until all the liquid is absorbed and the rice no longer tastes raw, about 20 minutes. Taste and adjust the seasonings, especially for salt and pepper. The rice can be prepared up to 3 hours in advance of serving.

• last-minute reheating

Preheat the oven to 325°F. Cover the pan and place in the oven. Reheat until the rice is piping hot, about 15 minutes. Serve at once.

•menu ideas

This is a good party dish to serve as an accompaniment with Braised Chicken Breasts with Saffron Ginger Sauce, Chinois Butterflied Leg of Lamb, or Barbecued Shrimp Brushed with Creole Butter.

Jade Rice

Jade Rice derives its name from the combination of fresh green herbs, spinach, and Asian seasonings that are liquefied in an electric blender, then stirred into the rice. The sauce's complex flavor profile, brilliant color, and simplicity of preparation make it one of the most versatile in this book. It is ideal to toss with boiled ravioli, spoon across broiled sole, or mix with ½ pound just-drained pasta. Although this recipe gives last-minute cooking instructions, the rice can be made entirely in advance, then reheated in a 325°F. oven for 15 minutes or zapped in the microwave. This do-ahead shortcut eases last-minute cooking efforts but diminishes some of the rice's bright green color.

- Easy
- Serves 6 to 8 as a side dish.

1½ cups long-grain white rice (not minute or converted rice)
1 tablespoon finely minced fresh ginger
3 cloves garlic, finely minced
¼ cup cooking oil or unsalted butter
2¼ cups Homemade Chicken Stock (page 70)

• jade sauce

½ cup firmly packed spinach leaves
1 teaspoon finely grated orange zest (colored part of skin)
¼ cup fresh mint leaves
½ cup fresh cilantro sprigs
12 large fresh basil leaves
2 small whole green onions, chopped
2 tablespoons dry sherry
2 tablespoons white distilled vinegar
2 tablespoons dark sesame oil
1 tablespoon thin soy sauce
2 teaspoons hoisin sauce
2 teaspoons sugar
½ teaspoon Asian chile sauce
½ teaspoon salt

• advance preparation

Place the rice in a sieve and rinse with cold water until the rinse water is no longer cloudy, about 2 minutes. Drain thoroughly. Set aside separately the ginger and garlic, oil or butter, and chicken stock.

Place all of the ingredients for the Jade Sauce in an electric blender. Blend until completely liquefied, then refrigerate.

Place a 2½-quart saucepan over high heat and add the oil or butter, ginger, and garlic. When the oil becomes hot, add the rice. Sauté the rice about 3 to 5 minutes, until well heated. Then add the chicken stock and bring to a low boil. Cover the pot, reduce the heat to the lowest setting, and simmer the rice 20 minutes, until all of the liquid disappears and the grains of rice are tender. Stir in the Jade Sauce. Serve immediately. Or, if prepared up to 2 hours in advance of serving, set aside at room temperature; if prepared further ahead, cool to room temperature, then cover and refrigerate.

• last-minute cooking

If reheating the rice, cover the saucepan and warm in a preheated 325°F. oven until piping hot, about 15 minutes. Taste and adjust seasonings. Serve at once.

• menu ideas

Serve Jade Rice with barbecued meats and fish.

Wild Rice with Currants, Pine Nuts, and Port

Wild rice is a wonderfully versatile ingredient. Not a "rice" at all, and not interchangeable with white or brown rice, this "water grass" grows wild in the Great Lakes area and is also grown commercially. Cooked in a copious amount of water, drained, rinsed with cold water, and drained again, it keeps well for up to 10 days in the refrigerator. Make cooked wild rice a kitchen resource by adding it to bread dough or pancake or muffin batter or stirring it into stews or braised chicken dishes. In addition, wild rice adds a nutty texture, "wild" taste, and exotic look to virtually any salad or soup, whether European or Asian. This dish can be cooked entirely in advance of serving, placed in a heat-proof bowl, covered, and reheated up to 8 hours later in a 325°F. oven for 20 minutes.

• Easy
• Serves 6 as a side dish.

2 cups wild rice
1 teaspoon salt plus additional salt, to taste
1 cup currants
1 cup port
½ cup pine nuts
4 cloves garlic, finely minced
2 shallots, finely minced
4 whole green onions
6 tablespoons unsalted butter
Freshly ground black pepper, to taste
About ¼ cup balsamic vinegar

• preparation and cooking

Place the wild rice in a sieve and rinse under cold water. In a 4-quart saucepan set over high heat, bring 12 cups water to a vigorous boil. Add the wild rice and 1 teaspoon salt. When the water returns to a low boil, reduce the heat to low and cook the wild rice, maintaining the very low boil, for about 45 minutes. The rice is done when about three fourths of the rice grains have puffed open and the rest of the grains are still closed and firm to the bite. Immediately transfer the rice to a sieve and rinse under cold water to prevent further cooking, then drain thoroughly. Transfer to a bowl and refrigerate. Makes about 8 cups.

In a small bowl, combine the currants and port and marinate for at least 30 minutes but for no longer than 2 hours. Drain the currants, reserving the port.

Preheat the oven to 325°F.

Toast the pine nuts on a baking sheet in the preheated oven until golden, about 8 minutes. Set aside the garlic and shallots. Cut the green onions on a sharp diagonal into ⅛-inch-thin pieces.

• last-minute cooking

Place a 12- or 14-inch sauté pan over highest heat. Add the butter and as it melts, add the garlic and shallots. When the butter sizzles but before the garlic begins to brown, add the wild rice, currants, port, and green onions. Sauté the wild rice mixture over high heat for about 6 minutes, until the wild rice is thoroughly reheated and the port has been completely absorbed by the wild rice. Stir in the pine nuts. Season to taste with freshly ground black pepper, salt, and sprinkles of balsamic vinegar. Serve at once.

• menu ideas

For a dinner in Sun Valley for 8, we served fresh caviar, Beef Tenderloin with Shiitake Cream Sauce accompanied by Wild Rice with Currants, Pine Nuts, and Port, a simple green salad, and Fantastic Raspberry Ice Cream with Velvet Chocolate Sauce.

Santa Fe Corn Bread

As a side dish for barbecued meats and stews, it would be hard to find an easier recipe. Serve the corn bread with butter, honey-butter, or Ancho Chile Jam. Or bake the corn bread hours in advance, split the bread in half horizontally, brush on garlic butter, and then, just before serving, toast under the broiler until crisp and reheated. Or, hours in advance, bake the corn bread in cast-iron pans indented with corn cob-shaped molds, then, when ready to serve, warm the corn-bread sticks in the oven. Freeze leftover corn bread and use it in place of bread crumbs the next time you make stuffing for chicken or turkey.

- Easy
- Serves 8 as a side dish.

1½ cups yellow cornmeal
½ cup unbleached white flour
2 teaspoons baking powder
1 teaspoon salt
3 eggs, well beaten
1¼ cups buttermilk
⅓ cup unsalted butter, melted
¼ cup honey
1 red bell pepper
¼ cup pine nuts
3 serrano chiles, stemmed, or 1 teaspoon
   Asian chile sauce (optional)
3 cloves garlic, very finely minced
Kernels from 2 ears of white corn
¼ cup chopped fresh cilantro

• preparation and cooking

Preheat the oven to 400°F. Lightly butter or oil an 8- to 10-inch cast-iron skillet and heat in the oven for 20 minutes.

Place the cornmeal, flour, baking powder, and salt in a large bowl and mix well. In a separate bowl, combine the eggs, milk, butter, and honey.

Chop the red pepper. Place the pine nuts on a baking sheet and toast in the oven until light golden, about 5 minutes. Very finely mince the chiles (including the seeds). Add the pepper, pine nuts, chiles, garlic, raw corn kernels, and cilantro to the milk mixture. Stir this into the corn-meal mixture. Mix only until the dry ingredients are moistened, leaving plenty of lumps.

Remove the cast-iron pan from the oven, then pour the batter into the pan. Return the pan to the oven and bake the corn bread until a knife blade pushed deep into the center comes out clean, about 25 to 30 minutes. Cut the corn bread into slices and serve at once.

Polenta Madness

Polenta madness is gripping the nation. Few side dishes are as easy to make or are better appreciated by dinner guests than broiled or grilled polenta matched with a stew or another dish that has plenty of sauce. The polenta can be made a day in advance, then brushed with extra-virgin olive oil and simply popped under the broiler flame or cooked in a fish screen on a grill until reheated and golden. For this recipe, a thin layer of pesto is sandwiched inside the polenta, but other flavor accents, such as Ancho Chile Jam and Thai Green Curry Paste, can be used as well. If, however, the flavor from the entrée does not complement the pesto, Ancho Chile Jam, or Thai Curry Paste, simply make the polenta without any filling.

- Easy
- Serves 4 to 6 as a side dish.

⅓ cup unsalted butter

⅓ cup Mascarpone cheese

½ cup freshly grated imported
   Parmesan cheese

½ cup New World Pesto (page 103) or
   store-bought pesto (optional)

2 cups polenta (not "instant") or yellow
   cornmeal

3 cups cold water

2 teaspoons salt

2 tablespoons extra-virgin olive oil

•advance preparation

Set aside the butter, Mascarpone, Parmesan, and pesto sauce. Combine the polenta with the cold water. Fill a 2½-quart saucepan with 3 cups water and bring to a vigorous boil. Add the salt and stir in the polenta-cold water mixture. Bring to a low boil, reduce the heat to low, and cook the polenta, stirring slowly but continually, for about 10 to 20 minutes, until the polenta thickens and pulls away from the sides of the saucepan with each stirring motion. Taste the polenta. There should be no raw or gritty taste.

Remove the pan from heat, add the butter, Mascarpone, and Parmesan, and stir until completely absorbed by the polenta.

Transfer half the polenta into a 7-inch-square metal pan or a 9-inch springform pan, then return the rest of the polenta to the stove over very low heat. Using a spatula, spread the polenta in the pan into a smooth layer, then immediately add a thin, even layer of pesto.

Immediately and gently top the pesto with the remaining polenta and spread into an even layer. Let the polenta cool for at least 1 hour, until firm. The recipe to this point can be completed up to a day in advance of last-minute cooking.

•last-minute cooking

Preheat the oven to 450°F. Cut the polenta into serving-size pieces, leaving the polenta in the pan, and brush the top surface with the oil. Turn the oven setting to broil, place the polenta 4 inches from the broiler heat, and cook until it turns golden and is well heated through, about 8 minutes. Do not turn the pieces over during broiling. (Alternatively, preheat a gas barbecue or indoor grill to medium, 350°F. If using charcoal or wood, prepare a fire. Cut the polenta into squares, triangles, or wedges, and place the pieces in a fish screen. Close the screen to secure the polenta, brush both sides of the polenta with oil, and lay the screen on the barbecue or grill. When the polenta turns golden, after about 5 minutes, turn the fish screen over and cook the polenta approximately 5 more minutes, until well heated and golden.) Transfer the polenta to serving plates and serve at once.

•menu ideas

We love serving grilled polenta with Braised Beef with Mushrooms, Thyme, and Asian Accents, Steamed White Corn with Szechwan Butter Glaze, and White Chocolate Mousse with Tropical Fruits.

Popovers Scented with Garlic, Cilantro, and Chile

The following is an example of what happens when a cook with a fondness for the Southwest gets hold of an old family recipe. The original recipe is from a handwritten cookbook begun in 1870 by my great-great grandmother, Marcia Lamberton Stevens, who kept the cookbook notes in her kitchen at "Riverview," North Hoosick, New York. Next to the original recipe, Marcia Stevens wrote "good." But we think that, with the addition of cilantro and crushed dried red chile to the batter, a more enthusiastic description is warranted. If possible, cook the popovers in a cast-iron muffin tin, which because of even heat distribution, causes the batter to pop over the edges.

• Easy
• Serves 4 as a side dish.

2 tablespoons unsalted butter or rendered bacon fat

3 cloves garlic, very finely minced

¼ cup finely chopped fresh cilantro

½ teaspoon crushed dried red chile

½ teaspoon grated orange zest (colored part of skin)

1 cup milk

1 cup unbleached white flour

½ teaspoon salt

1 egg

Flour and butter to rub on cast-iron muffin tin

• **preparation and last-minute cooking**

Preheat the oven to 450°F. Place a small saucepan over low heat. Add the butter and garlic and sauté until the butter begins to sizzle, then remove the pan from the heat.

Set aside the cilantro, chile, and grated orange zest. In a small bowl, combine the milk, flour, and salt, and beat just until smooth. In a separate bowl, beat the egg lightly. Stir the butter, garlic, egg, cilantro, chile, and orange zest into the batter.

Lightly butter a 10- to 12-hole cast-iron muffin tin, then dust the inside of the holes with a little flour, shaking out all of the excess.

Fill each hole no more than three-fourths to the top. Place in the preheated oven and bake 20 minutes. Reduce the heat to 350°F. and bake 10 more minutes. Do not open the oven door. After the final 10 minutes in the oven, immediately transfer the popovers to heated dinner plates or a basket lined with linen. Serve at once.

• **menu ideas**

Serve these popovers with barbecued meats, such as Red-Cooked Barbecued Lamb Shanks, or with a dish that has lots of sauce, such as Braised Chicken Breasts with Exotic Mushrooms.

Any Kind of Bread or Rolls

Any Kind of Bread is based on a recipe from my friend, Houston chef Magnus Hansson. It is a marvelous recipe that lends itself to "any kind" of variation. I have made excellent "any kind of bread" using a wide range of oils, such as extra-virgin olive oil, walnut oil, and Asian dark sesame oil, as well as by using many different combinations of flour.

Also try adding a combination of 1 cup chopped roasted red pepper, raw kernels from 4 ears of white corn, and 1 cup currants. Or stir in ½ cup any kind of chopped olives, 1 cup toasted pine nuts, and 1 cup dried cranberries. Or infuse the bread with flavor by adding 1 cup chopped fresh cilantro, ½ cup toasted sesame seeds, 2 teaspoons red chile flakes, and 6 finely minced garlic cloves sautéed in oil. Served with any kind of food, you'll never need to make any kind of excuse for the taste.

- Easy
- Makes 2 loaves or 24 rolls.

1 ounce quick-rising dry yeast (4 ¼-ounce packages)

2 cups warm water (110°F.)

⅓ cup honey or other sweetener, such as sugar, molasses, or maple syrup

1 tablespoon salt, any kind

¼ cup extra-virgin olive oil

5 cups white bread flour

Any kind of seasoning (see introduction to recipe)

•advance preparation and baking

In a large bowl, stir the yeast into the warm water. Stir in the honey or other sweetener. When bubbles form on the surface of the mixture, after about 5 minutes, the yeast has been activated. (Do not proceed if this does not occur.)

Stir the salt and oil into the yeast mixture. Then add 2 cups of the flour and beat vigorously for 2 minutes. Add any kind of seasonings. Gently stir in 2⅓ cups additional flour. Turn the dough out onto a floured surface, and knead about 5 minutes, working in about ⅔ cup more flour, until the dough is smooth and no longer sticky. Transfer the dough to a lightly oiled bowl, brush the top of the dough with more oil, cover with a towel, and let rise in a warm area until doubled in size, about 30 minutes.

When the dough has doubled in size, punch it down and transfer to 2 8½-by-4½-inch bread loaf pans. Or, shape the dough into 24 rolls, lightly flour, and place on a baking sheet. Let loaves or rolls rise 10 minutes.

Preheat the oven to 350°F. If desired, brush the dough with beaten egg or honey. Bake the bread about 1 hour and rolls about 20 to 30 minutes, until the bread or rolls make a hollow sound when tapped. Immediately transfer from the pan(s) to a wire rack and allow to cool. When cool, serve or wrap in plastic and refrigerate or freeze.

Southwestern Pasta with Grilled Vegetables and Goat Cheese

Grilled corn, tomato slices, asparagus, and red bell peppers add a wonderful depth of flavor to this spicy, Southwest-style pasta dish. If you are making this recipe for a group of 4 or fewer, barbecue the vegetables at the last moment along with boneless, skin-on chicken breasts or pieces of firm-fleshed fish. Then cut the meat or seafood into bite-sized pieces and incorporate them, along with the grilled vegetables, into the just-cooked pasta. Nothing else is needed for this dinner except a simple green salad and a premium store-bought ice cream topped with one of the dessert sauces from Chapter 10.

- Moderate
- Serves 4 as a side dish.

2 red bell peppers
3 vine-ripened tomatoes
1 bunch asparagus
3 ears white corn
4 whole green onions
East West Marinade (page 186)
½ cup chopped fresh cilantro
5 cloves garlic, finely minced
4 serrano chiles, stemmed and finely minced (including seeds)
½ teaspoon cinnamon
4 ounces soft goat cheese
8 ounces dried pasta
3 tablespoons extra-virgin olive oil
Salt and freshly ground black pepper, to taste

• advance preparation

Remove the stems and seeds from the bell peppers. Cut the tomatoes into ½-inch-thick slices. Snap off and discard the asparagus ends. Remove the corn husks. Trim off and discard the green onion ends.

Prepare the Grilled Vegetable Marinade. Place the marinade in a large bowl, add the peppers, tomatoes, asparagus, corn, and green onions, and toss to coat evenly. Marinate 1 hour.

Set aside the cilantro. Combine the minced garlic and serrano chiles. In a small bowl, set aside the cinnamon. Crumble the goat cheese.

If using a gas barbecue or indoor grill, preheat to medium (350°F.). If using charcoal or wood, prepare a fire. When the coals or wood are ash-covered or the gas barbecue or indoor grill is preheated, brush with oil, then grill the vegetables until they have a slight charred look, about 5 minutes, brushing on more marinade during cooking. When the vegetables are done, remove them from the grill and cool. Cut the kernels off the corn ears and cut the remaining vegetables into bite-sized pieces. Refrigerate all of the vegetables. Set aside ½ cup of the vegetable marinade. The recipe to this point can be completed up to 4 hours in advance of last-minute cooking.

• last-minute cooking

Bring 6 quarts water to a vigorous boil in a large pasta pot. Add the dried pasta and cook according to the directions on the package, until the pasta just loses its raw interior taste but is still firm. Immediately drain the pasta in a colander.

Meanwhile, place a 12- or 14-inch sauté pan over highest heat. Add the olive oil, garlic, and chiles, and sauté until the garlic begins to sizzle. Add the grilled vegetables and stir and toss until they begin to sizzle, about 5 minutes. Add the pasta, cinnamon, vegetable marinade, and goat cheese. Stir and toss until all of the ingredients are evenly combined and the goat cheese is melted. Stir in the cilantro. Taste and adjust the seasonings, especially for salt and pepper. Transfer to 4 heated dinner plates and serve at once.

Mushroom Fantasy Pasta

Although the pasta machine adds an aura of culinary expertise when positioned prominently on a kitchen counter, it is far better suited to pressing salmon for *gravlax* or anchoring a small boat than making pasta now that such a wide variety of quick-cooking dried pastas, both plain and flavored, is available. None of the pasta recipes in this book calls for the "fresh" pasta that is sold in the deli cases of most supermarkets. This product, extruded under great pressure from a machine, has a heavy texture and inferior taste.

• Moderate
• Serves 4 as a side dish.

3 shallots, peeled and minced

3 cloves garlic, finely minced

1 cup Homemade Chicken Stock (page 70)

½ ounce dried porcini or cèpe mushrooms

¼ pound fresh shiitake mushrooms

½ pound fresh portabello mushrooms

½ pound fresh button mushrooms

1½ cups chopped fresh parsley

2 tablespoons dry sherry

2 tablespoons oyster sauce

1 tablespoon dark sesame oil

2 teaspoons cornstarch

½ teaspoon sugar

¼ teaspoon freshly ground black pepper

1 cup finely grated imported Parmesan cheese

¼ cup unsalted butter

8 ounces dried mushroom-flavored pasta

• advance preparation

Combine the minced shallots and garlic. Bring the chicken stock to a boil, remove from the heat, and stir in the dried mushrooms. Soak the dried mushrooms until softened, about 20 minutes, then remove the mushrooms and chop. Using a fine-meshed sieve (lined with cheese-cloth, if necessary), strain the chicken stock into a bowl and set aside.

Cut off and discard the shiitake stems. Overlap the caps and cut into ¼-inch-wide strips. Cut off and discard the portabello stems. Cut the portabello caps in half, rotate the mushrooms a quarter turn, and cut the caps into ¼-inch-wide strips. Cut the button mushrooms through the cap into ¼-inch-wide slices. Set aside the parsley. In a small bowl, combine the chicken stock, dry sherry, oyster sauce, sesame oil, cornstarch, sugar, and pepper. Set aside the Parmesan.

Place a 12-inch sauté pan over high heat. Add the butter and when the butter melts, add the shallots and garlic. When the garlic sizzles, add the fresh and dried mushrooms. Sauté the mushrooms until their liquid is expelled and boils away and the mushrooms become densely textured, about 15 minutes. Remove the pan from the heat and stir in the chicken stock mixture. Transfer to a bowl and refrigerate up to 8 hours.

• last-minute cooking

Bring 6 quarts water to a vigorous boil in a large pasta pot. Add the mushroom pasta and a little salt. Cook the pasta according to the directions on the package, until it just loses its raw interior taste but is still firm. Immediately drain the pasta in a colander.

Meanwhile, in a large sauté pan, bring the mushrooms and sauce to a rapid boil. Transfer the pasta from the colander to the sauté pan and toss the pasta and sauce until well combined. Taste and adjust the seasonings. Transfer to 4 heated dinner plates. Sprinkle on the chopped parsley and grated Parmesan. Serve at once.

• menu ideas

Vegetarian dinner for 8: Bruschetta East and West, Grilled Vegetable Salad with Tortilla Threads, Mushroom Fantasy Pasta served with Addicted to Asparagus, and, for dessert, Ginger Banana Cream Tart Lined with Chocolate.

Two-Way Pasta

One of the easiest ways to make a pasta side dish for a quick meal is to place just-cooked pasta in a big bowl and toss it with olive oil, sautéed garlic, fresh herbs, grated cheese, salt, and freshly ground black pepper. The following recipe provides 2 simple variations: European and Chinese. But you can easily create additional variations by stirring into the cooked pasta ⅓ cup New World Pesto, Jade Sauce, or Southwest Salsa. Whether you stick to one of the recipes that follow or improvise your own pasta side dish, taste the pasta frequently while adding the seasonings to assure that you are achieving a blend of flavors that pleases you. Don't forget to add a generous amount of salt, which intensifies the tastes of all the ingredients and creates depth of flavor.

• Easy
• Each variation serves 4 as a side dish.

8 ounces dried pasta

• european

¼ cup extra-virgin olive oil
2 large cloves garlic, very finely minced
1 teaspoon dried herbes de provence
½ teaspoon crushed red chile flakes
1½ cups chopped fresh flat-leaf Italian parsley
1 cup freshly grated imported Parmesan cheese
2 tablespoons balsamic vinegar
Salt and freshly ground pepper, to taste

• chinese

3 tablespoons cooking oil
3 cloves garlic, finely minced
1 tablespoon finely minced fresh ginger
3 tablespoons thin soy sauce
1 tablespoon dark sesame oil
1 tablespoon unseasoned Japanese rice vinegar
1 tablespoon brown sugar
½ teaspoon Asian chile sauce
½ teaspoon grated orange zest (colored part of skin)
¾ cup chopped fresh cilantro

• preparation and cooking

Choose one of the pasta flavorings. For the European, combine the olive oil, garlic, dried herbs and red chile flakes. Set aside separately the parsley, Parmesan, and vinegar. For the Chinese, combine the cooking oil, garlic, and ginger. In a separate bowl, combine the soy sauce, sesame oil, vinegar, sugar, chile sauce, and orange zest. Set aside the chopped fresh cilantro.

Bring 6 quarts water to a vigorous boil in a large pasta pot. Add the dried pasta and a dash of salt. Cook the pasta according to the directions on the package, until the pasta loses its raw interior taste but is still firm. If you want a creamy pasta sauce, reserve ½ cup of the pasta water. Then immediately drain the pasta in a colander.

For European: Return the pasta pot to the stove over medium-low heat. Wipe away any water remaining in the pot. Add the oil mixture and sauté 15 seconds. Return the pasta to the pot, add the parsley and cheese, and toss to combine evenly. Sprinkle on the balsamic vinegar and toss again. Add the pasta water if you want a creamier taste. Taste and adjust seasonings, adding salt (about 1 teaspoon) and pepper. Serve at once.

For Chinese: Return the pasta pot to the stove over medium-low heat. Wipe away any water remaining in the pot. Add the oil mixture and sauté 15 seconds. Return the pasta to the pot, add the soy sauce mixture and chopped cilantro, and toss to combine evenly. Add the pasta water if you want a creamier taste. Taste and adjust seasonings and serve at once.

Salmon Pasta
with Sun-Dried Tomatoes

Stars and Supporting Roles with Pasta, Rice, and Breads

When creating this dish we tried to achieve a wide range of flavors, colors, and textures by sautéing bite-sized pieces of salmon with crunchy sugar snap peas, intensely flavored sun-dried tomatoes, roasted walnuts, and, for a burst of high flavor notes, fresh herbs. The addition of a little whipping cream and a judicious sprinkling of salt provides a rounded flavor, while the spaghetti acts as a neutral stage upon which the special attributes of all the ingredients can shine. If you plan on doubling this recipe, enlist a cooking partner to duplicate your actions in another 12- or 14-inch sauté pan.

• Moderate
• Serves 4 as a main entrée.

1 pound salmon filet, skinned and bones removed

1 cup walnuts

12 sun-dried tomatoes

2 cups sugar snap peas

4 cloves garlic, very finely minced

2 shallots, peeled and minced

1 cup whipping cream

½ cup dry vermouth

¼ cup thin soy sauce

½ cup grated imported Parmesan cheese

¾ cup chopped fresh herbs (such as basil, oregano, and/or thyme)

12 ounces dried linguine

3 tablespoons extra-virgin olive oil

Salt and freshly ground black pepper, to taste

•**advance preparation**

Cut the salmon into ¼-inch-thin bite-sized pieces, then set aside. Roast the walnuts as described on page 222. Place the sun-dried tomatoes in a small bowl and cover with boiling water. When the tomatoes soften, after about 20 minutes, drain and mince them. Cut the sugar snap peas in half on the diagonal and set aside. Combine the garlic and shallots and set aside. In a small bowl, combine the cream, vermouth, and soy sauce. Set aside the Parmesan cheese. The recipe to this point can be completed up to 8 hours in advance of cooking.

•**last-minute cooking**

Set aside the herbs. Bring 6 quarts water to a furious boil in a large stockpot. Add the linguine and cook according to the direction on the package, until it just loses it raw interior taste but is still firm. Immediately drain in a colander.

Meanwhile, place a 12- or 14-inch sauté pan over highest heat. When very hot, add the olive oil, garlic, and shallots. When the garlic sizzles, after about 15 seconds, add the tomatoes, herbs, and sugar snap peas. Stir and toss for 1 minute, then add the sauce. Bring to a vigorous boil, then add the salmon. Sauté the salmon until nearly cooked, about 1 minute, then add the pasta and walnuts. Toss all of the ingredients to combine evenly. Stir in the Parmesan. Taste and adjust seasonings, especially for salt and pepper. Serve at once.

•**menu ideas**

Accompany this main entrée with dishes that do not require last-minute work, such as Southwest Caesar Salad with Chile Croutons and fresh fruit with Chocolate Meltdown Cookies.

Garlic Mashed Potatoes with Mascarpone

For many of us, mashed potatoes are near the top of the list of dishes to eat that final night before, as Julia Child likes to say, "we slip off the raft." We have consumed hundreds of versions of mashed potatoes, but Garlic Mashed Potatoes with Mascarpone is our favorite: In this recipe, peeled, boiled potatoes are mashed very finely with lots of hot milk, butter, roasted garlic, and rich Mascarpone cheese, then packed into ramekins, sprinkled with grated Parmesan, and popped under the broiler until golden and bubbly across the surface. These mashed potatoes are so good that we always keep a few extra ramekins of them on hand to heat under the broiler in order to satisfy the inevitable requests for second helpings.

For this recipe you will need four to six 1½-cup heatproof ceramic ramekins or an 8-inch-square heatproof baking dish. The mashed potatoes can be refrigerated for up to 6 hours prior to running them under the broiler. Serve with any meat or seafood entrée.

• Easy
• Serves 4 to 6 as a side dish.

5 medium-sized baking potatoes, about 2½ pounds
1 teaspoon salt
8 cloves roasted garlic (page 220)
¼ cup unsalted butter, at room temperature
1 cup Mascarpone cheese or sour cream, at room temperature
¼ cup freshly grated imported Parmesan cheese
¼ cup chopped chives
½ cup milk
Salt and freshly ground black pepper, to taste

• advance preparation

Peel the potatoes, then cut each potato into 6 pieces. Place the potatoes and 1 teaspoon salt in a large saucepan and cover the potatoes with cold water.

Mash the roasted garlic. Set aside separately the butter, Mascarpone, Parmesan, and chives. Set aside the milk in a small saucepan.

Place the saucepan holding the potatoes over high heat, bring the water to a low boil, reduce the heat to medium, and boil the potatoes until tender, about 15 minutes. Drain all the water from the potatoes, then return them to the pan in which they were cooked. Warm the milk. Mash the potatoes in the pan with a potato masher or fork until the texture is completely smooth.

Mash in the garlic, butter, Mascarpone, chives, and milk. Taste and adjust seasonings, adding approximately 1 teaspoon each salt and freshly ground black pepper. Transfer the potatoes to four 1½-cup heatproof ceramic ramekins or an 8-inch-square baking dish. Cool to room temperature, then cover the potatoes with plastic wrap and refrigerate for up to 6 hours.

• last-minute cooking

Preheat the oven to 350°F. Remove the plastic wrap from the potatoes, place the ramekins or baking dish in the preheated oven, and bake the potatoes in the ramekins 15 minutes, and the potatoes in the baking dish 30 minutes. Sprinkle the surface of the potatoes with Parmesan. Turn the oven setting to broil, place the potatoes 4 inches below the broiler heat, and cook until the surface of the potatoes turns golden, about 5 minutes. Serve at once.

Panfried Potatoes with Rosemary

Potatoes were transported from Peru to Spain by the conquistadors in about 1535, and the popularity of this New World crop quickly spread throughout Europe and beyond. Today the range of potato varieties available in our markets is vast, having grown markedly in the last few years. On a recent early morning visit to a local farmers' market, we spotted, in addition to the common russets and red and white boiling potatoes, the following varieties: True Blue (blue skin and flesh), Caribe (purple skin with white flesh), Cherries Jubilee (red skin and flesh), and Yukon Gold (yellow skin and flesh).

Regardless of how common or exotic the variety of potato, the following recipe makes one of the most satisfying and easiest side dishes to serve alongside barbecued meats.

• Easy
• Serves 4 as a side dish.

2 pounds (about 20) small red potatoes
1 tablespoon mixed black, white, and green peppercorns
3 whole green onions
½ cup chopped fresh basil leaves
¼ cup tender fresh rosemary ends
8 cloves garlic, finely minced
2 tablespoons finely minced fresh ginger
2 tablespoons extra-virgin olive oil
Salt, to taste

• advance preparation

Scrub the potatoes, then cut them in half. If done more than 30 minutes in advance of cooking, cover the potatoes with cold water. Cut the green onions on a diagonal into ½-inch lengths. Set aside together the green onions, basil, and rosemary. Place the peppercorns in an ungreased skillet, place over high heat, and toast until they begin to smoke. Remove the peppercorns from the pan and crush or coarsely grind. Set aside the garlic and ginger. The recipe to this point can be completed up to 8 hours in advance of last-minute cooking.

• last-minute cooking

Place a 12-inch nonstick skillet over medium-high heat. Add the oil and when it becomes hot, add the potatoes and the crushed peppercorns. Cover, reduce the heat to low, and cook, stirring every 5 minutes (so the potatoes don't scorch), until the potatoes become light brown and tender in the center, about 15 minutes. During the last 8 minutes of cooking, stir in the garlic, ginger, green onions, basil, and rosemary. Season with salt and serve at once.

• menu ideas

Serve these potatoes with Barbecued Chicken Breasts Caribbean and Baby Greens with Blue Cheese-Pecan Dressing.

Magic with Vegetables and Eggs

Steamed White Corn with Szechwan Butter Glaze

Everywhere we travel in North America, local cooks tell us that no corn tastes as sweet as their local variety. They are, of course, mistaken, because no corn tastes as sweet or tender as the corn grown in the Napa Valley nor does any other corn have rows of kernels as perfectly straight, small, and white. Outside every kitchen door in the Napa Valley, rows of this perfect corn, planted in 2-week intervals, spring up thanks to the region's perfect marriage of rich soil, heat, and humidity. Nowhere else in the world do cooks train during the off-season to sprint the short distance between the rows of corn and pots of boiling water. And nowhere else is tender steamed corn rolled in a seasoned butter glaze or brushed with New World Pesto Sauce or Ancho Chile Jam.

• Easy
• Serves 4 as a side dish.

8 ears white corn, picked the day they will be cooked

½ cup unsalted butter

2 cloves garlic, finely minced

½ teaspoon crushed Szechwan peppercorns

½ teaspoon Asian chile sauce

½ teaspoon salt

¼ cup chopped fresh cilantro, basil, or mint

• preparation and cooking

Husk the corn. Place the butter, garlic, peppercorns, chile sauce, and salt in a 12-inch sauté pan. Set aside the cilantro, basil, or mint.

Place the sauté pan over medium heat. When the butter melts and the garlic begins to sizzle, remove the sauté pan from the heat and stir in the herb.

In a large stockpot or pasta pot set over highest heat, bring 3 inches water to a furious boil. Add the corn, cover the pot, and cook until the corn is just heated through, about 2 minutes.

Remove the corn from the pot. Place the corn, 1 ear at a time, in the seasoned butter mixture, roll quickly to coat evenly with butter, then transfer to a heated serving platter or individual plates. Serve at once.

•menu ideas

Fourth of July party Napa-style: Crisp Salmon Spring Rolls, Watermelon and Sweet Red Onion Salad, Chinese Barbecued Chicken with Ginger, Cinnamon, and Chiles served with Any Kind of Bread Rolls and Steamed White Corn with Szechwan Butter Glaze, and Black and White Bread Pudding served hot, accompanied by fresh strawberries.

PRECEDING PAGE

Roasted Baby Artichokes with Tomatoes and Basil

Magic with Vegetables and Eggs

Asian Black Bean Chile

This recipe, one of the easiest in the book, pairs black beans with a rich Asian sauce made with hoisin sauce, oyster sauce, bean sauce, chile sauce, and vinegar to produce a robust side dish with a multilayered taste. For variation, embellish the chile with extra chicken stock and leftover grilled chicken to create a one-dish meal. Or cook rabbit in the chile until tender, then cut the meat off the bone and return the meat to the chile for a gentle reheating. Or simmer the chile until no liquid remains, sprinkle on extra-sharp aged cheddar, and serve with tortillas as an appetizer. Any way you use it, this recipe will revolutionize the way you think about chile.

- Easy
- Serves 4 as a side dish.

1 cup dried black beans
1 large yellow onion
1 tablespoon finely minced garlic
1 tablespoon very finely minced fresh ginger
5 cups Homemade Chicken Stock (page 70)
¼ cup dry sherry
3 tablespoons hoisin sauce
1½ tablespoons oyster sauce
1 tablespoon bean sauce
1 tablespoon dark sesame oil
1 tablespoon white wine vinegar
1 teaspoon Asian chile sauce
½ teaspoon sugar
2 tablespoons light-grade olive oil
1 cup chopped fresh cilantro
1 cup grated sharp cheddar cheese

• advance preparation and cooking

Rinse the black beans carefully, discarding any grit or small stones. Place the beans in a saucepan, cover with cold water, bring to a boil, and boil for 2 minutes. Then remove the pot from the stove, cover, and let the beans cool in the water for 2 hours. Drain and rinse the black beans. Peel and chop the onion. Combine the onion, garlic, and ginger. In a medium bowl, combine the chicken stock, sherry, hoisin sauce, oyster sauce, bean sauce, sesame oil, vinegar, chile sauce, and sugar.

Place a 12-inch sauté pan or heavy skillet over medium-high heat. Add the olive oil, onion, garlic, and ginger, and sauté until the onions brown lightly, about 15 minutes. Then add the beans, sauce, and 2 cups water. Bring to a low boil, reduce the heat to low, and simmer until the beans are tender, about 3 hours. If most of the liquid disappears but the beans are not tender, add more water.

Taste and adjust the seasonings. Serve at once accompanied by chopped cilantro and grated cheddar cheese. Or cool and refrigerate. Reheat over low heat.

Roasted Vegetables
with Caramelized Glaze

As anyone who has scattered vegetables around meat roasting in the oven knows, roasting transforms even the most boring vegetables by concentrating the sugar and intensifying the underlying flavors. The next time you are stuck with rock-hard supermarket tomatoes, cut the tomatoes into ½-inch slices and give them a preliminary roasting in the oven for 30 minutes. Then chop them into small pieces and add to salsa, stew, or tomato sauce. Your gardening friends will think you yanked the tomatoes from the vine that morning.

- Easy
- Serves 4 as a side dish.

8 small red potatoes
4 small parsnips
1 bunch (about 12) small carrots
1 bunch small beets
½ pound medium-sized button
   mushrooms
2 red bell peppers
2 tablespoons unsalted butter
2 tablespoons extra-virgin olive oil
2 tablespoons white wine
2 tablespoons thin soy sauce
2 tablespoons balsamic vinegar
1 tablespoon light brown sugar
¼ teaspoon freshly ground black pepper
2 cloves garlic, finely minced
1 tablespoon finely minced fresh ginger
2 tablespoons chopped fresh herbs (such
   as cilantro, basil, chives, rosemary, tarragon, or oregano)

• preparation and cooking

Preheat the oven to 400°F. Scrub the potatoes. Peel the parsnips and carrots. Scrub the beets. Wipe the mushrooms with a damp towel. Stem and seed the bell peppers, then cut into 1-inch cubes. Place all of the vegetables together in a large mixing bowl. Line a shallow roasting pan with foil and spray the foil with nonstick cooking spray.

In a small saucepan, combine all of the remaining ingredients. Place the saucepan over medium heat and bring the sauce to a low simmer. Pour the sauce over the vegetables, stir to coat evenly, then lay the vegetables on the roasting pan.

Roast the vegetables until they become tender, about 1 hour, turning them over and brushing on more sauce every 15 minutes. Transfer the vegetables to 4 heated dinner plates and serve at once.

Two-Way Grilled Vegetables

Grilled or barbecued vegetables make a sensational accompaniment to practically every entrée. They can also be sprinkled across pizza dough, chopped to make salsa, placed inside vegetarian sandwiches, stirred into stews to provide a deeper flavor, combined with goat cheese for grilled vegetable quesadillas, or rolled next to Mango Salsa inside hot tortillas for an easy appetizer. Choose vegetables that lie flat on the grill and cut them large enough to prevent them from falling into the fire.

The following recipe provides two marinades, but all of the salad dressings in this book also work wonders with grilled vegetables. Always marinate the vegetables for 1 to 2 hours, then brush on more marinade every few minutes during cooking.

• Easy
• Serves 4 as a side dish.

About 8 to 12 cups vegetables, such as asparagus, carrots, eggplant, green beans, green onions, mushrooms, onions, bell peppers, potatoes, summer squash, tomatoes, yams, corn with the husk removed, or cooked and halved, chilled artichokes from which the thistle has been removed

• **east west marinade**

6 cloves garlic, finely minced
2 tablespoons finely minced fresh ginger
Grated zest (colored part of skin) from 2 limes
Juice from 2 limes
1 cup chopped fresh cilantro
½ cup chopped fresh mint leaves
½ cup chopped fresh basil leaves
3 whole green onions, minced
5 serrano chiles, stemmed and minced (including seeds)
½ cup extra-virgin olive oil
½ cup dry sherry
¼ cup oyster sauce
¼ cup thin soy sauce
¼ cup honey
1 tablespoon Asian chile sauce

• **basil parmesan marinade**

2 cups chopped fresh basil leaves
6 cloves garlic, finely minced
1 cup extra-virgin olive oil
1 cup white wine
½ cup freshly squeezed lemon juice
½ cup Dijon mustard
⅓ cup thin soy sauce
1 tablespoon juniper berries, crushed
1 teaspoon freshly ground black pepper
⅔ cup freshly grated imported Parmesan cheese

• **advance preparation**

Prepare your choice of vegetables. Snap off tough bottoms of asparagus spears. Peel carrots; if large, split in half lengthwise. Cut eggplant into long ¼-inch-thick slices. Trim green beans. Trim away green onion ends. If mushrooms are large, cut into halves or quarters. Peel and cut onions into ¼-inch-thick rings. Stem and seed peppers; then cut into long, 1-inch-wide slices. Cut potatoes into ¼-inch-thick slices. Cut squash into long ¼-inch-thick slices. Stem tomatoes, then cut into ½-inch-thick slices. Peel yams and cut lengthwise into quarters.

Combine the ingredients for one marinade. Combine the marinade and vegetables in a non-corrosive bowl and marinate 2 hours, rotating the vegetables occasionally.

• **last-minute cooking**

If using a gas barbecue or indoor grill, preheat to medium (350°F.). If using charcoal or wood, prepare a fire. When the coals or wood are ash-covered or the gas barbecue or indoor grill is preheated, brush the grill with oil, then place the vegetables on the grill. Grill the vegetables until they soften and begin to turn golden, turning the vegetables and brushing on more of the marinade every 5 minutes. Serve at once on 4 heated dinner plates.

Cajun Asian Ratatouille

According to *Larousse Gastronomique,* to make ratatouille, "the different vegetables should be cooked separately, then combined and cooked together until they attain a smooth creamy consistency." Recently, we have heard that some chefs precook the vegetables briefly, then simmer them for only a moment in the sauce to retain their crispness. We, however, prefer to simmer the vegetables until they create the creamy, blended flavor that is the essence of ratatouille, according to *Larousse.*

As a tiny variation on the classic recipe from Nice, in this recipe, the vegetables are marinated, grilled, and then simmered in a spicy, herb-infused Cajun sauce. The barbecue sauce contributes a special low-note flavor that raises classic ratatouille to an ethereal taste sensation!

- Moderate
- Serves 4 as a side dish.

2 yellow onions
4 Japanese eggplants
4 small zucchini
3 green bell peppers
4 vine-ripened tomatoes
East West Marinade (page 186)
6 cloves garlic, finely minced
2 tablespoons finely minced fresh ginger
2 tablespoons light-grade olive oil
¼ cup fresh oregano leaves
1 bunch thyme (tied into a bundle with kitchen string)
1 cup Homemade Chicken Stock (page 70)
1 cup white wine
2 tablespoons oyster sauce
2 teaspoons tomato paste
½ teaspoon sugar
Salt, to taste

• **preparation and cooking**

Peel the onions, then slice into ¼-inch-wide rings. Trim the ends off the eggplant and zucchini, then cut each lengthwise into 4 sections. Stem and seed the bell peppers, then cut into 1-inch-wide strips. Discard the tomato stems, then cut the tomatoes into ½-inch slices. Make the marinade for the vegetables, then marinate the vegetables for 1 hour, rotating them every 20 minutes.

Combine the garlic, ginger, and olive oil. In a small bowl, combine the oregano, thyme, chicken stock, wine, oyster sauce, tomato paste, and sugar.

If using a gas barbecue or indoor grill, preheat to medium (350°F.). If using charcoal or wood, prepare a fire. When the coals or wood are ash-covered or the gas barbecue or indoor grill is preheated, brush the grill with oil, then place the vegetables on the grill. Grill the vegetables until they soften and begin to turn golden, turning the vegetables and brushing on more of the marinade every 5 minutes. Reserve all of the extra marinade.

Remove the vegetables from the grill and cut into bite-sized pieces. Place a heavy 12-inch skillet over medium-high heat. Add the garlic-olive oil mixture. Sauté the garlic until it sizzles, then lay the grilled vegetables in the skillet. Add the wine sauce, bring to a low boil, reduce the heat to low, cover the pot, and simmer the vegetables for 30 minutes, stirring occasionally, until there is almost no liquid remaining. Remove the thyme. Taste and adjust the seasonings by adding salt or a little of the East West Marinade if needed. Serve on 4 heated dinner plates or refrigerate and reheat up to 2 days later.

Grilled Figs
Stuffed with Blue Cheese

The 100-year-old fig tree at the Napa Valley restaurant called Showley's not only forms a canopy across the entire outdoor eating area, but is the principal resource for a week-long fig festival featuring this dish along with Fig Pizza, Figs with Foie Gras, Salmon Filet Wrapped with Fig Leaves, and Fig Fritters with Mango Sauce.

If you can't find the Italian bacon called pancetta, substitute thinly sliced ham, such as prosciutto, but not American bacon, which is entirely different. Wrapped around the figs, pancetta or ham contributes flavor and prevents the figs from sticking to the grill.

- Easy
- Serves 4 as a side dish.

12 fresh figs, not fully ripe
4 walnuts
¼ pound blue cheese, at room temperature
1 tablespoon cognac
¼ pound pancetta, thinly sliced
¼ cup balsamic vinegar

• preparation and cooking

Cut the figs in half only halfway. Toast the walnuts as described on page 222. When toasted, cool to room temperature, then chop. Place the walnuts, blue cheese, and cognac in a small bowl and, using the back of a fork, blend together until evenly mixed. Stuff the figs with the cheese mixture, then wrap the pancetta around the figs and secure with a toothpick.

If using a gas barbecue or indoor grill, preheat to medium (350°F.). If using charcoal or wood, prepare a fire. When the coals or wood are ash-covered or the gas barbecue or indoor grill is preheated, brush the grill with oil. Brush the figs with the balsamic vinegar, then place the figs on the grill. Cover and cook about 2 minutes, rotate half a turn and cook another 2 minutes. Serve at once.

•menu ideas

These figs make a great appetizer, accompaniment to barbecued meat, or dessert when matched with a vintage port.

Roasted Baby Artichokes with Tomatoes and Basil

It is always fun to see the astonished looks on people's faces when they see their first artichoke plant. A perennial vegetable that grows to a diameter and height of 3 feet, the prickly artichoke plant yields tightly packed cones that are picked for eating, or, if left on the plant, open into flowery purple thistles. Originally farmed in Sicily, most artichokes sold in North America come from the tiny California town of Castroville, located a few miles from the coast and about 2 hours south of San Francisco, where the rich soil and frequent cool fogs provide the ideal growing climate.

• Moderate
• Serves 4 as a side dish.

6 cloves garlic, finely minced
1 small yellow onion, chopped
1½ cups seeded and chopped vine-
    ripened tomatoes, about 1½ pounds
1 cup white wine
½ cup chopped fresh basil leaves
2 tablespoons thin soy sauce
½ teaspoon Asian chile sauce (optional)
1 lemon
8 baby artichokes
¼ cup light-grade olive oil
Salt, to taste

•advance preparation

Combine the garlic and onions. Combine the tomatoes, wine, basil, soy sauce, chile sauce, and the grated zest (colored part of skin) from 1 lemon.

Remove the tough outer leaves of the artichokes. Cut off about ½ inch from the top of each artichoke. Using scissors, snip the thorns away from the remaining leaves. Split the artichokes in half, then scrape out the thistle with a melon scoop. Place the artichokes in a bowl, cover with cold water, and add the juice from the lemon. The recipe to this point can be completed up to 8 hours in advance of cooking.

•last-minute cooking

Preheat the oven to 375°F. Place a 12-inch sauté pan with ovenproof handles over medium-high heat. When hot, add the olive oil, garlic, and onions, and sauté until the onions begin to turn golden, about 10 minutes. Drain the artichokes and add to the pan along with the tomato mixture. Bring to a simmer, then transfer the sauté pan to the preheated oven and roast, covered, until the artichoke stems become tender and the leaves pull away easily, about 1 hour. Remove the pan from the oven. Transfer the artichokes to 4 heated dinner plates. Place the sauté pan over high heat and boil the sauce until it thickens, about 3 minutes. Taste and adjust seasonings. Spoon the sauce around the artichokes. Serve hot or cold.

•menu ideas

Serve these artichokes with Barbecued Veal Chops with Chinese Herb Marinade and Wild Rice with Currants, Pine Nuts, and Port.

Stir-Fried Asparagus with Tangerine and Pine Nuts

This recipe was inspired by a dish we ate at a Chinese restaurant recently. The Chinese chef cut medium-thick asparagus on a diagonal into 2-inch pieces, blanched them until they turned bright green, then briefly stir-fried them with tangerine zest and garlic. Here asparagus are steam-cooked in a covered wok. To prevent the asparagus from scorching, the wok is shaken vigorously. To add an extra richness, 1 tablespoon softened butter is stirred into the asparagus during the final moments of stir-frying. This is the perfect stir-fried vegetable dish to serve with any barbecued seafood or meat entrée.

- Easy
- Serves 4 as a side dish.

2 bunches medium-thick asparagus
½ cup pine nuts
3 cloves garlic, finely minced
½ cup dry sherry
2 tablespoons thin soy sauce
1 tablespoon dark sesame oil
2 teaspoons hoisin sauce
1 teaspoon cornstarch
1 tangerine or ½ an orange
Salt and freshly ground black pepper, to taste
2 tablespoons cooking oil
1 tablespoon unsalted butter, softened (optional)

• advance preparation

Snap off and discard the ends from the asparagus. If the asparagus spears are very thin, cut on a sharp diagonal into 2-inch lengths. If the asparagus spears are medium or thick, cut the asparagus on a sharp diagonal, rolling the asparagus towards you one-quarter turn after each diagonal cut.

Preheat the oven to 325°F. Place the pine nuts on a baking sheet and toast in the preheated oven until golden, about 8 minutes. Set aside the garlic. In a small bowl, combine ¼ cup of the dry sherry, the soy sauce, sesame oil, hoisin sauce, cornstarch, ½ teaspoon grated or finely minced tangerine or orange zest (colored part of skin), and the juice from the citrus. The recipe to this point can be completed up to 8 hours in advance of last-minute cooking.

• last-minute cooking

Place a wok over highest heat. When the wok becomes very hot, add the cooking oil to the center and roll it around the sides of the wok. Add the minced garlic. When the garlic begins to sizzle but has not turned brown, add the asparagus and stir and toss for 1 minute.

Add the remaining ¼ cup dry sherry, then immediately cover the wok. Cook the asparagus until they turn bright green, about 2 minutes, removing the cover and stirring them a few times. (If all the liquid disappears before the asparagus turn bright green, add a splash more dry sherry or water.) When the asparagus turn bright green, add the sauce and pine nuts. Stir and toss the asparagus until glazed with the sauce, about 1 minute. Stir in the butter (if using). Transfer to 4 heated dinner plates. Serve at once.

Addicted to Asparagus

Why overwhelm the pure, slightly grassy taste of asparagus with assertive seasonings or sauces when it is one of the glories of eating in its natural state. Here asparagus spears are rolled in garlic and extra-virgin olive oil, baked briefly, then sprinkled with balsamic vinegar, salt, pepper, and Parmesan cheese before being popped under the broiler for a final minute of cooking. It seems pointless for us to list specific menu ideas since asparagus are the perfect accompaniment to all meat and seafood entrées, night after night.

- Easy
- Serves 4 as a side dish.

2 bunches extra-thick asparagus, 3 to 4 spears per person
½ cup extra-virgin olive oil
3 cloves garlic, finely minced
¼ cup balsamic vinegar
Salt and freshly ground black pepper, to taste
½ cup freshly grated imported Parmesan cheese

•preparation and cooking

Preheat the oven to 400°F. Snap off the tough ends of the asparagus. Place the olive oil and garlic on a large plate or in a rectangular glass dish. Add the asparagus and roll them in the oil until thoroughly coated.

Place the asparagus on a baking sheet and bake until they turn bright green, about 6 to 9 minutes. Remove the baking sheet from the oven, then sprinkle the vinegar, salt, pepper, and Parmesan over the asparagus. Turn the oven setting to broil and broil the asparagus for 1 minute. Transfer to 4 heated dinner plates and serve at once.

Wild Mushroom Stew

After a winter rain and a few days of sun, we tramp through the forest near our home with eyes downcast, scanning the soil, circling tree trunks, and poking fallen limbs, in search of golden chanterelles, honey mushrooms, tree fungus, and giant boletus. Spoor print identifications, visits to local mushroom hunting experts, and absolute secrecy about newly discovered mushroom fairy rings are all part of our winter passion for mushrooms picked and cooked at the peak of flavor.

When shopping for mushrooms, only purchase those that feel very dense, with gills standing out distinctly and caps that retain their original shape. Wipe mushrooms with a damp cloth, or if covered with earthy compost, give the mushrooms the briefest washing followed by an immediate drying.

This mushroom stew, which is delicious made with store-bought button mushrooms, rises to gastronomic paradise if an assortment of edible mushrooms just pulled from the forest floor are included.

• Easy
• Serves 4 as a side dish.

4 cloves garlic, finely minced
3 large shallots, peeled and chopped
2 pounds assorted mushrooms (such as shiitakes, chanterelles, portabellos, or buttons)
1 cup red wine
1 cup Homemade Chicken Stock (page 70)
2 tablespoons heavy soy sauce
1 tablespoon oyster sauce
1 teaspoon tomato paste
½ teaspoon Asian chile sauce
1 bunch fresh thyme (tied into a bundle with kitchen string)
1 bay leaf
¼ cup unsalted butter
Salt, to taste

• advance preparation

Combine the garlic and shallots. Discard the stems from the shiitake mushrooms. Wipe the chanterelle, portabello, and button mushrooms with a damp towel. Cut the mushrooms into quarters or large pieces. In a small bowl, combine the wine, chicken stock, soy sauce, oyster sauce, tomato paste, chile sauce, thyme, and bay leaf. The recipe to this point can be completed up to 8 hours in advance of cooking.

• last-minute cooking

Place a 12-inch sauté pan over medium heat. Add the butter and when the butter melts, add the garlic and shallots followed by the mushrooms. Sauté the mushrooms until they absorb all the butter and begin to sizzle in the pan, about 4 minutes. Add the wine mixture, bring to a low boil, reduce the heat to low, and continue cooking the mushrooms until they absorb all of the liquid and acquire a very dense texture, about 15 minutes.

Remove the bundle of thyme. Taste and adjust seasonings. Transfer to 4 heated dinner plates and serve at once.

• menu ideas

Nearly vegetarian dinner for 6: Marinated Goat Cheese with Pepper Berries, Garlic, and Mint; Papaya and Avocado Salad; Wild Mushroom Stew served with Polenta Madness; and, for dessert, Fantastic Raspberry Ice Cream.

Magic with Vegetables and Eggs

Magic with Vegetables and Eggs

Napa-Style Eggs Sardou

Making eggs Sardou, a famous New Orleans egg dish, involves removing the center thistle from artichokes, then steaming the artichokes until tender, standing them upright on dinner plates, and filling the hollowed sections with layers of creamed spinach, poached eggs, and hollandaise sauce. Guests and hosts dip the leaves into the sauce and eventually eat the nutty-tasting artichoke heart blessed with the creamy spinach and soft-poached egg.

- Challenging
- Serves 4 as a main entrée.

4 large artichokes

1 lemon

2 large bunches spinach, about 12 cups leaves

5 tablespoons whipping cream

½ teaspoon freshly grated nutmeg

Salt and freshly ground black pepper, to taste

2 teaspoons whole cloves

2 tablespoons freshly squeezed lemon juice

1 tablespoon unsalted butter, at room temperature

7 tablespoons unsalted butter, melted

1 teaspoon finely minced fresh ginger

1 teaspoon grated or finely minced lemon zest (colored part of skin)

3 egg yolks

8 eggs

•advance preparation

Using a sharp knife or poultry scissors, cut the top third off each artichoke. Snip all the thorns from the remaining leaves. Using a melon scoop, scrape away the center thistle section of the artichoke. Rub the cut sections of the artichoke with lemon to prevent discoloration. Trim the artichoke stems so the artichokes will stand upright.

Wash the spinach leaves. In a 2½-quart saucepan, bring 1 inch water to a rapid boil. Add the spinach leaves and rotate them until they wilt, about 30 seconds. Immediately drain the spinach in a colander and rinse with cold water, then press the spinach in your fist to squeeze away all moisture. Chop the spinach finely. You should have about ⅔ cup chopped spinach. Place the spinach in a small saucepan with the whipping cream. Heat until warm, then add the nutmeg and salt and pepper. Cool and refrigerate until ready to assemble the artichokes.

•last-minute cooking

Place 2 inches water in a pot large enough to hold all of the artichokes in a single layer. Add the cloves. Bring the water to a boil over medium heat, add the artichokes, stem end down, cover the pot, and cook the artichokes until tender, about 45 minutes. Periodically add more boiling water to the pot to maintain the original water level. The artichokes are done when you can easily detach a leaf.

When the artichokes are nearly cooked, place the creamed spinach in a small saucepan and warm over very low heat. Set aside separately the lemon juice, room temperature butter, melted butter, ginger, and grated lemon zest.

Make the hollandaise sauce: Fill a medium-sized saucepan halfway with water and bring to a boil over high heat. Reduce the heat to low and keep the water at a simmer. In a very small saucepan, beat the yolks and 1 tablespoon of the lemon juice. Stir in the tablespoon of room-temperature butter. Place the saucepan over the larger pan of simmering water and beat the yolks with a whisk until the sauce thickens to the consistency of heavy cream. Remove from the heat and slowly beat in the melted butter. Season with the ginger, lemon zest, remaining 1 tablespoon lemon juice, and salt and pepper. Keep the hollandaise sauce warm for a few minutes by resting the saucepan over the larger pot of water, with the heat turned off.

Poach the eggs: Place 1½ inches water in a 12-inch sauté pan. Place over medium heat, bring to a low boil, and maintain at this temperature. Break each egg into its own saucer. Hold the saucers very close to the boiling water and slide the eggs into the water. Poach the eggs about 2 minutes, spooning more boiling water over them as they cook. Remove the eggs with a slotted spoon when the yolks are still runny. (Alternatively, cook the eggs in an egg poacher.)

Place the artichokes upright on 4 heated plates. In the hollow of each artichoke place a fourth of the creamed spinach, 2 poached eggs, and a fourth of the hollandaise sauce. Serve at once.

•menu ideas

Sunday brunch for 4: Firecracker Shrimp, Napa-Style Eggs Sardou, Any Kind of Bread Rolls, and Fresh Strawberries with Valrhona Cocoa Truffles.

Szechwan Huevos Rancheros

This is one of our favorite dishes to serve at Sunday brunch or to make as a quick dinner for just the two of us. Instead of using the Mexican "ranchero sauce" (made with tomatoes, chile, and garlic) that traditionally tops the eggs, or *huevos*, we sauté ground pork, garlic, and ginger with the Szechwan seasonings of dark sesame oil, heavy soy sauce, and Asian chile sauce. Simmered with chopped vine-ripened tomatoes, diced green bell peppers, and green onions, the sauce provides a dramatic contrast in taste, texture, and color to the soft-fried eggs and heated tortillas. For variation, toss this sauce with ½ pound cooked pasta, spoon it over barbecued mahi mahi, or ladle it across the surface of a platter before adding poached Asian dumplings and chopped cilantro.

- Easy
- Serves 4 as a main entrée.

1 green bell pepper
2 medium-sized vine-ripened tomatoes
2 whole green onions
¼ pound ground pork
4 cloves garlic, finely minced
1 tablespoon very finely minced fresh ginger
1 teaspoon Asian chile sauce
¼ cup dry sherry
¼ cup tomato sauce
1 tablespoon dark sesame oil
2 teaspoons heavy soy sauce
1 teaspoon red wine vinegar
½ teaspoon white sugar
8 6-inch corn or flour tortillas
½ cup chopped fresh cilantro
¼ cup light-grade olive oil
8 eggs
¼ cup sour cream

• advance preparation

Stem, seed, and chop the green pepper. Stem, seed, and finely chop the tomatoes. Mince the green onions. Mix the pork with garlic, ginger, and chile sauce until evenly combined. In a small bowl, combine the dry sherry, tomato sauce, sesame oil, soy sauce, vinegar, and sugar.

• last-minute cooking

Preheat the oven to 325°F. Wrap the tortillas in aluminum foil and place in the preheated oven for 8 minutes. Chop the cilantro.

Place a 10-inch sauté pan over high heat and add 2 tablespoons of the olive oil. Add the pork and sauté until it loses its raw color and breaks into little pieces. Add the pepper, tomatoes, and green onions, and sauté until the peppers brighten, about 1 minute. Add the sauce and bring to a low boil. Reduce the heat to low. Taste and adjust seasonings, especially for salt.

Place a 12-inch nonstick sauté pan over medium-high heat. Add the remaining olive oil. When the oil is hot, break 4 of the eggs into the pan without breaking the yolks. Soft-fry on one side about 30 seconds, then flip the eggs over and fry another 30 seconds. Remove the eggs while the yolks are still slightly runny. Repeat the frying process with the remaining 4 eggs.

Overlap the tortillas on 4 heated dinner plates. Place the eggs on top of the tortillas. Spoon the sauce over the eggs. Sprinkle on the chopped cilantro. Add a dollop of sour cream in the center and serve at once.

Spicy Wild Mushroom and Roasted Garlic Frittata

We like entertaining on weekend mornings rather than evenings since it frees us from the gourmet dinner menu trap and gathers the group in a more casual sunlit setting. Welcome your friends with a choice of beverages, such as Bloody Marys, sparkling wine, freshly squeezed orange juice, and extra-rich brewed coffee. Serve Watermelon and Sweet Red Onion Salad (dressing made a day in advance), then Spicy Wild Mushroom and Roasted Garlic Frittata accompanied by Mango Salsa, Asian Black Bean Chile (made a day in advance), and sliced and toasted Any Kind of Bread (kept stockpiled in the freezer for just such occasions). For a memorable dessert, serve White Chocolate Mousse (made up to a week in advance of serving).

- Easy
- Serves 4 as a main entrée.

10 small cloves roasted garlic (page 220)
1½ pounds mushrooms, such as shiitakes, portabellos, or chanterelles
2 whole green onions
¼ cup chopped fresh basil leaves
8 eggs
½ cup freshly grated imported Parmesan cheese
½ teaspoon salt
8 sun-dried tomatoes
2 fresh serrano chiles
¼ cup chopped fresh cilantro
2 ounces soft goat cheese
2 tablespoons pine nuts
¼ cup unsalted butter

• preparation and cooking

Preheat the oven to 325°F. Slip the roasted garlic cloves out of their skins and mash. Cut the mushrooms into ⅛-inch-thin slices. Mince the green onions and combine with the chopped basil. Break the eggs into a mixing bowl, beat very well, then stir in the grated Parmesan and salt. Cover the sun-dried tomatoes with boiling water and let sit 20 minutes; then discard the water and chop the tomatoes. Stem and finely mince the chiles (including the seeds). Set aside the cilantro and goat cheese. Place the pine nuts on a baking sheet and toast in the preheated oven until golden, about 8 minutes. Do not turn off the oven when the pine nuts are done.

Place a 12-inch cast-iron skillet over medium-high heat and add the butter. When the butter melts, add the mushrooms and garlic and sauté until the mushrooms soften and reduce in volume, adding a splash of water or white wine after 5 minutes to help the mushrooms soften. Continue to cook the mushrooms until no more liquid remains, for a total of about 15 minutes. Sprinkle the green onions and basil across the mushrooms. Pour in the egg mixture. Place the skillet, uncovered, in the preheated oven. Bake 15 minutes, until the egg mixture just begins to set across the top surface.

Turn the oven setting to broil. Scatter the chopped tomatoes, chiles, cilantro, goat cheese, and pine nuts across the surface of the egg. Place the skillet 5 inches below the broiler heat and cook about 3 minutes to melt the goat cheese.

Remove the skillet from the oven. Cut the frittata into wedges, transfer to 4 heated dinner plates, and serve at once.

Summer Omelet
with Vine-Ripened Tomatoes

Don't let the fancy folding and flipping techniques displayed by hotel chefs at Sunday morning buffets intimidate you from becoming an omelet master! Just make sure to cook the omelet in a nonstick sauté pan with short sloping sides so a spatula can slide easily under the omelet when it's time to fold it into an envelope shape. Although this recipe gives directions for individual omelets, we often make a single giant omelet in a larger pan, then divide the omelet into serving-size portions.

• Easy
• Serves 4 as a breakfast, brunch, or dinner entrée.

4 cloves garlic, finely minced
1 bunch fresh basil leaves, chopped
3 whole green onions, chopped
6 vine-ripened tomatoes, seeded and
   chopped
6 tablespoons extra-virgin olive oil
¼ teaspoon sugar
Freshly ground black pepper or Asian
   chile sauce, to taste
Salt, to taste
1 cup freshly grated imported Parmesan
   cheese, about 4 ounces
8 eggs
Chopped fresh basil, green onion, chives,
   or parsley, for garnish

• advance preparation

Set aside the garlic, basil, green onions, and tomatoes.

Place a 12-inch sauté pan over medium-high heat. Add 2 tablespoons of the olive oil and the garlic. Sauté 30 seconds, then add the basil, green onions, and tomatoes. Add the sugar, a couple of grinds of black pepper or a dash of Asian chile sauce, and a sprinkling of salt (about ½ teaspoon). Cook until all the liquid disappears, about 10 minutes. Taste and adjust the seasonings. This filling can be prepared up to 2 hours in advance of last-minute cooking and held at room temperature.

• last-minute cooking

Set aside the Parmesan. Crack the eggs into a bowl and beat with a fork or whisk until well blended. Set aside the garnish.

Heat a heavy 10-inch nonstick pan over high heat until hot. Add 1 tablespoon of the olive oil and roll around the sides of the pan. Add a fourth of the beaten eggs and quickly roll around the bottom of the pan to form a thin layer, about 15 seconds. Spread a fourth of the tomato mixture across the center of the omelet and sprinkle on a fourth of the Parmesan. When the egg surface is nearly cooked, gently roll or

fold the omelet over the filling, for a total cooking time of about 1 minute. Slide out onto a warm plate. Garnish, then repeat the process 3 more times with the remaining ingredients. Serve at once.

• menu ideas

Sunday brunch on the terrace: Spicy Gravlax with Mango Salsa, Summer Omelet with Vine-Ripened Tomatoes served with Popovers Scented with Cilantro and Chile (omit the garlic), and choice of Bloody Marys, champagne, freshly squeezed orange juice, coffee, or tea.

note: For variation, replace the tomato filling with the crab and shiitake filling on page 25, Hot and Sour Chicken Livers (page 23), or the stewed mushrooms on page 194.

Chocolate
Fantasies
for Life
Fulfillment

Kahlúa Passion Tiles

God created chocolate desserts first and, as an afterthought, added other desserts and the preliminary dishes. But not all chocolate was created equal. Most European chocolate has a much smoother texture and more complex taste than American-made chocolate. This can be explained by several factors. European chocolate manufacturers purchase the best quality cocoa beans, which grow in Ecuador and Venezuela, rather than the less expensive beans that grow in Mexico and elsewhere. Moreover, European chocolate "Blend Masters" are legendary for their preoccupation with achieving the perfect mix of cocoa beans and roasting the beans at an exact temperature for a precise amount of time. They are also meticulous about conching, one of the final processes of chocolate-making, which involves rolling the chocolate mixture under a heavy roller that moves back and forth continuously. Whereas American chocolate manufacturers limit the conching to just a few hours, European chocolate is conched for much longer, resulting in chocolate with an incredible smoothness. For all your chocolate recipes, choose from among the following European manufacturers: Valrhona, Lindt, and Callebaut. Begin your experiments with this recipe. Consume this dessert in tiny bites, savoring the silky richness. Intensify the flavors with glasses of fine vintage port.

• Easy
• Serves 10 to 12.

15 ounces bittersweet chocolate, preferably European
¼ cup unsalted butter
1 cup whipping cream
1 tablespoon freshly and finely ground coffee beans (optional)
4 egg yolks
½ cup powdered sugar
6 tablespoons Kahlúa
Raspberry Essence (page 204)
1 pint box fresh raspberries
½ cup whipping cream
Orange zest threads (colored part of skin), for garnish

• preparation and serving

Cut the chocolate into very small pieces. Place the chocolate, butter, and cream in a small metal bowl. Place the ground coffee beans in a coffee filter, then slowly pour 2 cups boiling water over the grounds; drink the brewed coffee or discard. Transfer all the grounds from the coffee filter into the bowl holding the chocolate.

Place the bowl of chocolate mixture over a saucepan holding 2 inches barely simmering water. Stir until the chocolate is melted and well blended with the other ingredients, then remove from the heat and cool to room temperature. (Alternatively, place the chocolate mixture in a microwave-safe bowl and melt in a microwave set on low power, stirring the mixture every 10 seconds.)

Beat the egg yolks well, then stir into the chocolate mixture. Sift in the sugar and stir to combine. Stir in the Kahlúa.

Line the bottom of a narrow loaf pan with nonstick cooking (parchment) paper. Pour the chocolate

mixture into the loaf pan and freeze for at least 4 hours. (Note: Removing the chocolate from the loaf pan and slicing it takes some finesse.) Alternatively, pour the melted chocolate mixture into individual ½-cup dessert cups. Freeze or refrigerate. The recipe to this point can be made 4 weeks in advance of serving if kept in the freezer.

Make the Raspberry Essence.

To serve (may be done several hours in advance): If Raspberry Essence is very thick, thin it by stirring in a little Grand Marnier or other liqueur.

If the chocolate mixture has been frozen in a narrow loaf pan, place ¼ cup Raspberry Essence in the center of each plate. Dip the loaf pan into very hot water for 30 seconds, then invert and unmold on a work surface. Cut the chocolate into ¼-inch-thick slices, running the knife under hot water after each cut. Position 1 tile in the center of each plate so that the raspberry sauce is pushed around the tile in a neat circle. Decorate the sauce with fresh raspberries. Beat the whipping cream until thick, then place in a pastry bag fitted with a small star tip and make a little whipped cream flower in the center of each tile. Sprinkle on the orange zest threads.

If the chocolate mixture has been frozen or refrigerated in individual dessert cups, decorate the top of each one with a little raspberry sauce, fresh raspberries, a whipped cream flower, and orange zest threads, if desired. Refrigerate dessert plates or cups for up to 4 hours before serving.

PAGE 201 *Valrhona Cocoa Truffles*

Fantastic Raspberry Ice Cream with Velvet Chocolate Sauce

Homemade ice cream, one of the most delicious, versatile, and appreciated desserts, tastes best eaten straight out of the ice cream machine or, if one is forced to share it with family and friends, then served within a few hours of churning. Since most cookware and department stores sell inexpensive ice cream machines that require neither ice nor salt, there is no excuse for postponing making this recipe. If you are in a cheating mood, however, substitute 2 pints high-quality store-bought French vanilla ice cream for the home-made ice cream, soften it slightly, stir in the Raspberry Essence, and freeze.

The idea to use crème fraîche in the Velvet Chocolate Sauce is from Peter Kump's Cooking School in New York. You can make your own crème fraîche by mixing 1 cup whipping cream with 2 tablespoons buttermilk. Let the mixture sit in a warm place for 24 hours, then refrigerate for at least 4 hours but for no longer than 10 days.

- Challenging
- Serves 8.

• velvet chocolate sauce

8 ounces bittersweet chocolate,
  preferably European
¾ cup whipping cream or crème fraîche
¼ cup unsalted butter, at room
  temperature
1 teaspoon pure vanilla extract

• raspberry essence

12 ounces frozen raspberries
1 bottle reasonable-quality red wine
  (750 milliliters)
1 cup sugar
¼ teaspoon finely ground black pepper
•
6 egg yolks
¾ cup sugar
3 cups whipping cream
1 pint fresh raspberries
Mint sprigs, for garnish

• advance preparation

Prepare the Velvet Chocolate Sauce: Cut the chocolate into little pieces. In a small metal bowl, combine the chocolate and cream or crème fraîche. Place the bowl over a larger saucepan holding 2 inches barely simmering water and stir until melted. (Alternatively, place the chocolate and cream or crème fraîche in a microwave-safe bowl and melt in a microwave set on low power, stirring every 10 seconds.) Remove the chocolate mixture from the heat and whisk in the softened butter and vanilla. The sauce will keep for up to 1 month in the refrigerator. It must be warmed slightly before using.

Prepare the Raspberry Essence: In a 12-inch sauté pan (not aluminum or cast iron), combine the raspberries, wine, sugar, and pepper. Place over high heat, bring to a vigorous boil, and boil until 2 cups remain. Immediately pour the sauce through a medium-meshed sieve, forcing all the pulp through the sieve by scraping the sieve with a metal spoon. The sauce lasts indefinitely in the refrigerator. It may need to be thinned slightly with a liqueur or water before using.

Prepare the ice cream: In a copper or thin-gauged stainless steel mixing bowl, combine the egg yolks and sugar and beat vigorously with a whisk until the egg yolks absorb the sugar and the mixture falls from the whisk in a smooth pale yellow ribbon, about 3 minutes. In a 2½-quart saucepan, heat 2 cups of the whipping cream until bubbles form around the edges. Stir the cream into the egg mixture, then immediately pour the mixture back into the saucepan. Place the empty mixing bowl in a sink or larger bowl filled with cold water and ice. Place the saucepan over high heat and beat the egg mixture vigorously with a whisk until it thickens and its volume nearly doubles, about 4 to 6 minutes. Immediately tip the mixture into the chilled mixing bowl. Stir occasionally until chilled.

Set up the ice cream machine. Add the remaining cup of whipping cream to the ice cream custard. Churn in the ice cream machine according to the manufacturer's instructions, adding all of the Raspberry Essence when the mixture is very thick, then continuing to churn until well set. Transfer the ice cream to a chilled bowl and freeze.

• **to serve**

Place the Velvet Chocolate Sauce in a small metal bowl and place over barely simmering water. When hot, place a pool of chocolate sauce on 6 to 8 dessert plates. Add a large scoop of ice cream to the center of the chocolate sauce, then place the fresh raspberries on the chocolate sauce and garnish the ice cream with mint sprigs. Serve at once.

Chocolate Sorbet with Mangoes

The only disappointment in our move from Los Angeles to Napa was the realization that we would no longer be able to eat at Joachim Splichal's restaurant, Patina, on a regular basis. Enormously talented and disciplined, Splichal creates food of a quality rarely found in restaurants in North America. For purely professional reasons, because of our pursuit of a Doctorate of Chocolate Degree, we always order Patina's chocolate dessert plate, which includes a magical chocolate sorbet, perfected by Joachim and Pastry Chef Bruno Feldeisen. To assure that the sorbet will churn to the proper consistency in a home ice cream machine (as opposed to the commercial ice cream machine operated at Patina), we had to, alas, reduce the amount of chocolate in the original recipe.

• Easy
• Serves 8.

12 ounces bittersweet chocolate, preferably European
2 cups water
1 cup sugar
¼ cup very strong coffee
¼ cup Grand Marnier or Kahlúa
1 teaspoon pure vanilla extract
3 ripe mangoes
Juice from 1 lime
Mint sprigs, for garnish

• **advance preparation**

Chop the chocolate into very small pieces. In a 2½-quart saucepan, bring the water and sugar to a boil and cook until the sugar dissolves, about 30 seconds. Place the chocolate in a bowl and pour the boiling syrup over it. Stir the chocolate until completely melted. Cool to room temperature, then stir in the coffee, liqueur, and vanilla. Churn the sorbet in an ice cream machine following the manufacturer's instructions, then transfer to a bowl, press a layer of plastic wrap across the surface, and place in the freezer.

Peel the mangoes. Cut all of the flesh off 1½ mangoes, then place in a food processor and purée. Add the juice from 1 lime. Chill thoroughly. Cut the flesh from the remaining mangoes, cut into bite-sized pieces, and set aside.

• **last-minute assembly**

Place the mango sauce on each dessert plate. Add scoops of chocolate sorbet to the center of each plate. Place the chopped mango around the sorbet. Garnish with mint sprigs. Serve at once.

White Chocolate Mousse with Tropical Fruits

Made with cocoa butter, sugar, vanillin, and other flavorings, white chocolate contains no chocolate liquor and, in truth, is not chocolate at all. Sweet and buttery, it has its own unique attributes, and while not interchangeable with "real" chocolate, it has its own devoted following. In the following recipe, a rich, ethereally silky, and intensely white mousse is positioned on a dark chocolate lace cookie, garnished with fresh fruits, and surrounded by a fruit sauce. It is sure to satisfy white chocolate connoisseurs and even the most stubborn "real" chocolate purists.

- Challenging
- Serves 6 to 12.

• chocolate lace cookies

Exactly 4 ounces raw almonds
¾ cup sugar
2 tablespoons unsweetened cocoa powder, preferably Valrhona
6 tablespoons unsalted butter, melted
3 tablespoons milk
•
8 ounces white chocolate, preferably European
4 eggs, separated into yolks and whites
⅓ cup sugar
¼ cup Grand Marnier
1 teaspoon pure vanilla extract
1 cup whipping cream
1 mango
2 kiwis
1 pint strawberries
Raspberry Essence (page 204)

• advance preparation

Make the lace cookies: Preheat the oven to 325°F. Spread the almonds on a baking sheet and toast in the oven until golden, about 15 minutes. Cool the almonds for 15 minutes, then place in a food processor and grind until they take on the texture of sand. Add the sugar and cocoa powder and process briefly. Transfer to a small bowl and stir in the melted butter and milk. Mix thoroughly. This dough can be refrigerated for 1 week or frozen indefinitely.

Preheat the oven to 375°F. Cut nonstick cooking (parchment) paper into 6-inch squares. Place 4 squares of paper on a baking sheet, then place 1 tablespoon cookie dough in the center of each square. Bake the cookies until they become very thin and bubbly across the surface, about 8 to 12 minutes. Remove from the oven. Slide the paper with the cookies off the baking sheet and let the cookies cool completely on the paper. Continue baking the cookies. Leave the cookies on the paper and store at room temperature for up to 8 hours, or in the freezer indefinitely. Makes 12 to 20 cookies.

Cut the white chocolate into small pieces. Place the chocolate in a small metal bowl and place over a larger saucepan holding 2 inches barely simmering water. Turn off the heat. Stir the chocolate until melted, then remove the bowl from the saucepan. (Alternatively, place the white chocolate in a microwave-safe bowl and melt in a microwave oven set on low power, stirring the chocolate every 10 seconds.) Keep the chocolate at a warm room temperature.

Place the egg yolks and sugar in the bowl of an electric mixer and beat at highest speed until the mixture becomes very thick, about 4 minutes. Add the Grand Marnier and beat 2 more minutes. Transfer the mixing bowl holding the egg mixture to a saucepan one-fourth full of simmering water and stir until the mixture becomes hot to the touch and almost as thick as mayonnaise, about 5 minutes. Remove the bowl from the heat and stir in the melted chocolate. Stir in the vanilla extract. Beat the egg whites until stiff. Stir a third of the egg whites into the chocolate mixture, then fold in the remaining egg whites. Refrigerate the mousse until chilled, about 30 minutes. Beat the whipping cream until stiff, then gently fold the cream into the mousse. Transfer the mousse to an ice cream machine and churn until the mousse has the consistency of ice cream, about 15 minutes. Transfer the mousse to a bowl and freeze for at least 6 hours but no longer than 5 days.

Peel the mango and kiwis, then cut the fruit into bite-sized pieces. Stem the strawberries and cut into slices.

Prepare the Raspberry Essence.

• last-minute assembly

Remove the cookies from the paper squares and place each cookie in the center of a large dessert plate. Place a scoop of white chocolate mousse in the center of each cookie. Add a little Raspberry Essence around the edges of the cookies. Place the fruit on top of the sauce. Serve at once.

Chocolate Nut Tart

Currently Americans consume 14 pounds of chocolate per person per year as compared to the Swiss who nibble away at 22 pounds per person. Perhaps if we served more chocolate desserts, such as the following chocolate tart covered with a thin layer of roasted nuts tossed in a caramel butter sauce, we would surpass the Swiss in our quest for life fulfillment.

- Moderate
- Serves 8.

1 cup unbleached white flour
1 tablespoon granulated sugar
½ teaspoon salt
½ cup unsalted butter, cut into small pieces, plus 3 tablespoons butter
About 4 tablespoons ice water
12 ounces bittersweet chocolate, preferably European
1 cup whipping cream
2 teaspoons pure vanilla extract
1 egg white plus 2 additional egg yolks
⅓ cup whole raw shelled almonds, skin on
⅓ cup raw shelled hazelnuts, skinned
⅓ cup raw shelled walnut halves
⅓ cup raw shelled pecan halves
⅓ cup raw cashews
2 cups cooking oil

- caramel butter sauce

1 cup granulated sugar
¼ cup water
½ cup whipping cream
2 tablespoons unsalted butter

- advance preparation and assembly

Make the pastry dough: Place the flour, sugar, salt, and ½ cup butter in a food processor fitted with the chopping blade. Pulse on and off very briefly until the flour mixture resembles cornmeal. Add a little ice water, processing again until the dough holds together when pressed between your fingers.

Turn the dough out onto a lightly floured board and press into a ball. Wrap the dough in plastic wrap and refrigerate 30 minutes. Preheat the oven to 375°F. On a lightly floured board, roll the dough into a ⅛-inch-thin circle. Butter a 10-inch diameter fluted tart pan with removable sides, then gently fit the dough into the tart pan, pressing the dough up around the sides of the pan. Cover the pastry with foil and place a layer of pastry weights or raw rice or beans on top of the foil. Bake until the edges turn light golden, about 15 minutes. Remove the foil and bake until the pastry turns golden, about 15 minutes. Remove from the oven and cool to room temperature.

Melt 2 ounces of the chocolate with ½ tablespoon butter. Brush a paper-thin layer of chocolate across the entire inside surface of the pastry shell. Place the pastry shell in the freezer briefly in order to harden the chocolate layer.

Cut the remaining 10 ounces of chocolate into small pieces. Place the chocolate, cream, and remaining 2½ tablespoons butter in a small metal bowl. Place this bowl over a saucepan holding 2 inches of barely simmering water and stir until the chocolate is completely melted. Remove the bowl and let the chocolate cool to room temperature. (Alternatively, place the chocolate mixture in a microwave-safe bowl and melt on low power, stirring the mixture every 10 seconds.) Stir in the vanilla. Beat the eggs very well, then stir into the chocolate mixture.

Remove the tart from the freezer and pour the chocolate mixture into the tart shell. Refrigerate the tart for at least 1 hour before adding the nut topping.

Place the almonds, hazelnuts, walnuts, pecans, and cashews in a medium saucepan. Add the cooking oil, then place the saucepan over medium heat. Stir the nuts until the oil begins to bubble and the nuts turn a very light golden, about 4 minutes, then immediately tip the nuts and oil into a sieve placed over another saucepan. Cool the nuts to room temperature, about 45 minutes; then pat dry with paper towels.

Make the Caramel Butter Sauce: Place the sugar and water in a heavy saucepan and bring to a rapid boil over high heat without stirring. Boil, without stirring, until the sugar caramelizes and turns a very dark amber. When the sugar just gives off the first hint of smoke, remove the saucepan from the heat. Immediately, using a long-handled whisk, whisk in 1 tablespoon whipping cream. Be careful, because the caramel syrup will bubble up dramatically. Continue whisking in the whipping cream, 1 tablespoon at a time, until all of it is incorporated into the caramel syrup. Stir in the butter. Transfer the caramel sauce to a glass jar and refrigerate for up to 3 weeks.

To finish the tart, place the nuts in a bowl. Heat ⅔ cup Caramel Butter Sauce until very warm. Add the sauce to the nuts and stir to evenly combine. Using your hands, place the nuts in a single layer, very close together, across the surface of the tart. Refrigerate the tart until ready to serve. The tart may be assembled a day in advance of serving and stored in the refrigerator.

Chocolate Ginger Mousse with Raspberry Essence

Successful recipes boast a spectrum of flavors that constantly intrigue the palate, bite after bite. For example, chocolate desserts are made more complex and interesting when the intense flavor of fine chocolate is matched with such ingredients as grated orange and lemon zest, mint, cinnamon, very strong coffee and the coffee grounds used for brewing the coffee, finely ground black pepper, raspberries, strawberries, intense reduction fruit sauces, and liqueurs, particularly Grand Marnier, Kahlúa, Framboise, and dark rum. The following mousse, proof of the effectiveness of this technique, calls for several of these flavorings plus shredded crystallized ginger.

• Moderate
• Serves 8.

10 ounces bittersweet chocolate, preferably European

¼ cup strong coffee

6 tablespoons unsalted butter, cut into small pieces

¼ teaspoon very finely ground black pepper

4 eggs, separated into yolks and whites

½ cup sugar

¼ cup Grand Marnier

2 teaspoons pure vanilla extract

1 teaspoon grated orange zest (colored part of skin)

⅛ teaspoon cream of tartar

1 cup whipping cream plus ½ cup for garnishing

¼ cup Raspberry Essence (page 204)

¼ cup finely shredded crystallized ginger, for garnish

Mint sprigs, for garnish

• advance preparation

Cut the chocolate into very small pieces. Place the chocolate, coffee, butter, and black pepper in a small metal bowl and place over a saucepan holding 2 inches barely simmering water. Stir the chocolate mixture until it is completely smooth and melted. Remove the chocolate mixture from the saucepan and keep warm. (Alternatively, place the chocolate mixture in a microwave-safe bowl and melt in a microwave oven set on low power, stirring the chocolate every 10 seconds.)

Place the egg yolks and sugar in a medium-sized copper or metal mixing bowl and beat with a whisk until the mixture turns a pale yellow and all signs of the sugar crystals disappear, about 3 minutes. Beat in the Grand Marnier. Place the bowl over simmering water and beat slowly with a whisk until the mixture becomes hot to the touch and becomes as thick as heavy whipping cream, about 5 minutes.

Stir the melted chocolate mixture into the egg yolk mixture. Stir in the vanilla and the grated orange zest. Remove the mixture from the saucepan.

Beat the egg whites until stiff but not dry. During the last few minutes of beating, sprinkle in the cream of tartar. Stir one fourth of the egg whites into the chocolate mixture. Then fold in the rest of the egg whites one third at a time. When the mousse is at room temperature, beat 1 cup cream until stiff, then fold into the mousse mixture.

Carefully portion the mousse mixture into 8 large wineglasses and refrigerate for at least 6 hours, or overnight.

Prepare the Raspberry Essence. The recipe to this point can be prepared up to 1 day in advance of serving.

• last-minute assembly

Set aside the crystallized ginger. Within 5 hours of serving, beat the remaining ½ cup whipping cream until stiff, then place in a pastry bag fitted with a fine rosette tip and pipe a little into the center of each wineglass. Add ½ tablespoon Raspberry Essence as a garnish to each glass. Garnish with a mint sprig and crystallized ginger. Serve within 5 hours.

Ginger Banana Cream Tart Lined with Chocolate

A good technique when making any tart filled with pastry cream is to brush the entire inside surface of the pastry with a paper-thin layer of melted chocolate. Not only does this prevent a soggy crust, but the chocolate adds another dimension of flavor and texture. For variation, make this chocolate-lined tart with a wide range of other fruits, such as kiwi, grapes, tree-ripened peaches, and all types of berries. Although the tart tastes best the same day it is made, the pastry dough and pastry cream can be made a day in advance and refrigerated.

• Challenging
• Serves 8 to 10.

1 cup unbleached white flour
1 tablespoon sugar
½ teaspoon salt
½ cup chilled unsalted butter, cut into small pieces, plus ½ tablespoon butter
About 4 tablespoons ice water
2 ounces bittersweet chocolate, preferably European

•

3 egg yolks
⅓ cup sugar
2 teaspoons pure vanilla extract
1 tablespoon unbleached white flour
1 tablespoon cornstarch
1 cup milk
1 tablespoon dark rum
½ cup whipping cream
4 ripe bananas
½ cup apricot jam
2 tablespoons very finely minced fresh ginger
1 tablespoon cognac
Fresh berries, for garnish

• **advance preparation and cooking**

Make the pastry dough: Place the flour, sugar, salt, and ½ cup butter in a food processor fitted with the chopping blade. Pulse on and off very briefly until the flour mixture resembles cornmeal. Add a little ice water, processing again until the dough holds together when pressed between your fingers.

Turn the dough out onto a lightly floured board and press into a ball. Wrap the dough in plastic wrap and refrigerate 30 minutes. Preheat the oven to 375°F. On a lightly floured board, roll the dough into a ⅛-inch-thin circle. Butter a 10-inch fluted tart pan with removable sides, then gently fit the dough into the tart pan, pressing the dough up around the sides of the pan. Cover the pastry with foil and place a layer of pastry weights or raw rice or beans on top of the foil. Bake until the edges become light golden, about 15 minutes. Remove the foil and bake until the pastry becomes golden, about 15 minutes. Remove from the oven and cool to room temperature.

Cut the chocolate into little pieces. Place the chocolate and the remaining ½ tablespoon butter in a small metal bowl and place over a larger saucepan holding 2 inches barely simmering water. Stir the chocolate until melted. (Alternatively, place the chocolate and butter in a microwave-safe bowl and melt in a

microwave set on low power, stirring every 10 seconds.) Brush a paper-thin layer of chocolate across the entire inside surface of the pastry shell. Place in the freezer briefly in order to harden the chocolate layer.

Prepare the pastry cream: Beat the egg yolks and sugar until the mixture turns a pale yellow. Beat in the vanilla, flour, and cornstarch. In a saucepan, heat the milk until bubbles appear around the edges, then stir the hot milk into the egg mixture. Pour the mixture back into the saucepan and place over medium-high heat. Beat with a whisk until the mixture becomes very thick, about 2 minutes. Turn out into a bowl and cool. Stir the rum into the pastry cream, then refrigerate the pastry cream until thoroughly chilled, at least 30 minutes.

Beat the whipping cream until stiff. Gently fold the whipping cream into the pastry cream. Thinly slice 1 banana and stir it into the pastry cream. Fill the pastry shell with the pastry cream.

Thinly slice the remaining bananas and place across the surface of the tart. Heat the apricot jam until hot; strain through a sieve into a bowl, then stir in the finely minced ginger and the cognac. Brush the apricot sauce across the bananas. Refrigerate the tart until ready to serve. Garnish with fresh berries, if desired.

Valrhona Cocoa Truffles

There is nothing more exciting to a chocolate lover than a chocolate recipe that leaves chocolate coating every piece of kitchen equipment, including both hands, as well as kitchen counters and the knobs on cupboard doors. Such is the case with this recipe, contributed by the talented pastry chef Keith Schauffel, who with his brother, Craig, owns Pairs Parkside Café in the Napa Valley town of St. Helena. While you can vary the recipe by adding 1 cup chopped roasted hazelnuts or ½ cup liqueur to the chocolate ganache, don't vary the cocoa powder if you can help it. Try to find the world's best, which is made by Valrhona and is sold at specialty food shops and through gourmet food catalogs.

- Moderate
- Makes 3 to 6 dozen truffles, depending on the size.

1½ **pounds bittersweet chocolate, preferably European**
1 **cup whipping cream**
2 **tablespoons sugar**
¼ **cup unsalted butter, at room temperature**
¼ **pound Valrhona cocoa powder**

•advance preparation and assembly

Cut the chocolate into small pieces. Set aside ½ pound of the chocolate.

Prepare the chocolate ganache: Place the whipping cream, sugar, 1 pound chocolate pieces, and butter in a medium metal bowl. Place this bowl over a saucepan holding 2 inches of barely simmering water. Stir the mixture until the chocolate melts and the mixture is smooth. (Alternatively, place the ingredients in a microwave-safe bowl and melt in a microwave set on low power, stirring every 10 seconds.) Lay plastic wrap directly across the chocolate mixture so that it is completely covered. Refrigerate until thoroughly chilled, about 2 hours or overnight.

Using a teaspoon, melon baller, or 1-ounce ice cream scoop, scoop out balls of chocolate and place on a baking sheet covered with nonstick cooking (parchment) paper. Use your hands to round all the chocolate scoops into perfect balls. Refrigerate until thoroughly chilled.

Place the remaining ½ pound bittersweet chocolate pieces in a small metal bowl and set over a saucepan holding 2 inches barely simmering water. Stir the chocolate until melted. (Alternatively, place the chocolate in a microwave-safe bowl and melt in a microwave set on low power, stirring every 10 seconds.)

Remove the chocolate balls from the refrigerator. Place the cocoa powder on a small baking sheet or shallow tray. Place nearby a clean baking sheet lined with nonstick cooking (parchment) paper. Place a little melted chocolate in the palm of one hand. Using your clean hand, transfer a chocolate ball to your "chocolate palm" and roll the ball until well coated with the melted chocolate. Place the ball in the cocoa powder. When you have placed all the balls on the tray holding the cocoa powder, gently shake the tray until the balls are evenly covered with the cocoa powder. The truffles should be smooth and no specks of chocolate should show through the cocoa powder. Transfer the truffles to the baking sheet lined with nonstick cooking (parchment) paper and refrigerate. Sift the remaining cocoa powder to remove any bits of chocolate, then transfer the cocoa to an airtight container for future use. The truffles can be made up to 4 days in advance of serving. Bring them to room temperature before serving.

Angels in Heaven

One of the high points of our travels thus far was a stay at the Lodge at Koele located on David Murdock's private Hawaiian island called Lana'i. Situated on a mountainside and surrounded by Norfolk pines, ironwood, giant banyans, euphorbia, and Chinese lantern trees, the country manor and the acres of exotic botanical landscape provide a magical setting for a dream vacation. Believing that nothing concludes a dinner on a more luxurious and festive note than a dessert soufflé, every night we finished our dinner with one of Pastry Chef Gary Wald's fantastic soufflés. His endless flavor variations served as the inspiration for this white chocolate soufflé. When the individual soufflés arrive at the dining table, each person makes a little hole in the center of their mini masterpiece and pours an ethereal dessert sauce into the hollow. Angels ascend to heaven with each and every bite.

• Moderate
• Serves 6.

4½ tablespoons unsalted butter
4½ tablespoons unbleached white flour
1½ cups milk
6 whole eggs plus 2 additional egg whites
2 teaspoons pure vanilla extract
8 ounces white chocolate, preferably European
Caramel Butter Sauce (page 208), Velvet Chocolate Sauce (page 204), or Raspberry Essence (page 204)
1 tablespoon each butter and sugar, for dusting soufflé molds
½ cup sugar

• advance preparation

Make the soufflé base: Melt the butter in a saucepan. Remove from the heat and stir in the flour until thoroughly blended. Bring the milk to a low boil, then using a whisk, stir the milk into the butter-flour mixture. Return the saucepan to medium heat and cook until very thick, stirring continually, about 3 minutes. Remove from the heat and cool for 2 minutes. Separate the egg yolks from the whites. Stir the yolks into the soufflé base mixture. Stir in the vanilla. This mixture may be held at room temperature for up to 4 hours.

Using a sharp knife, cut the chocolate into small pieces, then cut into very fine shavings. Set aside.

Make one or more of the sauces.

Butter the sides of six 2-cup soufflé ramekins. Add a little sugar to each one, then shake and turn to coat the sides, shaking out the excess.

Beat the egg whites until they form soft peaks. Gradually add the sugar and beat until the whites stiffen. Stir a fourth of the whites into the yolk mixture, then fold in the remaining whites. Gently fold in the white chocolate shavings. Fill each ramekin to within 1 inch of its top lip. The unbaked soufflés can be stored at room temperature for 1 hour.

• last-minute cooking

Preheat the oven to 400°F. Place the ramekins on a baking sheet and bake for approximately 25 minutes, until the soufflés have risen about 2 inches above the lip of the ramekins.

Warm the sauces. When the soufflés are done, immediately take them to the table. Instruct each person to make a little hole in the center of the soufflé and pour the sauces into the hollow.

Black and White Bread Pudding

Jean Carey, one of America's top food stylists, worked with us on our first two cookbooks and shares our passion for chocolate. So with very little cajoling, she volunteered to devote months to creating this recipe, cooking and eating thousands of bread puddings in order to achieve perfection.

If you are using very densely textured bread, soak it overnight in the chocolate sauce so that the bread is completely saturated. For instant Nirvana, serve this bread pudding right out of the oven, gently positioned on dessert plates, encircled with one of the dessert sauces from this chapter, dusted with cocoa powder, and topped with white chocolate curls.

- Moderate
- Serves 6.

¾ cup walnuts
½ pound high-quality French bread (to yield about 6 cups ½-inch cubes)
1 cup raisins
¾ cup Grand Marnier
8 ounces bittersweet chocolate, preferably European
2 cups light cream
6 eggs
½ cup sugar
2 teaspoons ground cinnamon
1 teaspoon pure vanilla extract
½ teaspoon freshly and finely ground black pepper
4-ounce chunk white chocolate, preferably European
1 tablespoon unsweetened cocoa powder, preferably Valrhona

•advance preparation

Spray an 8-cup ovenproof bowl with nonstick cooking spray. Cut enough bread into ½-inch cubes to fill 6 cups. Place the cubes in the prepared container. Soak the raisins in the Grand Marnier for 30 minutes or heat in a microwave oven at high power for 2 minutes. Drain the raisins, reserving ¼ cup Grand Marnier.

Cut the bittersweet chocolate into small pieces. Combine the chocolate and 1 cup of the light cream in a small metal bowl and place over a larger saucepan holding 2 inches barely simmering water. Stir until completely melted. (Alternatively, place the chocolate and cream in a microwave-safe bowl and melt in a microwave set on low power, stirring every 10 seconds.)

In an electric blender, combine the remaining 1 cup light cream, the ¼ cup Grand Marnier, the eggs, sugar, cinnamon, vanilla, and black pepper. Blend at high speed for 1 minute. Then, at low speed, slowly add the melted chocolate mixture, blending well.

Pour the chocolate mixture over the bread cubes. Let sit at room temperature for 30 minutes, stirring every 10 minutes. Then cover with foil and refrigerate until the bread is completely saturated with the chocolate sauce. Using a potato peeler, "peel" curls from the chunk of white chocolate and set them aside.

•last-minute cooking

Preheat the oven to 325°F. Place the ovenproof bowl, still covered with foil, in a larger baking dish and fill halfway with hot water. Bake in the oven for 50 to 60 minutes, until the bread is firm to the touch. Remove the foil and spoon onto warm dessert plates. Place the cocoa powder in a sieve and dust over each serving. Garnish with the white chocolate curls and serve at once.

Chocolate Meltdown Cookies

Chocolate is extremely sensitive to heat and to small amounts of liquid and must be melted carefully. Cut the chocolate into very small pieces, place in a metal bowl just big enough to fit inside a saucepan containing barely simmering water, and stir it as it melts. (Using a larger bowl that extends beyond the saucepan results in the sides of the bowl becoming so hot that the chocolate scorches.) Alternatively, melt chocolate in a microwave as follows: Cut the chocolate into small pieces, place in a microwave-safe bowl, and melt on low power, stirring every 10 seconds. When chocolate is melted alone, there must be absolutely no moisture either in the bowl or on the knife used to cut the chocolate or the chocolate will "seize" into a dull, sticky ball. Alice Medrich, the Chocolate Czar, has the most sensible advice: Always keep extra chocolate on hand in case you inadvertently scorch the chocolate or the chocolate seizes. It would be a terrible fate to plan to make a temptation like this one and then be denied the pleasure because you don't have enough chocolate.

- Easy
- Makes 2 dozen cookies.

6 tablespoons unsalted butter
¾ cup sugar
2 eggs
4 ounces bittersweet chocolate, preferably European
2 tablespoons unsweetened cocoa powder, preferably Valrhona
¼ cup Kahlúa
1 teaspoon pure vanilla extract
¾ teaspoon baking powder
½ teaspoon salt
½ cup chopped roasted walnuts (page 222)
½ cup chocolate chips
¾ cup unbleached white flour

• preparation and baking

Preheat the oven to 350°F. Cut the butter into small pieces. Place the butter and sugar in a food processor fitted with the chopping blade and process until thoroughly blended. With the processor on, add the eggs, one at a time, through the feed tube. Cut the chocolate into small pieces. Transfer the chocolate to a small metal bowl placed over a saucepan holding 2 inches simmering water and warm until melted. (Alternatively, place the chocolate in a microwave-safe bowl and melt in a microwave oven set on low power, stirring every 10 seconds.) With the processor on, pour the melted chocolate through the feed tube.

Remove the processor lid, add the cocoa powder, and process again until well blended. Transfer the mixture to a mixing bowl and stir in the Kahlúa, vanilla, baking powder, salt, walnuts, and chocolate chips. Add the flour and stir until thoroughly mixed.

Line baking sheets with nonstick cooking (parchment) paper. Transfer the dough, in 2-tablespoon portions, to the baking sheets, leaving 2 inches between each cookie. Bake for 12 minutes, then cool on the paper on the baking sheets.

Flavor Resources to Enrich Our Everyday Food

The quality of our cooking is dependent not only on purchasing the freshest vegetables, seafood, meats, and herbs, but also on choosing the best brands of bottled condiments and spices that have been stored properly to ensure their intense original flavor. This section provides a review of ethnic ingredients that are playing an increasingly important role in American cooking. Descriptions include the names of preferred brands, where applicable, as well as storage information and suggestions on how to use these ingredients to enliven the flavors of everyday food.

bean sauce: Bean sauce is a pungent Chinese condiment made from yellow beans, flour, salt, and water. Purchase only bean sauces in which fragments of beans are visible, since this guarantees that top-quality beans were used to make them. Preparations containing bean sauce always include a little sugar to counter the sauce's slight salty taste.

Suggested Uses: Add 1 tablespoon bean sauce plus a pinch of sugar to meat stews to achieve a deeper, more earthy flavor.

Storage: Sold in both cans and in glass jars. If canned, transfer to a jar and seal tightly. Keeps indefinitely in the refrigerator.

Substitute. None.

Best Brand: Koon Chun Bean Sauce.

butter: Always try to use "unsalted" butter when specified throughout this book. In recipes where just a small amount of butter is used for cooking, lightly salted butter or

cooking oil can be substituted. You may, however, have to reduce the amount of salt in the recipe, and if using oil, the dish may not have as rich a flavor. As for margarine, from a gastronomic point of view, it has no place in modern American cooking.

cheeses: The many small manufacturers of American goat cheese and blue cheese produce excellent products. Unfortunately, American-produced Parmesan and Asiago cheeses have a nasty scalded-milk taste. Always buy imported Parmigiano-Reggiano and Asiago cheeses. Coarsely grated over salads, pasta dishes, and stews, they add a deep, nutty, slightly salty taste that is unrivaled by other cheeses. Tightly wrapped, these cheeses will last for months in the refrigerator, or indefinitely in the freezer.

chiles, dried: Dried chiles have a more intense flavor and sweetness than fresh chiles. To use for cooking, seed and stem them, then cover with boiling water until softened, about 30 minutes. Next the chiles can be placed in an electric blender (a food processor does this poorly) with a little liquid and liquefied. As Mark Miller noted in *The Great Chile Cookbook,* dried chiles have a complex taste profile including low notes from the toasting, middle notes from their fruity flavor, and high notes from the slight citrus aftertaste.

Suggested Uses: If you have not cooked with dried chiles before, begin your experimentation with ancho and chipotle chiles. Seed,

soak, and purée a chile; then add to stews, pot roasts, curries, soups, salad dressings, bread or muffin batters, and even to melted chocolate to be used for desserts.

Storage: In an airtight container placed in a cool, dark place. Use within 6 months.

Substitutes: Use fresh chiles or a small amount of one of the chile sauces described below.

chiles, fresh: The smaller the chile, the spicier its taste. As the chile ripens on the vine, its color reddens and its flavor becomes milder and sweeter. The "heat" that characterizes chiles is from capsaicin (an alkaloid), 80 percent of which is concentrated in the inside ribbing and seeds. However, since seeding chiles is a tedious matter, all the recipes in this book call for just stemming the chile, and then finely mincing it with its seeds. Mince fresh chiles in a mini-chopper rather than by hand in order to avoid spreading the searing capsaicin onto sensitive areas of the skin. During the warm summer months, grow chiles in a garden or in a pot near a sunny window.

Storage: Placed in a paper bag in the refrigerator, fresh chiles will last a month. Discard chiles when they begin to wrinkle.

Substitutes: Use dried red chiles or a small amount of one of the chile sauces listed below.

chile sauces: There are dozens of brands of Asian, Cajun, Mexican, and Caribbean chile sauces. Most are made with chiles, garlic, salt, and oil.

Usually ½ teaspoon is sufficient to contribute a mild spiciness to a dish. Asian chile sauce is a general term covering many sauces, variously labeled as chile paste, chile sauce, and chile paste with garlic. A milder chile sauce, called Sriracha, is manufactured in Thailand and sold under the brand name Swan Brand. Unlike many other Asian chile sauces, it is mild enough to be used as a table condiment. Don't confuse Swan Brand Sriracha sauce with the very spicy sriracha sauces manufactured in Hong Kong and America.

Suggested Uses: Add it to everything!

Storage: Keeps indefinitely in the refrigerator.

Best Brand: Rooster Brand Delicious Hot Chile Garlic Sauce, which is sold in an 8-ounce clear plastic jar with a green cap.

chipotles in adobo sauce: This wonderful ingredient, chipotles (smoked jalapeños) stewed in a sauce of vinegar, tomatoes, onions, and garlic, is sold in 4-ounce cans in Mexican and Latin American markets. To use, purée in an electric blender, then strain out the seeds.

Suggested Uses: Add to barbecue and other sauces, stews, curries, and ground meat.

Storage: Once opened, transfer to a glass jar and store in the refrigerator up to 2 weeks.

Substitute: 8 dried chipotles, 1 chopped small yellow onion, 4 cloves minced garlic, ¼ cup cider vinegar, ¼ cup ketchup, and 3 cups water. Combine all ingredients and simmer in a covered saucepan for 1 hour; then liquefy in an electric blender and strain out the seeds.

citrus zest: The oils contained in citrus zest (the colored part of citrus skin) contribute an intense flavor to a recipe that it is not possible to achieve when using just the juice; never use the white part of the skin, which is bitter. Grate the zest just before using because the flavor dissipates quickly. Either grate against the fine mesh of a cheese grater (very time-consuming) or with a zester (very easy to do), then finely mince the zest by hand or in a mini-chopper.

Suggested Uses: Add to salad dressings, marinades, sauces, and desserts to achieve a fresh citrus taste. Use judiciously, for even ½ teaspoon has a powerful flavoring effect.

Substitute: There is no substitute. Citrus oils and other extracts add an artificial taste to food.

coconut milk: Excellent canned unsweetened coconut milk is sold by every Asian market and by many American supermarkets. Purchase a Thai brand whose ingredients are just coconut and water. Occasionally, coconut milk is so thick it needs to be diluted with a little additional water before using.

Suggested Uses: Substitute coconut milk for whipping cream in any non-dessert recipe. Coconut milk contributes a rich taste when added to soups, stews, curries, and gravies.

Storage: Once opened, coconut milk keeps for a week in the refrigerator. Do not freeze coconut milk because the oil separates, giving the coconut milk a curdled look.

Best Brand: Chaokoh brand from Thailand. Whatever brand you buy, look for the word "gata" on the label, which indicates that the coconut milk is extra rich.

crème fraîche: Crème fraîche, a sour-tasting cream with nutty undertones, is used extensively in French cooking and is sold by many American supermarkets. If unavailable, a simple recipe for it is given on page 204.

Suggested Uses: Stir into sauces and soups, and spoon over fresh fruit.

Storage: Keeps for 2 weeks in the refrigerator.

Substitute: Sour cream, although it does not have the rich, nutty flavor that sets crème fraîche apart.

curry paste, indian: Indian curry paste, a blend of many different seasonings mixed with oil, has a much more complex taste and longer shelf life than curry powder. For improved flavor in recipes, substitute 1 teaspoon curry paste for every 1 tablespoon curry powder.

Best Brand: Madras Indian Curry Paste, which is sold by most supermarkets.

curry paste, thai: Thai cooks use only curry pastes (never powders) and make them with complex combinations of fresh herbs and spices. Thai green curry paste is made with green chiles and basil, red curry paste with fresh and dried red chiles, and yellow curry paste with chiles and fresh turmeric. While freshly made Thai curry pastes have a marvelously intriguing taste, store-bought Thai curry pastes have a salty, stale, artificial flavor. As such, there is no substitute for freshly made Thai curry pastes (see page 100).

dijon mustard: One of the great flavor resources, Dijon mustard lends a complex taste when added to salad dressings, mayonnaise, marinades, and barbecue and other sauces.

Suggested Uses: Its flavors work very well when combined with such Asian condiments as hoisin sauce, thin soy sauce, and dark sesame oil.

Storage: Keeps indefinitely in the refrigerator.

Best Brand: Maille Dijon Mustard.

dry sherry and wines: Always use good-quality dry sherry, rice wine, and wine for cooking; a poor-tasting sherry or wine will result in an inferior-tasting dish.

Substitutes: For recipes that call for dry sherry, substitute dry vermouth or a good Chinese rice wine, such as Pagoda Brand Shao Xing Rice Wine or Pagoda Brand Shao Hsing Hua Tiao Chiew.

egg roll skins (or wrappers): These 6-inch square wrappers are made from the same egg noodle dough used for making won ton wrappers. Always purchase egg roll skins that are a light yellow color.

Suggested Uses: Use for making large entrée-sized ravioli.

Storage: For as long as a month in the refrigerator or indefinitely in the freezer.

fish sauce: Fish sauce is used in Thai and Vietnamese cooking the way soy sauce is used in Chinese cooking. It is made by layering fresh anchovies or squid in large containers, covering them with brine, and fermenting them for several months to yield a watery, golden, and very flavorful liquid. Always buy fish sauce produced in Thailand, which is far superior to the very salty tasting fish sauces from other countries.

Suggested Uses: Add a dash to soups, stews, curries, and sauces in place of salt. It will add a more complex flavor than salt as well as heighten the flavors of the other ingredients.

Storage: Lasts indefinitely at room temperature.

Substitute: None.

Best Brands: Three Crab Brand and Tiparos Brand Fish Sauce.

five-spice powder: This powdered blend of anise, fennel, cinnamon, Szechwan pepper, and cloves is sold in 1-ounce bags in Asian markets and in the spice section at all supermarkets.

Suggested Uses: Contributes a complex spice taste when added to marinades, poultry, and fish. Because of its potent flavor, don't use more than ¼ teaspoon at a time.

Storage: Keeps indefinitely at room temperature if tightly sealed in a jar.

Substitute: None.

Best Brand: Buy the five-spice powder made in Asia and sold by Asian markets.

galangal: Known variously as *laos, ka,* and Thai ginger, galangal is botanically part of the ginger family. It has a smoother and lighter colored skin and a thicker root than ginger, and a wonderfully flowery flavor. It may be found in the produce section at Asian markets in cities with large Southeast Asian populations.

Suggested Uses: Use in all recipes that call for fresh ginger, substituting an equal amount of galangal, or thinly slice and add to simmering soups and stews (in this case the slices are not meant to be eaten).

Storage: Lasts indefinitely if placed in a bottle filled with dry sherry, then refrigerated. Lasts for about a week, on its own, in the refrigerator.

garlic, fresh: Fresh garlic is an indispensable seasoning. Always purchase garlic heads that feel very hard and are of medium size. The huge "elephant garlic" has too mild a taste to satisfy any garlic lover. To peel a clove, cut off the stubby end, then lay a Chinese knife on the clove, and gently tap the blade with your hand. Pick the garlic up by the tail end and shake out the garlic clove. If the garlic clove has a green shoot, remove it. Garlic should be minced either by hand or in a mini-chopper or food processor. Forcing garlic through a garlic press gives it a bitter taste.

Storage: Stored at room temperature, garlic will not soften and spoil for several months. To keep minced garlic on hand, peel several dozen cloves. Mince these finely in a food processor, stir in a few tablespoons of cooking oil to moisten, then bottle and refrigerate for up to several months. Alternatively, roast the garlic as described below.

garlic, roasted: Roasted garlic boasts a mellow, nutty flavor and can be stored indefinitely in the refrigerator. To roast: Using a sharp knife, cut the top quarter off each head of garlic. Place the heads on a piece of aluminum foil or in a small baking dish, pour extra-virgin olive oil into the exposed garlic cloves, seal, and roast in a 400°F. oven for 1 hour. Cool to room temperature, wrap in a plastic bag, and refrigerate.

Suggested Uses: When ready to use, squeeze the garlic skins to slip out the cloves, then spread on bread, crackers, or pizza dough; mash and add to dips, stews, curries, or sauces; or pack underneath chicken skin before roasting.

ginger, crystallized: These are slices of fresh ginger that are candied and coated in sugar. They have a sweet, sharp ginger flavor. They are available in most supermarkets and all Asian stores. The slices should feel slightly soft when squeezed. If they feel rock hard, they are stale and should be discarded.

Suggested Uses: Excellent chopped and sprinkled over ice cream or served as a candy with fresh fruit.

Storage: Keeps indefinitely at room temperature sealed in jar.

Substitute: None.

ginger, fresh: Absolutely indispensable for modern American cooking, these pungent and spicy, knobby brown rhizomes are sold in the produce section of all supermarkets. Buy firm ginger with smooth skin. Never peel ginger unless the skin is wrinkled. To use, cut ginger crosswise into paper-thin slices, then very finely mince by hand or in an electric mini-chopper.

Storage: Store ginger in a dark cupboard, where it will stay fresh for up to a month. Discard ginger when it begins to wrinkle and soften.

Substitute: None, since powdered ginger has an entirely different taste, and crystallized ginger is too sweet.

ginger, red sweet: Sold in glass jars at most Asian markets, these are pieces of bright red ginger in a heavy syrup and are not to be confused with Japanese pickled ginger.

Suggested Uses: Red sweet ginger, finely minced and combined with a little of its syrup, makes a great taste contribution to salad dressings.

Storage: Keeps indefinitely at room temperature provided the syrup covers the ginger pieces.

Substitute: None.

Best Brands: Mee Chun Preserved Red Ginger Slices (or Threads) in Syrup and Koon Chun Red Ginger in Syrup.

herbs, dried: Dried herbs are used in this book only to season meat and seafood before browning in oil.

Storage: Store dried herbs in a cool, dark place. They gradually lose what little flavor they have and should be discarded every 12 months.

herbs, fresh: Nearly all recipes in this book use fresh herbs, which have a far more intense bouquet than their dried cousins. Although fresh herbs are available at most supermarkets throughout the year, whenever possible, grow your own. Requiring only a little sunlight and occasional watering, freshly pickled herbs have an unmatched intensity of flavor.

Storage: Wrap fresh store-bought herbs in damp paper towels and store in plastic bags in the vegetable compartment of the refrigerator. Pick homegrown herbs the day you plan to use them.

Substitute: In an emergency, substitute 1 to 2 teaspoons dried herbs for the fresh herbs that are specified.

hoisin sauce: This thick, sweet and spicy, dark brownish red condiment is made with soybeans, chiles, garlic, ginger, and sugar, and is one of the Chinese condiments most loved by

Americans. It is sold by Asian markets both in glass jars and in cans.

Suggested Uses: Great spread across tortillas, as the foundation of barbecue sauces, for enriching salad dressings, and for many stir-fry sauces, stews, and curries.

Storage: If canned, open and transfer to a glass container. Keeps indefinitely at room temperature.

Substitute: None.

Best Brand: Buy only Koon Chun Hoisin Sauce, which is far superior in taste to all other brands.

kaffir lime leaves: These dark green leaves, which come from a special variety of Thai limes and are available fresh at Asian markets, have a floral-lime fragrance totally unlike any other leaf. They are used by Thai cooks to season soups, curries, and stews in much the same way that Americans use bay leaves. Kaffir lime leaves are also available dried and frozen, but neither of these has the wonderful intense flavor of the fresh leaves. Use frozen (not dried) leaves only as a last resort.

Suggested Uses: Cut leaves into shreds or leave whole and add to soups, stews, and sauces.

Substitutes: None.

lemongrass: One of the most important seasonings for Thai and Vietnamese cooking, lemongrass, a 3-foot-long greenish plant with an 8-inch woody stem and long slender leaves, is beginning to appear in the produce section of big-city American supermarkets. Only buy lemongrass that has firm, smooth stems and green leaves without any brown edges. Or, if you live in a temperate climate, purchase a lemongrass plant in the herb section of a nursery and grow it in your garden at home.

Suggested Uses: Finely mince the woody stem, which has a faint lemon-balm flavor, and add it to dishes the same way you would minced ginger, or cut it on a sharp diagonal into ½-inch pieces and add the pieces to stews, curries, and soups; large pieces of lemongrass are meant to flavor a dish but not to be eaten.

Storage: Lemongrass loses its flavor within a few days of being picked. Store in the refrigerator.

Substitute: ½ teaspoon finely grated lemon zest (colored part of skin), though the flavor is not quite the same. Never substitute dried or frozen lemongrass, which have no flavor.

mushrooms, dried asian and european: Dried mushrooms have an intense flavor and dense texture that are lacking in fresh mushrooms. Softened in hot water, then chopped finely, dried mushrooms contribute an earthy flavor to dumpling fillings, soups, stews, pasta and rice dishes, and sauces. To use, pour just enough hot or boiling water over the mushrooms to cover them, submerge them by placing a small saucer on top, and soak until softened, about 30 minutes. Finely chop the mushrooms, discarding any tough sections. Strain the "mushroom water" through a fine-meshed sieve, place in a sealable plastic bag, and freeze; the mushroom water makes a great addition to soups, stews, and sauces. Chinese black mushrooms, Japanese forest mushrooms (shiitakes), morels, porcinis, and cèpes can all be used interchangeably.

Storage: Indefinitely in a cool, dark pantry.

noodles, dried american and european: The number of dried American and European pastas sold in supermarkets is ever-increasing. I prefer the flavored pastas that cook in 2 to 4 minutes because they have a wonderful light texture. Other good pastas are the multicolored bow-tie, shell, and corkscrew-shaped pastas. Avoid the so-called "fresh" pastas sold in the deli case of many supermarkets because they have a dense texture and inferior taste.

Storage: Indefinitely at room temperature.

nuts, how to roast: The taste of all recipes that call for nuts, whether entrées or desserts, is improved if the nuts are first roasted because roasting intensifies the nuts' flavor. Almonds: Roast slivered, sliced, and whole almonds in a 325°F. oven until golden, about 15 minutes. Hazelnuts (filberts): Roast shelled hazelnuts in a 325°F. oven for 15 minutes; when nuts cool to room temperature, rub vigorously between your palms to loosen the exterior skin. Pecans: Roast pecans in a 325°F. oven for 15 minutes. Pine Nuts: Roast pine nuts in a 325°F. oven until golden, about 8 minutes. Walnuts: All shelled walnuts have a rancid taste before they are roasted. Place walnuts in a saucepan, cover with cold water, bring water to a vigorous boil, and boil 5 minutes. Immediately tip walnuts into a sieve, spread on a baking sheet, and roast in a 325°F. oven for 30 minutes, turning walnuts over using a metal spatula after the first 15 minutes of roasting. When the walnuts cool, they will have an intense walnut flavor without any

bitter, rancid taste. Cashews, Peanuts, Macadamia Nuts: When raw cashews, shelled raw peanuts, and raw macadamia nuts are dry-roasted in the oven, their internal nut oil evaporates, creating a tasteless, mealy nut. Instead, place nuts in a small saucepan, then add enough room-temperature cooking oil to submerge them completely (preheating the oil before adding the nuts will cause the nuts to cook unevenly). Place the saucepan over medium-high heat and stir the nuts slowly and continually with a long wooden spoon. The moment the nuts turn a light golden, tip them into a sieve placed over another saucepan. The nuts will continue to darken and cook as they cool. When the nuts return to room temperature, pat them dry with paper towels. The nuts will have an intense flavor and crispness without any oiliness.

Storage: All roasted nuts will last indefinitely if sealed tightly in a plastic bag and frozen.

oil: Several types of oil are specified in the recipes in this book. The term cooking oil refers to any tasteless oil that has a high smoking temperature, such as peanut oil, canola oil, safflower oil, or corn oil. Light-grade olive oil has virtually no olive oil taste nor a green tint and can be used interchangeably with cooking oil. Extra-virgin olive oil is a green, very fruity olive oil made from the first pressing of olives. Its rich flavor and heavy grade make it a perfect oil for bread-dipping and for salads, where its rich flavor matches the assertiveness of vinegar and seasonings. (We rarely use extra-virgin olive oil as a cooking oil because its flavor is too dominating.) Walnut oil from France, a specialty oil sold in small cans by gourmet markets and cookware shops, is also wonderful in salad dressings. (Avoid American walnut oil, sold in glass bottles, because it has no flavor.) Dark sesame oil is a nutty, dark golden brown oil made from toasted crushed sesame seeds. Do not confuse dark sesame oil with clear-colored sesame oil, which has no flavor, or black sesame oil, which has far too strong a taste. Dark sesame oil contributes a deep rich taste when added in very small amounts ($\frac{1}{2}$ teaspoon to 1 tablespoon) to salad dressings, marinades, and sauces, but should not be used as a cooking oil, because its low smoking temperature causes it to burn easily. The quality of dark sesame oil varies greatly. Always purchase dark sesame oil labeled "pure" (to avoid those adulterated with cottonseed oil), such as Kadoya Sesame Oil. Do not buy Dynasty Brand Sesame Oil, sold by many supermarkets, because it has a rancid taste.

Storage: Store all oils, except walnut oil, in a cool, dark pantry. Store walnut oil in the refrigerator.

oyster sauce: Also called "oyster-flavored sauce," this oyster "ketchup" gives dishes a marvelous rich taste without a hint of its seafood origins. A pinch of sugar is usually added to dishes flavored with oyster sauce to counteract its slightly salty taste.

Suggested Uses: Try adding 1 tablespoon oyster sauce to meat loaf mixes, 2 tablespoons to stews, curries, and sauces, and $\frac{1}{4}$ cup to barbecue sauces.

Storage: Keeps indefinitely in the refrigerator.

Substitute: None.

Best Brands: Sa Cheng Oyster Flavored Sauce, Hop Sing Lung Oyster Sauce Factory Oyster Flavored Sauce, and Lee Kum Kee Oyster Flavored Sauce, Old Brand.

peppercorns, black and white: Black peppercorns are the dried unripe fruits of a tropical vine. White peppercorns are the mature fruit of the same vine from which the outer coating has been removed. Always grind peppercorns just before using (commercially ground black and white pepper should be banished from all kitchens). In order to accent their peppery taste, place them in an ungreased skillet and toast over medium heat until they begin to smoke lightly. Cool to room temperature, then transfer to a pepper grinder. House Pepper Blend: For a more complex-tasting pepper blend, combine equal amounts of white, black, and Szechwan (see below) peppercorns. Toast, cool, and transfer to a pepper grinder.

peppercorns, szechwan: These small, reddish brown seeds, all partly open, are the product of the prickly ash tree and are available at all Asian markets. They have a beautiful aromatic flavor without the spice of black or white peppercorns. To use, toast Szechwan peppercorns in a sauté pan until they smoke lightly, grind in an electric spice grinder, then sift through a medium-meshed sieve to remove the brown exterior shells. Confusingly, some Asian markets label white peppercorns as "Szechwan pepper."

peppers, roasted: Roasting red, yellow, and green bell peppers and chiles gives them a smoky, earthy, and complex taste. To roast: Place

the whole peppers or chiles, uncut, over a gas flame or barbecue. When the peppers blacken on the underside, rotate a third of a turn. Continue roasting peppers until they are entirely blackened. (The peppers will not explode!) Alternatively, cut off and discard both ends from the peppers. Cut open the peppers, discard the ribs and seeds, and flatten the peppers. Lay the peppers, skin side up, directly on an oven rack. Place the rack as close to the broiler as possible, turn the oven on to broil, and broil the peppers until their skins blister and blacken. Do not turn the peppers over. Once peppers have blackened, place them in a plastic or paper bag, close the bag, and let them "steam" for 5 minutes. It is a simple matter, then, to rub the peppers with your fingers and remove all the blackened skin. Do not rinse it off because this washes away some of the essential oils and flavor.

Suggested Uses: Roasted peppers and chiles contribute a deep, intriguing flavor when they are stirred into guacamole, dips, salsas, and soups; when they are tossed with salad greens or simmered in stews and curries; and when they are used as a garnish and flavor accent.

Storage: Tightly fitted in a glass jar and covered with light-grade olive oil, roasted peppers will last for at least 1 month in the refrigerator.

Substitute: None.

plum sauce: This chutney-like condiment is made with plums, apricots, garlic, red chiles, sugar, vinegar, salt, and water. It is different than a condiment found only on the East Coast called "duck sauce," which is made with plums, apples, and spices. Plum sauce is available in cans and glass jars at all Asian markets and in many supermarkets.

Suggested Uses: The thick consistency and sweet, spicy flavor of plum sauce makes it an ideal addition to barbecue sauces and an excellent dip for crisp, deep-fried won tons or chilled shrimp.

Storage: If canned, once opened, transfer to a glass jar and seal. Keeps indefinitely at room temperature.

Substitute: Any kind of chutney.

Best Brand: Koon Chun Plum Sauce.

rice sticks: Rice sticks are long, thin, dried rice-flour vermicelli. When they are transferred directly from the package into hot oil they puff up instantly into a huge white mass many times their original size. They are the essential ingredient in many of the salads in this book and can also be used as a foundation on which to place stir-fries, stews, and curries. For cooking instructions, see page 58. Rice sticks are available at most supermarkets and all Asian markets.

Storage: Keep indefinitely at room temperature.

Substitute: None.

Best Brand: Be sure to purchase the Chinese-manufactured Sailing Boat Brand Rice Sticks, which are sold in 1-pound packages. Do not buy Thai rice sticks, which when deep-fried are too thick and coarse, or Dynasty or China Bowl brand rice sticks, which are so thin that they contribute no crunchy texture.

saffron: Nothing contributes a more luxurious look to a dish than bright yellow threads of saffron, actually the stigmas of the saffron crocus,

which grows in Spain, Turkey, and India. The world's most expensive spice, one ounce of saffron is made up of 13,000 stigmas, to which a single plant contributes three. Saffron needs to be simmered a minimum of 15 minutes in a dish in order to contribute its marvelous yellow tinge and delicate flavor. Always purchase saffron threads rather than the less expensive powdered saffron, which lacks both flavor and coloring ability.

Suggested Uses: Add 1 or 2 big pinches of saffron to light-colored soups, sauces, stews, and rice and pasta dishes.

Storage: Keeps indefinitely in the freezer.

Substitute: Turmeric will add a similar color but a slightly different flavor.

salt: More than any other ingredient, salt is the most essential flavoring agent for all foods. A small amount of salt accents the flavors of all other ingredients and creates a round, lingering flavor with each bite. Always taste every dish during the final moments of cooking. At that point, if food tastes flat with no long aftertastes, add a little salt to develop the full flavor.

Best Types: Kosher salt and sea salt, both of which are nothing but pure salt. Never use the common American "table salt," which has a strong metallic iodine taste.

Substitutes: To bring out the complex flavors of a dish, other salt intense condiments, such as oyster sauce, fish sauce, and soy sauce, can be substituted.

soy sauce, thin and heavy: "Thin" or "light" soy sauce is the most common soy sauce used in Asian cooking. Made from soy beans, roasted wheat, yeast, and salt, good thin soy sauce is available at all Asian markets and in most supermarkets. Heavy (also known as dark or black) soy sauce, to which molasses or caramel has been added, is not as watery as thin soy sauce and coats the neck of the bottle when shaken. Use it to add a rich flavor and color to sauces, stews, and curries. Never confuse "heavy" soy sauce with "thick" soy sauce, a syrup-like molasses that is sold in jars and will ruin the taste of any recipe in this book.

Storage: Keeps indefinitely at room temperature.

Substitute: None.

Best Brands: For heavy soy sauce, buy Pearl River Bridge Brand Mushroom Soy Sauce. For thin soy sauce, purchase Pearl River Bridge Brand Golden Label Superior Soya Sauce, Koon Chun Brand Thin Soy Sauce, or Kikkoman Regular Soy Sauce. If you are concerned about sodium, it is better to reduce the quantity of soy sauce in a recipe, rather than use the inferior-tasting, more expensive low-sodium "lite" brands.

spices: Many recipes in this book call for spices, such as cinnamon, allspice, cloves, coriander seeds, nutmeg, and star anise. It is always better to grind your own whole spices because freshly ground whole spices have a more intense flavor than preground spices. To intensify the flavor of whole spices further, place them in an ungreased sauté pan and dry-fry until they just begin to smoke lightly. Next grind them in an electric spice or coffee grinder and use immediately.

Storage: Store spices in a cool, dark pantry. Discard whole spices after 2 years, and ground spices after 1 year.

tamarind: Tamarind pods, which grow on a large tropical tree, contain a reddish brown pulp that when soaked in hot water has a delightful fruity, sour taste. Tamarind paste is sold in 8-ounce and 1-pound blocks at all Asian markets. To use, break off a thumb-sized piece of pulp and place in a bowl with just enough hot water to cover. After 10 minutes, rub the softened pulp, still in the water, with your fingers in order to extract all of its flavor, then strain the liquid through a sieve into a bowl. Discard the remaining pulp and use the liquid.

Suggested Uses: Add the tamarind "water" to soups, stews, and sauces; it will contribute a gentle sour flavor with undercurrents of tropical fruit.

Substitute: None. Do not buy tamarind concentrate or juice.

Storage: Tamarind pulp lasts indefinitely if stored in a cool, dark pantry.

tomatoes, vine-ripened: Vine-ripened tomatoes are an essential flavoring in many of the recipes in this book. Always pick the tomatoes from your garden or purchase the tomatoes at a farmers' market. (Unfortunately, even in the peak of the summer growing season, most supermarkets still carry only "Cement Brand Tomatoes.") If good tomatoes are unavailable, substitute dried tomatoes (see above right) or the superb-tasting Pomi brand "Chopped Tomatoes," sold in 26-ounce containers by most supermarkets.

tomatoes, dried: Dried tomatoes are sold in 3-ounce bags and by the ounce in the produce section at most supermarkets. To use, cover dried tomatoes with just enough boiling water to submerge, then soak until softened, about 10 minutes.

Suggested Uses: Use dried tomatoes that have been soaked and chopped for pizza toppings, to flavor dips, to enrich the taste of all tomato sauces, and to flavor stews, curries, breads, muffins, and rice and pasta dishes. Never purchase the expensive bottled dried tomatoes packed in oil. These tomatoes are always hard and need to be soaked in hot water in the same way as the inexpensive dried tomatoes.

tortillas, corn and flour: Corn and flour tortillas are sold by most supermarkets in North America. However, unless you live on the West Coast or in the Southwest, the corn tortillas available are usually tough and stale. Since much better quality 6- and 8-inch flour tortillas are widely available, all recipes in this book specify flour tortillas.

Storage: Tightly wrap and refrigerate for a week or freeze indefinitely. To reheat, stack tortillas, seal in an airtight aluminum foil envelope, and place in a 325°F. oven until hot, about 10 minutes.

vinegars: Vinegar is an essential flavoring in all salad dressings and in many other recipes. In general, the more expensive the vinegar, the better the flavor and the better the final dish will taste. This is especially true for the famous Italian vinegar called "balsamic vinegar," of which the best is the boiled down must of white grapes that are aged in wooden barrels for many years. As

for Japanese rice vinegar, its mild flavor makes it particularly good for pickling and in salad dressings and sauces. Never purchase rice vinegars labeled "seasoned" or "gourmet," adjectives that indicate that sugar and often monosodium glutamate have been added. Do not confuse Japanese rice vinegar with Chinese rice vinegar, which has too mild a taste for the recipes in this book.

Storage: All vinegars last indefinitely stored in a cool, dark pantry.

won ton skins: Measuring about 3 inches square (when sold in circles the skins are labeled gyoza wrappers), these thin egg-noodle wrappers are sold by every Asian market and by most supermarkets in the produce or deli sections. Purchase the thinnest ones, preferably fresh not frozen. (When frozen, won ton skins dry out and become brittle, increasing their tendency to tear when folded for dumplings. To make thawed skins more pliable, lightly moisten the surface with a little water, then add the filling and fold.)

Suggested Uses: Use won ton skins for all European and Asian dumplings. Or cut the won ton skins into ¼-inch widths, shallow-fry until golden, then toss gently with torn lettuce to produce a salad with an intriguing taste and texture.

Storage: Keep for 1 month in the refrigerator.

Substitute: None.

Acknowledgments

So many people contributed their special gifts to *Fusion Food Cookbook*. Our publisher, Leslie Stoker, who worked with us on our first two cookbooks, believed passionately in the project and worked unceasingly to transform our material into a masterful book. Graphic designer Jim Wageman made the book come to life. Melanie Falick, our text editor, spared no effort editing the manuscript.

The book glows because of the efforts of our food stylists. Erez, who works in San Francisco and Israel, shows his talents on the prepared foods and the cover photograph. Carol Cole, who works from Sebastopol, California, styled the photographs that open each chapter. Thank you for sharing our vision.

We want to thank the artists and galleries that were such rich sources for the art glass tabletop ware. Mary B. White, Dan Fenton, Debbie Young, Michael and Ann Nourot, Joseph and Debbie Morel, Penny Waller, and Shelby all opened their studios to us. Thank you to Jim Hegarty, Bill Sliney, and Van Hull of Gump's, San Francisco, who encouraged and supported us from day one because of their love of beautiful art glass.

Ronda Vosti of Rasberry's, Napa Valley, and Federico de Vera, Joan Shain, Art Options, and Mosaic Gallery, all of San Francisco, opened their doors and shared their artwork with us for the photography. Thank you all.

Many friends helped bring this book into print and we are deeply appreciative for their support. Our attorney, Susan Grode, helped us refine the book proposal. Jack and Dolores Cakebread, by generously making their winery kitchen available, provided us with the opportunity to perfect many of these recipes among a small group of cooking friends. Viking Range Corporation and John Helms increased our cooking pleasure when creating these recipes at home and preparing the food for photography. Most of the beautiful produce was raised by Jeff Dawson and his crew at the Fetzer Valley Oaks Organic Garden in Hopland, California. The delicious mushrooms were grown by Malcolm Clark and Richard Wu of Gourmet Mushrooms, Inc., in Sebastopol.

We are indebted to the following chefs who contributed recipes or provided key ideas: John Ash for the Watermelon and Sweet Red Onion Salad; John Barrett for Tropical Isle Bouillabaisse; Jean E. Carey for Black and White Bread Pudding; Robert Del Grande for Mussel Soup with Cilantro and Serrano Chiles; Magnus Hansson for Any Kind of Bread; Steve Kantrowitz for Rabbit Potpie; Peter Kump for Velvet Chocolate Sauce; Keith Schauffel for Valrhona Cocoa Truffles; Grant and Sharon Showley for Grilled Figs; Don Skipworth for Candied Walnuts; Hiro Sone for Crisp Won Tons with Shiitake Cream Sauce; Joachim Splichal and Bruno Feldeisen for Chocolate Sorbet; Harrison Turner for Marinated Goat Cheese; and Gary Wald for inspiration with soufflés.

After the recipes were tested at our home and used in cooking classes, they were given a final evaluation by the following home cooks. This book gained much from their special insights. Thank you Florence Antico, Kathleen Bergin and David Lampkin, David and Peggy Black, Pam Blair, Ginny Bogart, Jan and Russ Bohne, Betty Bohrer, Jo Bowen, John Bragg, Judy Burnstein, Lynda and Bill Casper, Karen and Don Cerwin, Nora Feune De Colombi, Megan and David Cornhill, Tobey Cotsen, Kris Cox, Kim and George David, Claire Dishman, Judy Dubrawski, Cary and Kim Feibleman, Peter Feit, Suzanne Figi, Sharie and Ron Goldfarb, Robert Gordon, Blanche and Sy Gottlieb, Donna Hodgens, Sally and Robert Hunt, Linda and Ron Johnson, Lynnette and Bob Kahn, Bettylu Kessler, Jeannie Komsky, Susan Krueger, Betty Mandrow, Jeremy Mann, Cynthia McMurray, Amy Mitten and Douglas Stevens, Patricia Niedfelt, Michele Nipper, Kathleen Sands, Mary Jo and Paul Shane, Ellie Shulman, Karen Sickels, Barbara and Scott Smith, Phil Stafford, Suzanne Vadnais.

Artwork Credits

Pages 2–3: bowl by Correia, glasses by Kosta Boda; pages 12–13: dishes by Nourot Glass Studio; page 16: pastel drawing by Teri Sandison; page 21: recycled glass plates by Mary B. White; page 24: recycled glass tumblers by Mary B. White; page 29: fused glass plate by Penny Waller; pages 32–33: bowls by Nourot Glass Studio; page 36–37: plate by J. Crew; page 40: Sugihara plates, DeVera Gallery; page 45: plates by Kosta Boda; page 53: plate by Annieglass, flatware by George Jensen; page 56–57: fused glass rondel by Dan Fenton; page 60: recycled glass plate by Mary B. White, glasses by R.P.M. Studios; page 64: platter by Fineline Studios, glasses by Off Center; page 69: bowls by Joseph Morel, Zellique; page 72–73: bowl by Gilvey Glass; page 76–77: bowls designed by Federico DeVera; page 80: bowl by Correia, glasses by Kosta Boda; page 85: bowl by Correia, pastel drawing by Teri Sandison; page 91: platter by Correia; page 94: plate by J. Camp; page 99: plate by Annieglass, glasses by Randy Strong, watercolor painting by Teri Sandison; page 106: plates by Annieglass, glasses by Ecologia; page 111: fused glass plate by Shelby; page 112: glass by Dale Chihuly; page 117: plate by Cobweb Studios, Cynthia Thompson; page 120: fused glass plate by Debbie Young and Bill Kasper; pages 124–25 and jacket front: fused glass plate by Dan Fenton, glasses by Orrefors; page 128: recycled glass plates and tumblers by Mary B. White; page 135: plate by David Lindsay, Nourot Glass Studio; pages 138–39: fused glass plate by Dan Fenton; page 144: bowls by Merry Morrison; page 148: fused glass plate by Dan Fenton; page 155: plate by J. Camp; page 159: bowls by Joseph Morel, Zellique; page 162: bowls by Merry Morrison; page 168: plate by Sherry Schuster; page 173: platter by Bruce Bortin; page 176: plate by Zellique Glass; page 181: fused glass plate by Penny Waller; page 184: platter by Roberto Niederer; page 189: bowl by Correia, glass figs by Gozo; page 192–93: plate by Susan Ward Designs; page 194: fused glass bowl by Debbie Young; page 201: plate by Annieglass; page 202: plates by Merry Morrison; page 207: dish by Nourot Glass Studio; page 209: plate by Merry Morrison

Conversion Chart

Butter
Some confusion may arise over the measuring of butter and other hard fats. In the United States, butter is generally sold in one-pound packages that contain four equal "sticks." The wrapper on each stick is marked to show tablespoons, so the cook can cut the stick according to the quantity required. The equivalent weights are:

1 stick = 115 g / 4 oz
1 tablespoon = 15 g / ½ oz

Flour
American all-purpose flour is milled from a mixture of hard and soft wheats, whereas British plain flour is made mainly from soft wheat. To achieve a near equivalent to American all-purpose flour, use half British plain flour and half strong bread flour.

Sugar
In the recipes in this book, if sugar is called for it is assumed to be granulated, unless otherwise specified. American granulated sugar is finer than British granulated; in fact, it is closer to caster sugar. British cooks should use caster sugar throughout.

Ingredients and Equipment Glossary
Although the following ingredients and equipment have different names in British and American English, they are otherwise the same or interchangeable.

American	British
arugula	rocket
baking soda	bicarbonate of soda
beans (dried)—lima, navy, Great Northern	dried white (haricot) beans
Belgian endive	chicory
bell pepper	sweet pepper (capsicum)
Bibb and Boston lettuce	soft-leaved, round lettuce
broiler/to broil	grill/to grill
cheesecloth	muslin
chile	chilli
cornstarch	cornflour
eggplant	aubergine
kitchen towel	tea towel
lowfat milk	semi-skimmed milk
parchment paper	nonstick baking paper
peanut oil	groundnut oil
pearl onion	button or baby onion
romaine lettuce	cos lettuce
Romano cheese	pecorino cheese
scallion	spring onion
shrimp	prawn (varying in size)
skillet	frying pan
tomato purée	sieved tomatoes or pasatta
whole milk	homogenized milk
zucchini	courgette

Volume Equivalents
These are not exact equivalents for the American volume measurements, but have been rounded up or down slightly to make measuring easier.

American Measures	Metric	Imperial
¼ t	1.25 ml	
½ t	2.5 ml	
1 t	5 ml	
½ T (1½ t)	7.5 ml	
1 T (3 t)	15 ml	
¼ cup (4 T)	60 ml	2 fl oz
⅓ cup (5 T)	75 ml	2½ fl oz
½ cup (8 T)	125 ml	4 fl oz
⅔ cup (10 T)	150 ml	5 fl oz (¼ pint)
¾ cup (12 T)	175 ml	6 fl oz
1 cup (16 T)	250 ml	8 fl oz
1¼ cups	300 ml	10 fl oz (½ pint)
1½ cups	350 ml	2 fl oz
1 pint (2 cups)	500 ml	16 fl oz
1 quart (4 cups)	1 litre	1¾ pints

Oven Temperatures
In the recipes in this book, only Fahrenheit temperatures have been given. Consult this chart for the Centigrade and gas mark equivalents.

Oven	°F	°C	Gas Mark
very cool	250–275	130–140	½–1
cool	300	150	2
warm	325	170	3
moderate	350	180	4
moderately hot	375	190	5
	400	200	6
hot	425	220	7
very hot	450	230	8
	475	250	9

Weight Equivalents
The metric weights given in this chart are not exact equivalents, but have been rounded up or down slightly to make measuring easier.

Avoirdupois	Metric	Avoirdupois	Metric
¼ oz	7 g	12 oz	350 g
½ oz	15 g	13 oz	375 g
1 oz	30 g	14 oz	400 g
2 oz	60 g	15 oz	425 g
3 oz	90 g	1 lb	450 g
4 oz	115 g	1 lb 2 oz	500 g
5 oz	150 g	1½ lb	750 g
6 oz	175 g	2 lb	900 g
7 oz	200 g	2¼ lb	1 kg
8 oz (½ lb)	225 g	3 lb	1.4 kg
9 oz	250 g	4 lb	1.8 kg
10 oz	300 g	4½ lb	2 kg
11 oz	325 g		

Index

Designed by Jim Wageman

*Typefaces in this book are Bauer Bodoni, based on designs by
Giambattista Bodoni, and Frutiger, designed by Adrian Frutiger
The type was set by Laura Lindgren, New York*

*Printed and bound by Toppan Printing Company, Ltd.
Tokyo, Japan*